Kuhl, David.

What dying people want.

$25.00

WHAT DYING PEOPLE WANT

WHAT DYING PEOPLE WANT

Practical Wisdom for the End of Life

David Kuhl, M.D.

PublicAffairs *New York*

Book design by Mark McGarry, Texas Type & Book Works.
Set in Weiss

Library of Congress Cataloging-in-Publication Data
Kuhl, David
What dying people want: practical wisdom for the end of life/David Kuhl.
Includes bibliographical references and index.
ISBN 1–58648–119–3
1. Death—Psychological aspects. 2. Terminally ill—Psychology.
3. Terminally ill—Family relationships. 4. Death—Psychological aspects—
Case studies. 5. Terminally ill—Psychology—Case studies. 6. Terminally ill—
Family relationships—Case studies.
I. Title.
BF789.D4.K84 2002   155.9'37—dc21   2002024928

FIRST EDITION
10 9 8 7 6 5 4 3 2 1

*To the people who participated in my research project
and thereby became my teachers. In some way they gave voice to the
thousands of people who have died while receiving care on the Palliative
Care Unit at St. Paul's Hospital; and*

To Nancy, my sister.

Contents

Acknowledgments

A ten-year project requires many acknowledgments. Words don't do justice to the gratitude I feel to a large number of people who have supported my work, professionally and personally, over the past decade. All are important for different reasons.

Above all others, I thank the people who participated in the study on which the themes of this book are based. I dedicate this work to them. I thank them for their time, their words, their insights which helped me to understand what it means to face death and to embrace living.

I am grateful for the sponsorship of the research and the writing of the book provided by St. Paul's Hospital, Providence Health Care and the Department of Family Practice, Faculty of Medicine, University of British Columbia. In that context, I especially thank Jim Thorsteinson, Head, Department of Family and Community Medicine at St. Paul's Hospital, who for many years listened, encouraged, and helped to create the space for me to be able to complete the work. Robert Woollard, Head, Department of Family Practice at the University of

British Columbia, has also believed in the value of this work doing all he could to make certain that it was completed.

I thank George Soros. Without his vision and commitment to changing the culture of death and dying, this research project would not have happened. I will be forever grateful to him for his gift to me through the Soros Faculty Scholar Program, Project on Death in America (PDIA). Thanks to Geri Frager, a friend since we met in medical school, who informed me about PDIA and provided moral support throughout the project. Thank you to Balfour Mount and Robin Cohen who served as mentors for the project. Cohen provided valuable insights to the design and work of the research; Mount not only provided emotional encouragement through the difficult times of the project, but has over the years had a strong influence on my work in caring for people at the end of life. Thank you to Kathy Foley, as the leader of the Project on Death in America, for supporting the research as well as the concept and effort in writing this book. Thanks to PDIA Board Member Patricia Prem for the personal interest and quiet assurance that this work had value. And thanks to other Faculty Scholars who have been particularly supportive, Harvey Chochinov (especially for the strong recommendation to pursue a Ph.D.), Frank Ferris, Joseph Fins, Diane Meier, Daniel Sulmasy, and Charles von Gunten. Thanks to Mary Callaway for her belief in this project, her encouraging words, and her supportive emails.

I thank Marv Westwood, the supervisor of my doctoral program for listening and for teaching me how to listen, for being a mentor and a role model, for guiding me through a great program, for reading the manuscript so often he could likely recite parts of it, and for being a healing source of strength in my life. I also thank the other members of my supervisory committee: Carol Herbert, Bill McKellin, and Terry Anderson, each of whom provided support in a unique fashion. I thank Joan Anderson for the hours of consultation, for teaching me about the reality of qualitative research, and for challenging me to trust my understanding of bearing witness to the experiences of people who were living with dying. I thank Rhodri Windsor Liscombe for believing in the inherent value of this research project, as well as in its value as the basis of an interdisciplinary doctoral program.

I thank my colleagues at St. Paul's Hospital: Jacqueline Fraser for the years of working together to translate a vision into reality, for listening to me talk about this project for years, and for believing that it would happen long before it was started; Millie Cumming, Daphne Lobb, and Fraser Black for doing some of my clinical work and for being on call so I could do the research. Thank you also for referring the patients to the research project. Thank you to Pamela Miller for assuming some of my administrative responsibilities so I could complete the research and do the writing. Thanks to the Palliative Care Team at St. Paul's Hospital who provided care for the people in this study as well as thousands of other people at the end of life.

I thank other colleagues at St. Paul's Hospital: Warren Murschell who invited me to join him, the Sisters of Providence, and others in designing and developing the Palliative Care Program at St. Paul's Hospital; Betty Calam for our many conversations; Bill Irvine for the encouragement given to me since I was a resident in Family Practice; Jack da Silva for being a supportive colleague and friend; and Eva Knell for promoting the work that follows a study such as this. I extend a special expression of gratitude to Jean Kozoway who transcribed most of the interviews. Also, thank you to Adrian Westwood for doing a portion of the typing. Thanks to Diane Doyle for believing this book would happen by buying the first copy even before I had an agent.

I thank Paddy Rodney and Michael Burgess for counsel regarding ethical principles relevant to this work.

Thanks to Patricia Wilenski for providing insights, myths, poems, friendship, and a lot of encouragement. Thanks to Dianne Westwood for a treasured copy of *Collected Poems* by T.S. Eliot as well as for honest feedback, broadened perspectives, and multiple reviews of the same chapters. Thanks to the many family and friends who helped me make the transition from writing my dissertation to writing for the general public: Rod Andrew; my parents, Dave and Kate Kuhl; Alison, Bev, and Carl Pauls; Hilary Pearson; Eleanor McIntyre; and Don and Mary Renaud. Thanks to David Williams for asking questions and sharing his insights regarding the content. Thanks to Ray deVries for helping me make connections that were important to this work and to Murray Hastings for his immediate and friendly response whenever my computer needed help.

A unique thank you to the members of a rock band, Roadkill, for tolerating my inexperience as a singer. The times to "express" myself with the band provided a wonderful balance to the intensity of the work I was doing in my day job. (And I know it's a good idea to keep my day job!)

I thank the people of St. Jude Resources: Mike Terrell who was very generous with regard to time and office space, Mary Jane Hamula for assistance with computer problems, and Larry Brock for sharing his stories and humor.

I thank the librarians at the Library of the British Columbia College of Physicians and Surgeons who consistently and with a pleasant manner provided a great deal of reading material for this project, and the administrative secretaries at Delta Hospital who ensured that I received the material in a timely fashion.

Thanks to Gabor Maté for suggesting that I write a book regarding the research project. Thanks to Denise Bukowski, my literary agent, who recognized the concept of the book as important to the well-being of those who would some day know they were living with a terminal illness; thanks to Meg Taylor, senior editor at Doubleday Canada who accepted the proposal the day before she started her job with Doubleday and who gently added her skills to improving the text; thanks to Lisa Kaufman, marketing director and editor at Public-

Affairs, who understood what this work was all about from the first moment we talked about it and who challenged me to write and rewrite as though I was talking to someone with a terminal illness in my living room. Thanks to Ann-Marie Metton for her work on the references and permissions.

Thanks to my family for teaching me in a new way that the real value in family meetings happens when people speak from the heart. Thanks to Ray, Darcy, Denise, Cory, and Carolyn for understanding my relationship with Nancy and for giving me permission to write about that relationship in the midst of their grief about her death.

I conclude by thanking Jean, Jennifer, and Sarah for their love, their patience, and their presence—Jean who shares my journey like no other, who believes in this work from the core of her being, and who spent many hours making corrections before the manuscript was submitted for editing; and to Jennifer and Sarah who embrace life in their songs, in their laughter, in their dancing, and in their hope.

Introduction

Facing Death

Talking about dying is very difficult. We are afraid that talking about death beckons it. We all know death is inevitable; death fascinates and disturbs us; but we don't want it to happen. Maybe, we think, if we don't talk about death, death might not notice us. Maybe if we ignore death, we might delay or even elude it.

For more than fifteen years I have worked, as a doctor, with people who were dying. They taught me many things—for example, that I didn't know how to talk to them about dying. And peculiar as it may seem, they taught me a lot about living.

Ten years ago, I sat next to a dying woman and wondered about the pain she was experiencing. Her name was Alice. She had cancer. She had been on the palliative care unit of St. Paul's Hospital in Vancouver for a considerable amount of time, and I felt that I knew her well. Every day I went in to hear her report of the nagging pain in her chest. It was no surprise that she had such pain, for she had lung cancer—inoperable, untreatable lung cancer. But very often we could control patients' pain with medication. Alice's pain seemed not to respond to anything we tried. I experienced a growing sense of frustration and an increasing wish to avoid witnessing her pain. Her anguish was so real, so apparent in her eyes and in the tone of her voice. I didn't want to give in to the sense of emerging incompetence I felt about not being able to help her. Alice was facing death, and I was facing a sense of failure.

Team members asked, "Isn't there anything else we can do—increase her medication, add another drug, call in the music therapist, pastoral care, or perhaps physiotherapy?" The team had cared for many other people with lung cancer. Those people were testimony to the fact that cancer pain could be controlled, shortness of breath usually managed. Logically, we could only assume that Alice's pain was just like that of the other patients, and yet its effect on her was very different. This seemed to be a rare case of pain that could not be controlled. What were we missing? What was different about Alice? What was I to do? How could I understand and treat this woman's pain in a way that could free her of it or at least reduce her suffering?

With a sense of desperation, I entered her room one more time. Her grimace told me that she was still in terrible pain. I decided to ask a question I had never asked a patient before. Holding Alice's hand, I said, "We haven't been too successful in decreasing your pain. I wonder whether it's possible that the pain in your chest isn't a pain that's coming from the cancer. I have a sense that it is a pain in your heart, one I can't touch." Her eyes told me I had said something that rang true for her. She said, "Yes, the pain is in my heart. It has to do with my daughter, Ruth. She is marrying a man I do not approve of, and I told her so. My daughter, my only child, did not want to hear that message. I had to tell her because by the time she realizes that he's no good for her, I will no longer be alive. I don't expect ever to be free of this pain, and what's more, unless circumstances change for Ruth, I don't want this pain to be taken away." As we talked, it became clear that she was relieved to finally be speaking with someone about her "real" pain.

Caring for Alice resulted in an "Aha!" for me. As soon as she responded to my question, I knew that unless the situation changed between her and her daughter, Alice would die suffering the loss of relationship with her only child. There were no medications for the anguish she was feeling. It was preposterous to think that I could affect the pain that had resulted from a broken relationship between a mother and her daughter.

Alice, like others before her and many since, taught me that dying is more than just a physical event. It is a process that includes one's whole being—physical, psychological, and spiritual. But Alice's situation in particular resulted in a new insight for me, namely, that I was ill-equipped as a palliative care physician to address or understand what psychological and spiritual pain was all about. Medical school and residency training had not prepared me to meet that challenge. The best I could do was acknowledge that her pain experience was beyond my skill and training at that time. Why had it been so difficult for me to ask Alice about the "pain in her heart"? Why had it taken me so long to recognize the complexity of her pain? We actually experienced similar emotions (similar in kind but not in degree): her sense of failure as a mother, my sense of failure as a palliative care physician; her anxiety about dying, my anxiety about being incompetent. We also shared a deep sense of relief that the unspeakable had finally been spoken.

Alice also taught me that dying is hard work and that for the most part dying includes suffering, some of which may never be resolved. Interestingly, my grandfather said the same thing. He spent the last days of his life in an extended care facility. It was there that he said, "Dying is hard work—not the physical part, but that part which is the inside of me, the work about who I am, who I have been, and who I will be." Dying presents a challenge we would rather avoid or ignore.

Alice longed for a peaceful death, a time of serenity and completeness. At times, she did appear to experience the peace she longed for.

There were also times of grief, anger, and sadness. People who are dying experience all the emotions people feel through the course of a lifetime. As much as they might know fear, loneliness, guilt, shame, and despair, they can also experience hope, joy, and intimacy. Dying is not void of the painful emotion we experience in living. At the same time, dying, like living, presents opportunity for personal growth and development. Dying involves choice. And for some people, the moment of realizing that death is inevitable, that their time is limited, marks the beginning of a new way of being. People generally die as they have lived. They can choose to embrace a particular event, or exist passively as though the inevitable—in this case death—is avoidable.

Is the experience of dying any different from that of living? Living is hard work, and for most people life includes suffering. Living presents challenges many would rather avoid or ignore. Living, like dying, includes choice.

As a physician, I have worked to control people's pain and to decrease their suffering. For some people, suffering includes depression and/or anxiety, both of which can often be treated with appropriate medication like antidepressants and antianxiety medication. Often I feel some relief if my patients' suffering is diagnosed in this way, because I know I can prescribe something that will diminish the intensity of their suffering. But there are no medications for loneliness, grief, fear, and despair. How do I respond to the suffering that results from those emotions?

Alice raised my level of awareness. What I learned from her made me think and feel differently about "whole-person care." I started to ask different questions. How could I begin more effectively to address the spiritual and psychological pain and suffering of the people I met in my practice every day? How could I address it if I didn't even understand it? What would it be like to know that I would die within hours, days, weeks, months, or even in a year or two? If my doctor told me I had a terminal illness, would I live differently? If I had a "true" understanding of the experience of living with a terminal illness as conveyed to me by my patients, would I practice medicine differently? Are we transformed once we have been told we are going to die? Do we see our relationships from a different perspective? Does our understanding of God influence us during that time? Who could and would answer these questions?

Only people with a terminal illness know what it is like to live with such an illness. They are the people who hold the knowledge, who know the lived experience of having a terminal illness. They are our best teachers. They are the ones who could answer my questions. How might they be heard and understood? How could I learn to listen, to really listen to what people were saying rather than to listen for the information I wanted to hear?

Before Alice, when I saw patients in pain I focused primarily on the *physical* components of pain. Many times I felt that I was doing the work of a detective, finding the cause of the pain and working to understand its every detail. I worked to identify the disease, ordering tests and prescribing appropriate medications or treatments to stop or reverse the disease process and enhance the quality of life. I had a vague sense that there must be more to what my patients were experiencing, but I was not certain how to address it. I wonder now whether my patients, during the course of my questioning, ever felt interrogated. I rarely asked questions about the impact of the disease on their life, their hopes and dreams, their relationships with others, or their belief system. Practically speaking, I wasn't even sure how I *could* ask those questions in the very limited amount of time I had during a scheduled appointment. But more important, what would I do with the answers?

In order to understand what it meant to live with a terminal illness such as cancer or AIDS, I decided to research the following question: What is the lived experience of knowing you have a terminal illness?

What is it like to get up every day knowing that the disease within you will likely cause your death? The methodology I used was that of existential phenomenology. What does that mean? It means that I had to stop being a detective. I had to learn to listen, not only with my ears but with my heart as well. I had to set aside biases, to stop seeking to predict, explain, or control the disease's progression. I had to suspend judgment and hear the testimony, to bear witness to the experience of living and dying with a terminal illness.

Personally, that was a difficult process. In addition to the type of judging we do almost automatically in many of our relationships and encounters every day, my training as a physician had taught me that my job was to judge, in the name of assessment, what was happening with regard to the disease process for which the patient was seeking my professional expertise. Now I had to relearn how to "be with" another person, how to hear what was *really* being said. This was something I could not learn on my own, and I realized that I needed additional training in listening and in understanding the psychological and spiritual experiences of the people I knew as patients.

Six years after meeting Alice, I enrolled in an interdisciplinary doctoral program to study the spiritual and psychological issues at the end of life as experienced and described by people who knew they had a terminal illness. This was supported through the Soros Faculty Scholar Program's Project on Death in America, based in New York, St. Paul's Hospital in Vancouver, and the University of British Columbia.

One of the first courses I took was an undergraduate course in counseling psychology. Its purpose was to develop skills in communication, primarily in listening. My grade in the first portion of that course was poor. The professor kept reminding me that I was very good at asking questions (being a detective) and equally limited in my ability to listen (bearing witness) to the real message that the speaker was attempting to get me to understand. The set of skills I needed to bear witness was very different from the skill set required to be a detective.

That course marked the beginning of the development of new skills that changed my understanding of what an effective doctor-patient relationship is. I learned to see a person experiencing an illness, rather than a patient in some stage of a disease process. In time, I would be able to combine the skills of being a witness with those of being a detective, but while exploring the spiritual and psychological issues at the end of life I made being a witness a priority. I had to focus on the personal experience of those who were living with an illness that would eventually result in death. I had to respect that whatever those people were saying was *their* truth, *their* reality, *their* experience of living with a terminal illness. They were, indeed, living with dying. This was the basis of my research project, and it is the primary theme of this book.

More important than any of the courses I took was the time I spent with people living with a terminal illness. They had learned from their doctors that their disease could not be cured. They had been told that the disease within them would likely cause their death, that they had less than a year to live. As a physician, I had been at the bedside of hundreds of people who were dying, some in my presence, others who would die in their own time—that is, in minutes, hours, days, weeks, or months. I had many impressions of what that experience was like. Now I wanted to confirm or dispel those impressions by hearing and observing the words, the descriptions, the direct experiences of individuals with cancer or AIDS. I wanted to understand the complexities of the physical, psychological, and spiritual components of knowing what it is to live with a terminal illness.

Before I became a physician I had the opportunity in the early 1980s to be with two people who were dying: my roommate and my father-in-law. I will always remember Rob, my roommate, for his generosity, his humor, and his pain. I benefited from his generosity when I moved from Winnipeg, Manitoba, to Halifax, Nova Scotia, after completing my undergraduate degree in sociology. I had been assured of a job in Halifax before moving there and learned upon my arrival that the job had been given to someone else. I met Rob through some friends. His roommate had just moved out. He invited me to join him, adding that he would absorb the rent until I found a job. I experienced his humor every day as I looked for work and then as we became good friends.

And I witnessed his pain after he was diagnosed with cancer. If I had known in 1980 what I know now, I would have spent more time with Rob, talking about his fears, his sense of failure in not being able to hold on to the belief that his cancer was curable, his confusion about the injustice he felt about being so young and terminally ill, his anger toward his friends who didn't want to hear his truth, his questioning who and where God was in all his pain and suffering. I would have been silent with him, and laughed even more with him, because he was one of the funniest people I have ever known. I would have held him when he felt so alone with his questions, his pain, his losses, his shattered dreams. Rob was one of the reasons I chose to work in palliative care.

In the case of my father-in-law, my wife and I would not have left his room the last night of his life just because the hospital staff told us to go home. The change in his breathing pattern was such that they must have known that he was dying. We left without saying the goodbye we would have said, without speaking the truths we would have spoken. We were not there to hold his hand even in his unconsciousness. That time was so precious, but the opportunity to complete our relationship evaded us because we didn't know what to do or to say—other than to believe the doctors and nurses. That was such a frightening time; death was so close, and we didn't understand what was going on.

The time of dying is a frightening time. We fear death. We have a sense of anxiety and panic that life is beyond our control, passing us by. We are awkward in speaking our truth, just as we have been awkward in speaking the truth to each other before the dying process started. For my wife and I, it seemed at the time that silence might be more appropriate than conversation. We could speak later. But later never comes. Death comes and, with it, silence, a permanent, implacable type of silence. Oh, for just one more hour, five more minutes! But silence fills the space. Questions go unanswered, feelings of love and affection are never expressed, never shared.

Grief sets in. My wife and I deeply regret not having had more conversations, direct and intimate conversations, with my father-in-law. The missed opportunity seems so final, so sad, so irreversible. Twenty years later, that sense of incompleteness lingers in our memories and causes my wife considerable pain. She still longs to bring the death of her father to a better resolution, a more dignified closure, a farewell that would honor who he was in her life.

How might the last days of my father-in-law's life have ended differently? What might the nurses or the doctors have said to us, rather than suggesting we go home? What might a conversation at the end of a loved one's life be like? I wish I had known then what I know now about the process of dying. I wish someone had talked to us about dying and living, about being present at his bedside even when he could no longer communicate. The most important thing I know now that I didn't know then is this: *People who are dying are still living.* This simple insight is my primary message.

The purpose of this book is to provide a guide for people who have a terminal illness, who know someone who has a terminal illness, or who choose to enhance their understanding of the dying process. It will provide:

- direction in speaking the truth
    before your own death
    with family members and close friends who are dying

- ways of encouraging another person to speak their truth
- methods for listening when someone is speaking their truth
- information to enhance your understanding of the doctor-patient relationship
- how to speak about difficult subjects
- how to ask questions pertaining to your illness or that of a friend or family member
- what to consider in making decisions regarding treatment, care plans, and end-of-life issues
- how pain is assessed and treated
- methods for exploring personal psychological issues and concerns
- a process by which you will be able to review your life—and leave a legacy of your story for others—if you choose to do so
- examples of the experiences of others who lived with a terminal illness
- the means by which you can do some of the work (unfinished business) that needs to get done before you or someone close to you dies

This book is based on stories, the stories of people who knew they were dying. By confiding in me, some of them experienced healing, and others realized the extent of their despair. As Clarissa Pinkola Estés, an international scholar and a psychoanalyst, says of stories, "A story is not just a story. In its most innate and proper sense, it is someone's life. It is the numen of their life and their first-hand familiarity with the stories they carry that makes the story 'medicine' . . . a medicine which strengthens and arights the individual and the community."

These stories are combined with my personal experience of being with friends and family members at the end of their lives; my education in medicine, counseling psychology, and theology; my clinical experience as a palliative care physician; and my research experience of bearing witness to those who told me what it was like to live with the knowledge that they would very likely die from the disease they had. From these people I wanted to hear about the experience of living with a terminal illness, particularly the spiritual and psychological issues at the end of life. I wanted to hear from people who were willing to speak openly about their experience and to have them confirm, modify, or reject the themes I identified in the stories they told me. I listened to their stories, recorded our conversations, transcribed the tapes, identified themes, and checked back with them so they could confirm that what I had heard and identified was accurate. In some instances I had not heard or understood them correctly. In that case, I would either correct or exclude the information. I sought to integrate what I heard from them into a book for people who have a terminal illness or who are caring for someone who does, a book that offers insight and understanding as well as approaches, strategies, and actions for facing death—and thus for embracing life.

The people who agreed to speak to me about their experience of living with a terminal illness had been diagnosed with either cancer or AIDS. They knew what it meant to be dating, married, partnered, separated, divorced, widowed. Some were gay, some straight. Some of them were childless, others had children; some adopted children, some were themselves adopted, and some had grandchildren. Their ages ranged from the mid-twenties to the mid-eighties. They were teachers and students, blue-collar workers, businesspersons, health care providers, government employees, and retirees. They were both rich and poor. Some lived on welfare, and others were able to do anything they pleased financially. They spoke of their roles as parents, as children, as employees, as friends. A few of them spoke of being spouses or lovers. They described their favorite times, their painful times, their favorite places and fondest memories.

What did they want others to know about their experience? For the most part, they wanted to be heard and to be understood simply for who they were in the world—in their families, in their work, in their pain, in their isolation, in their grief, suffering, and hope. In this book, you will find the words and stories of people who knew they would die before too long. Their emotions, concerns, and experiences are described in their own words. Their words are quoted at length, their identities disguised. In some instances I have combined the experiences of several people; in others I have divided the varied experiences of an individual.

I learned from these people by spending time in their homes. Many of the interviews lasted for an hour or more. I visited many of them numerous times over several months. A few were interviewed in the hospital. I wanted to hear whatever it was they wanted to tell me about their experience. Although I had specific topics to raise in case they could not be spontaneous in telling their stories, I rarely asked questions. The people simply wanted to tell their stories, to relate to someone about living with dying. And as I interviewed them, their descriptions of their experiences all seemed to focus around nine concerns or themes:

- their changing perceptions of time, what it means, and how to spend it
- the suffering that resulted from the experience of hearing their terminal diagnosis for the first time and the need to communicate effectively with health care professionals
- physical pain, its reality, and its effect on who they were
- the importance of being touched and being in touch
- the natural process of reviewing one's life (looking back) once one understands that dying is a reality
- speaking and hearing truth

- longing to belong, that is, to understand who they were, in the past with regard to their original families, as well as in the present with regard to their chosen (adult) family
- asking the question Who am I? in the search to know who they were in the present, free of the expectations of others
- experiencing transcendence—meaning, value, God, spirituality, a higher being greater than oneself

Each of these themes forms the core of a chapter in this book. The first half of the book (chapters 1–4) includes stories about the experience of having a terminal illness and of dealing with it on a practical level. The second half (chapters 5–9) pertains to the psychological and spiritual experience of that journey.

The people who participated in this study did so with the hope and expectation that the lessons I learned from them would be passed on to others who had a terminal illness, to the families and friends of others who had a terminal illness, and to those who give care to terminally ill people as professionals and as volunteers. They hoped that by speaking about their experience they could make a difference in society and that the suffering of others in a similar situation might be reduced, eliminated, or given new meaning. Specifically, they wanted the information they offered to contribute to changes in the care that doctors and nurses provide to people who are dying. They believed that their truth could serve as a key to unlock the knowledge, compassion, and commitment needed to provide a more comprehensive method of caring for people at the end of life. They longed for others to know about them: the difficulties they experienced in being taken seriously by doctors and other health care providers; the uncomfortable memories that surfaced during the last period of their lives and the truths that had never been spoken; their legacy in terms of children, work, students; and their sense that spiritual strength was increasing as their physical body weakened.

It is because of their courage and their deep desire and commitment to contribute to change that I felt compelled to write this book. In fact, many of them asked me to do exactly that. I do so as a conduit, a messenger, a bearer of information that at some time or another will be relevant to each of us. I have taken their stories to heart. Their truth must be spoken. It is a truth about their reality, their closeness to death, their desire to be fully alive, to be healed in their psychological and spiritual wounds if not cured of their physical disease. Their stories mean you don't have to be alone in your experience of dying or of living. For in our aloneness we are broken, and in our standing with others we cannot be broken, as is described in this story by Clarissa Pinkola Estés:

One Stick, Two Stick: The Way of the Old African Kings

An old man is dying. He calls his people to his side. He gives a short, sturdy stick to each of his many offspring, wives and relatives. "Break the stick," he instructs them. With some effort, they all snap their sticks in half.

"This is how it is when a soul is alone and without anyone. They can be easily broken."

The old man next gives each of his kin another stick, and says, "This is how I would like you to live after I pass. Tie your sticks together in bundles of twos and threes." He waits quietly as his family ties the sticks together. There are many bundles, some of two sticks, some of three sticks. "Now, break these bundles in half."

No one can break the sticks when there are two or more in a bundle. The old man smiles. "We are strong when we stand with another soul. When we are with others, we cannot be broken."

In this book, the stories of my "teachers," my "coresearchers," as I call them—people who knew they were dying—are combined with other stories from wisdom literature, folktales, myths, and religious traditions. In addition, each chapter includes what I call "practical wisdom," which consists of ideas, strategies, and methods for making use of the information and evidence these dying people provided. It is my hope that in reading the stories and in integrating the practical wisdom healing can occur for you.

✺ ✺ ✺ ✺

CHAPTER ONE

Time and Anxiety

A lot of people want time.

Brent

As time is the most valuable thing we have, because it is the most irrevocable, the thought of any lost time troubles us whenever we look back. Time lost is time in which we have failed to live a full human life, gain experience, learn, create, enjoy, and suffer; it is time that has not been filled up, but left empty.

Dietrich Bonhoeffer

Time is constantly in us and around us; nevertheless, we cannot grasp it.

Kurt R. Eissler

Gilgamesh and the Tree of Life

Young Gilgamesh and his friend Enkidu fought many hard battles against monsters and demons, and always returned victorious. But Enkidu incurred the wrath of the great goddess Ishtar, who persuaded the other gods that Enkidu must die. When Gilgamesh found out about the unexpected and unfair death of this bravest and most beloved of comrades, the hero mourned deeply. He mourned not only because he missed his friend, but also because Enkidu's death reminded him that he too was mortal and would one day die.

Being a hero, Gilgamesh could not sit about pondering the ultimate fate of humanity. He decided to go in search of immortality. He knew that his ancestor, Utnapishtim, the survivor of the Great Flood sent by the gods to punish humankind, was the only earthly creature ever to have achieved immortality. He was determined to find this man and learn from him the secrets of life and death.

At the outset of his journey, he came to the foot of a great range of mountains guarded by a scorpion-man and his wife. The scorpion-man told Gilgamesh that no mortal had ever crossed the mountains and braved their dangers. But Gilgamesh told him the purpose of his quest, and the scorpion-man, full of admiration, let the hero pass. Gilgamesh traveled for twelve leagues in darkness and eventually, arrived at the abode of the sun-god. The sun-god warned the hero that his quest was in vain, but Gilgamesh would not be dissuaded and went on his way.

At last, he arrived at the shores of the sea of the waters of death. There he met a guardian, a woman with a jug of ale, who, like the scorpion-man and the sun-god, endeavored to dissuade him from his quest. The ale-woman reminded him that life was to be enjoyed:

> Gilgamesh, where do you wander?
> You shall not find what you seek.
> When the gods created human beings,
> Death is what they allotted to mortals,

Retaining the secret of life in their own hands.
Let your belly be full, Gilgamesh,
And make a feast of rejoicing each day.
Day and night, dance and play.
Bathe yourself, and pay heed to the child who holds your hand,
And let your wife delight in you.
For this is the task of humankind.

But Gilgamesh could not forget Enkidu or his own eventual demise. He pushed on to the end of his perilous journey. By the shore he met the ancient boatman who had been the steersman of Utnapishtim's boat when the Great Flood destroyed most of the world, and he commanded this old man to ferry him across the waters of death. But the boatman told him to make a boat himself and never to touch a drop of the waters of death as he rowed across the sea. Gilgamesh did as he was instructed and, finally, arrived on an island where dwelt the survivor of the Great Flood.

But Utnapishtim only repeated what all the others had told the hero: the gods have declared immortality for themselves and have assigned death as the lot of humankind. Gilgamesh, abandoning hope at last, prepared to depart. But Utnapishtim took pity on him and told him of a secret Tree that grew at the bottom of the sea, which had the power to make the old young again. Gilgamesh rowed out to the middle of the sea, dived into the waters of death and found the Tree, bringing a branch back to his boat. He crossed safely to land again and began to make his way home with his treasure concealed in a sack. On his way home, he stopped by a pool to bathe and change his clothes. But a serpent, creeping near, smelled the heavenly scent of the Tree of Immortality and carried the branch off and ate the leaves. This is why the serpent is able to renew itself by shedding its skin.

Gilgamesh the hero knelt down by the pool, put his face in his hands and wept. He understood now that what he had been told was true: even the mightiest and most courageous of heroes is human and must learn to live with joy in the moment and acceptance of the inevitable end.

※

Time is. Time never stops. But we live our lives as though we will endure forever and, like Gilgamesh, believe on some level that we are immortal. Gilgamesh witnessed Enkidu's death and yet denied his own mortality. He saw his closest friend die yet imagined that he could escape human destiny. Like young men going to war, he believed that only those beside him would be killed and that he would be spared.

The *Mahabharata*, the great Indian epic, asks this question: What is the most wondrous thing in the world? The response is that people growing old and dying can be seen all around us yet we think it will not happen to us. Death happens only to others, those who are older, those of our parents' generations, those who are sick, our neighbors—but not to us. We have time to spend, time to spare, time to procrastinate, time to waste.

Sixty seconds in a minute, sixty minutes in an hour, twenty-four hours in a day, seven days in a week—this is *chronus*, the chronological marking of time. It is the same for each of us, day after day, season after season, year after year, generation after generation. *Chronus* is linear time. But there is also personal time, psychological time, the experience of life—this is *kairos*, time noted for its dimension of depth. When asked to define time, Augustine responded, "If no one asks me, I know; if I want to explain it to a questioner, I do not know."

The moment someone is told that their illness will likely result in death, time changes. Paradoxically, for a period time stops. Some may hear the message when they are feeling well, unaware of the disease process advancing within their body. Others may actually welcome the information in some strange way because it gives legitimacy to their experience of the previous days, weeks, and months. It helps to make sense of the fatigue, the pain, and the other symptoms that initially infringe on, then intrude on, and eventually seem to invade their lives. Some people deny those symptoms initially; others deny them indefinitely. Some people recognize that the symptoms mark the beginning of the end and that their time is limited—that they are running out of time. You may feel that way, especially if you have already been told that you have a terminal illness, that you only have a certain amount of time remaining.

As much as the diagnosis of a terminal illness marks the end, it also serves as a beginning—an opportunity to ask what the time remaining in your life means to you. *How important is the present, how important is now? What am I able to do and say in the time and with the energy that remains in my lifetime?*

Although you likely picked up this book because you already know that you have a terminal illness, imagine for a moment that you have not yet received that information. You have been experiencing pain in one area of your body and made a recent visit to the doctor, who ran some tests. You are scheduled to see her today to discuss the test results. If you have recently been given the diagnosis of a terminal illness, you can skip this story or compare it to your own experience:

You wake up this morning and go about your usual morning routine. You go down to the kitchen and make coffee, then stand at the window, looking out at the morning sunrise. You remember the adage—"Red sky in the morning, sailors take warning"—something your grandfather used to say to you when you spent your summer holidays on the East Coast. Is it a memory or a premonition?

You go upstairs to shower. The water is particularly refreshing, the scents of the shampoo and soap unusually intense. The towel feels soft today, even over the painful area—the reason you went to see your doctor a week ago. You hope you didn't wait too long to make that appointment. Even after you phoned, you had to wait six days for an appointment. She would likely have seen you sooner if you had expressed concern, but you didn't want to make a big deal of it. She's busy, too, her time important. You wrap the towel around yourself and begin combing your hair. You avoid looking in the mirror for fear of the message you might see. You have the same apprehension about stepping onto the bathroom scale. You substitute the towel for a bathrobe.

Walking back to the kitchen, you notice that the pain seems to be less severe than it was a week ago. Perhaps it was just your imagination. Perhaps you could have avoided the doctor's visit altogether. The smell of coffee invites you to read the paper. Usually this is your favorite time of day—really, your only time to be alone in the house. But today it is strangely quiet, and you are too alone. You place the newspaper on the kitchen table, scan the headlines, and read a few columns. Briefly, you get lost in the scores and stats of yesterday's hockey games. You turn a few pages and try to occupy your mind with the clues for the crossword puzzle in front of you, unable to fill the numbered squares at your usual pace. It's difficult to concentrate. At some level, you are aware of what the day might bring, despite the effort to avoid such thoughts.

Periodically, alarm clocks go off throughout the house; one sounds like a rooster, another plays a tune, a third, a powerful buzzer, seems loud enough to rouse the neighbors. The alarms are set to wake the other members of your household; they'll fight for their turn in the bathroom and prepare for the day. The musical alarm sounds every five minutes, as your teenage son keeps hitting the snooze button for that extra few minutes of sleep, that sense of suspension in time, the time between being asleep and becoming wakeful, the time that precedes responsibilities. Eventually everyone is up and dressed. Your youngest daughter talks a lot at the breakfast table. She's excited about the day's activities—school, friends, soccer, dance lessons. It's a welcome diversion from your thoughts. The other family members eat in their usual silence. You and your spouse review appointments, kids' activities, and other responsibilities. Then the kids are off to school, adults off to work—everyone is on time today.

The morning at work is uneventful—meetings, projects, telephone calls. Just before lunch, your work is set aside for your doctor's appointment. You are reminded again that this is test-result day. Since undergoing the tests, you have vacillated between ignoring and dreading the possible diagnosis. Arriving a few minutes early, you sit in the waiting room, next to a woman with a newborn. A toddler plays with the toys in the children's corner. While you wait, you leaf through one of the magazines on the table beside you. You see the words but don't really take them in.

The receptionist calls your name once, twice, then you hear her. She shows you to your room and says the doctor will be with you shortly. Still waiting, you look at the pictures on the wall—a Norman Rockwell painting, a nutrition guide, a poster about the dangers of smoking. Your doctor knocks lightly on the door and walks in. After a warm greeting and a very brief exchange about your families, she says, "I have some information for you today, which is difficult for me to share with you. I have received the results of the tests we ordered last week. I am sorry to have to tell you that you have cancer."

Time stops. Instantly, you are emotionally numb and frozen in thought; you don't hear, you don't feel. The doctor's lips are moving, but you don't hear what she is saying. Later, you look at a piece of paper the doctor handed you. It contains the diagnosis and another appointment time. You don't remember the conversation. From the moment you hear the word "cancer," something inside changes. Despite the wish to wind back the clock or to keep hitting the snooze button, it can't be done; time is irreversible. You cannot go back to the breakfast table to start the day again, you cannot go back to change other events or recapture moments of the past.

A sense of ambivalence begins to set in, characterized by two questions: *Do I embrace living, or do I prepare to die? Surely, there must be something that can be done to reverse the disease process. My doctor is wrong, they mixed up the specimens at the lab, somehow my name got mixed up, it's not me.* As much as you dread the diagnosis, you know on some level that it's true. The doctor's message that you have cancer will have a profound effect on you and on your family.

You stop at home before returning to the office. Again, you make a cup of coffee and sit at your spot at the table. While the silence and your aloneness were apparent this morning, now they scream at you. The reality of death, of mortality, interrupts your thoughts for the first time. Like a dog emerging from a swim, working to shake the water from his coat, you work hard to free yourself from the intruding reality. You wait for your spouse to come home for lunch. You don't remember having ever experienced time such as this. You're waiting for your spouse to come and yet you dread that moment. When shared with your life partner, the news will ascend to a new level of pain. The sound of a car door ends your speculation of what the next minutes will bring. Waiting ends, at least for the moment.

Waiting

In the context of our lives we often wait. We may even forget to appreciate the present because we are waiting for some event in the future. We tolerate the mundane features of our work in anticipation of a vacation months away, the cramped space of a small apartment in the hope of more space in the future, or the inconvenience of a long-distance relationship with the hope of living together in due course. The experience of living with a terminal illness includes a great deal of waiting.

Consider the waiting that characterized the experience of my coresearchers, that is, the people who participated in the study.

First, you wait to see the doctor:

I had a shower one afternoon in the summer. One side of my bath-room is all mirror. As I dried myself, I noticed the left groin area was full and the right looked normal. I put my hand on the protuberance in my left groin. It seemed to be the size of a large egg. I was alarmed. I tried moving my leg in several different positions and decided that indeed I did have the lump there. I felt panic and fear. It was Friday afternoon—everything happens just before the weekend, just when you can't do anything about it. Monday was a holiday, I wouldn't be able to see my doctor until Tuesday.

Next, you wait for the disease to progress:

They did two needle biopsies, both of which were clean so my doctor said, "Well, we'll just watch it for awhile." It continued to grow, so finally he said, "I think you'd better see a surgeon." I was on my way to see the surgeon within a week. The surgeon examined me and said, "What we're going to do is watch this." He measured the lump. I saw him every three or four weeks. I kept saying, "Let's find out what it is." I guess he didn't feel there was any urgency because I had a negative result from the needle biopsy. Finally he said, "I'd better have a look at this." He did a surgical biopsy. It was negative. He said, "We'll just keep watching it." We watched it for three months until the surgeon said, "We'd best have it out, no matter what it is." I went in for surgery and he removed it.

Then you wait for test results:

Waiting for information is probably the biggest drain on your nervous system because you can't do anything. I blame no one. It's just that the situation is that you have to expect to wait, that's all there is to it. Information is very, very important. I have to sit here and wait. I guess perhaps I'm a little impatient, but I don't think that's bad; I think that's a good thing sometimes. Waiting very much adds to people's suffering, and with waiting comes a loss of control.

You wait for the diagnosis:

> After the open biopsy was performed, I waited and waited. They
> sent me down to pathology. I'm waiting some more. Days are click-
> ing by. This is very stressful not only for me but for my family, who
> have essentially given up their vacations to sit in the hospital with
> their son and brother. I got tired of waiting.

You wait for support:

> He gave me the diagnosis, adding, "But don't worry you've got a
> good five years left," patted me on the arm, and walked out of the
> room. He just left me there. He left me alone in the room for two
> hours. He probably thought he was doing the right thing, but to say
> that and then to leave me alone for two hours affected my mind-set.
> I didn't have to live for five more years. I could take my life and just
> call it quits now.

You wait for the right time to speak to someone: Waiting for your
doctor to do rounds even though the visit will only last a few minutes,
you hope that she'll ask the right questions so you can explain how
you really feel; you hope you'll be taken seriously, that you'll be
understood. Waiting for the nurse to bring you the medication for
your pain, your nausea, your shortness of breath. Waiting for someone to speak the unspeakable, to speak of dying, of limited time and
energy, of relationships that are important to you, of the pain you feel
because you have to say goodbye. Waiting for family and friends to
arrive. Then waiting for them to leave. Waiting takes time. To wait is
to suffer.

You wait for suffering to end:

> Right now, mostly I want it to be over, as quickly as possible. The

lack of control, lack of success, lack of energy and completeness—it is intolerable.

You wait for death: Now is the only time available.

Anxiety

When you are waiting for the doctor's appointment, or the diagnosis and prognosis, you are in uncertain circumstances. And with uncertainty you can experience anxiety; the two coexist. James Hollis, a Jungian psychologist, defines anxiety as "a free-floating dis-ease which may be activated by nearly anything, may even light for a while on something specific, but which usually originates from the general insecurity one feels in one's life. The level of that insecurity, the amount of anxiety that may be tapped, is partly a function of one's particular history. The more troubled one's environment, family of origin and cultural setting, the more free-floating anxiety will be generated." Hollis differentiates anxiety from fear, describing fear as being specific, such as the fear of dogs because of being bitten by one as a child, the fear of water because of a near-drowning experience, the fear of heights because of an awareness of the dangers of falling.

It is not surprising that anxiety is part of waiting. You may feel that waiting fills your life with a degree of uncertainty—and so fills your life with anxiety. Ambivalence, that is, the reality of opposites, may add to the anxiety: *Are these symptoms real, or are they a feature of my imagination? Am I sick? Will I ever be well again? Is there medication available for this disease? Will the medication work? Am I living my life, or am I dying? Do I continue working? Do I resign? Do I tell someone how I really feel, or do I contain my anxiety and fear in silence?* The ambivalence is exaggerated if someone has a terminal illness and is taking medication or receiving treatment that *might* reverse the disease process or lead to remission.

For some people, waiting fosters impatience and breeds anxiety.

Anxiety flourishes amid uncertainty. If you are not familiar with this anxiety because you do not have a terminal illness, think back to your childhood when you were learning to swim. At that point, you were most comfortable in the water when you were able to touch the bottom without being in over your head.

The deep end of the pool is a scary place if you are unable to swim to the poolside. Likewise, the deeper part of a lake is frightening, unless you are wearing a lifejacket and are in the company of trusted swimmers or near a boatrail. There is no certainty as to where the bottom might be. If as a beginner you were taken by boat to the deepest part of the lake and dropped off to swim to shore, the uncertain depth of the water below you would likely result in considerable anxiety ("dis-ease"). And if for some reason you were in the middle of an ocean, unable to see the shore, not knowing the depths or what might be swimming in the water beneath you, you would likely be very anxious. If you were able to return to the shallow end of the pool or to the lakeshore, your anxiety would subside and linger only in your memory. The more extreme experience in the ocean, however, might result in a long-lasting fear of water. This type of fear can generally be ignored, although it is likely to recur if you ever find yourself in a similar situation. It can also be confronted. After all, it was not only the distance from the shore, the depth of the water, or the creatures of the sea that resulted in this fear. It was also the inability to swim, the absence of other swimmers, lifejackets, boats, navigation equipment.

This fear can be addressed by learning to swim, by understanding the ocean, by using a buddy system if you ever venture out again. It could include training in navigation on the ocean and education about sea creatures. As you mature in your ability to swim and come to understand what it means to exist in the deep end, so to speak, the uncertainty is diminished, and anxiety decreases. The very place you feared most can even become a welcome challenge as you test your skills. Eventually it might become a place of enjoyment, associated with fond memories of the challenge you met head-on. But that cannot happen without facing the fear.

For many people, learning that they have a terminal illness is akin to the bottom falling out, of being in deep water, uncertain as to how you will get to shore, a shore that is not visible. Anxiety and fear are part of the experience.

Ambivalence

When I began my study, AIDS was regarded as a terminal illness. Every participant who had been diagnosed with AIDS had been informed that they would likely die within six to twelve months. During the study, medications became available that changed the course of the disease. When the AIDS patients took the medication, what's known as the "viral load"—that is, the amount of virus in the body—decreased and the ability of the immune system to fight infections increased. As the prognosis changed from that of being a terminal illness with life expectancy of months to the possibility of being a chronic disease with a life expectancy of years, people's level of ambivalence became more apparent. *Does the disease raise issues of life and/or death, or of quality of life? Are the effects of the medication the same for everyone? Is it in my best interest to see this as a terminal illness or as a chronic disease?* This is similar to the ambivalence experienced by persons with cancer who have been told that the disease they carry usually results in death but that with a new research drug the disease process might be reversed. Do these people prepare to die, or do they embrace living?

Bob had AIDS and was all too familiar with the disease. His partner had died of AIDS. Several of his friends had AIDS, and several of them had died. He lost his hearing in one ear and experienced the usual series of infections associated with the illness.

Bob grew up in Montreal. When he was in his mid-twenties, his sister suggested he join her for a vacation in Vancouver. Bob did exactly that. They were in Vancouver for two weeks. And although it was one of the wettest Novembers on record, there was something about the place that Bob found appealing. He worked for a national bank in Montreal and requested a transfer, which was granted. He never regretted the move.

After living in Vancouver for a few years and developing a strong sense of community, he met Clarence, who became his partner. Even after Clarence's death, Bob spoke of him as his life partner. They were together for six years. It was after meeting Clarence, who was HIV-positive at the time they met, that Bob got tested for HIV and learned that he, too, was HIV-positive.

I met Bob two years after Clarence died. He spoke of the ambivalence that filled his life.

> I look at myself in two ways. The one way is taking the pills, and the other way is not taking them. There's no cure around the corner. What's the point of taking all these pills for another fifteen or twenty years, or however long I'm around, and then having to do my intravenous [IV] medication every day? Cramming all these pills into my body, doing the IV, that just doesn't make sense to me—to have to do all that just to keep living. I'm not going to have the quality of life that I think I should have.

The medication and the IV served as a lifeline for Bob. But because he couldn't skip a day, he also experienced them as a ball and chain. The prognosis, that is the outcome, was unknown and uncertain.

> I don't know what to think, even the doctors don't really know. What should I plan for? Everyone I talk to, my nurse, my doctor, they seem to be confident that I'm going to get sick and die. Well, I don't feel like I'm sick, and because I'm not feeling sick, it makes me

question whether I'm dying. It's really confusing. Maybe if I stopped eating so well it would weaken my system and I'd die quicker. It's just really bizarre to me. When I start thinking about life and some of the good things about life, I get worried. And there's the whole financial thing. I get a certain amount of money each month for ten years. What if I live beyond that point? Then I'll be in the poorhouse; what fun is that? When that money stops coming in, there's no way I'd be able to afford anything on what I make. And all those years lost in contributing to a retirement savings plan. All this stuff comes at you. It's awful. I don't know which is better—life or death.

Before the illness robbed him of the energy to continue, Bob enjoyed his work and his colleagues. They had learned to work well together and to party heartily at the end of the workday. His job had been important to his self-esteem. At times he thought about going back to school to complete his degree.

Last night I was thinking that maybe I should go back to work, and then when I woke up this morning I thought, *Oh god, I don't know if I could*. I'm not doing anything with my life—just hanging out here at home and going to appointments. I get very depressed when I start thinking of how old I am and where other people my age are in their lives, with degrees and decent jobs, raising families. I feel a lot of pressure that I should be doing something for a future I don't even know if I'm going to have. I feel helpless and just so empty. I'm this little person, standing still, and everything else is revolving around me, but I'm not a part of any of it at all. I just feel totally lost and not a part of anything. Sometimes I feel guilt for being a strain on society. I'm costing so many different organizations so much.

When you have a terminal illness, it is difficult to know where you might be on the trajectory of life from birth to death. What are the indications that someone is dying? Is it in the lab results, personal appearance, the doctor's opinion, the amount of energy you have, your dreams and aspirations? It is difficult to know whether to pursue living and life or to prepare for dying and death. As Bob relates, "The lab values pertaining to my immune system improved. On the one hand I'm happy, but on the other hand, I don't know. It makes me feel like I'm fine, and maybe I'll even go back to work. It makes you look at your life on a bigger scale."

Bob also spoke to the ambivalence he experienced:

I feel like I'm going crazy. I have to get out of here. I just really feel the need to go somewhere, anywhere. I want to take a chance and experience something new and different. I want to go and have an adventure in my life instead of sitting around this apartment all day popping pills every few hours. I feel like I'm in a no-win situation and that I've been that way for years. I'm sick of it. While I might be dying, I want to live to the fullest capacity I can. I want to go on an adventure with an open mind, an open spirit, an open heart and just make the best of what I can do. But I'm afraid that I'll get into some kind of trouble without anyone around to help me get through it. I might get mugged in the airport or something like that. I don't feel strong enough to go out and do something for myself because I have this disease. I have to take care of myself. Traveling can take a lot of energy out of you and wear you out while you're there. Then you'll get sick and you won't have anywhere to go. You'll be all alone. It would just be awful.

I don't know how much time I have, and this is something I've been wanting to do since I was in high school. I have a bit of money left; I'm in relatively stable health. My doctor has always told me, "You should go when you're having a stable period because if you wait until you're sick, you won't go." I just want to be at peace with myself. I want to do things and learn, and do as much as I can in the years I have, in the days that I have left.

Death Anxiety

Ours is a time-conscious society. Ours is also a death-denying society. Like Gilgamesh, we search for immortality—in diets, exercise programs, plastic surgery to keep us looking youthful, treatments to cure incurable diseases. Through your experience of having a life-threatening disease, you become aware of death. It is important to continue living, yet death—and your anxiety about it—can no longer be ignored. It is not happening to the world outside you, to others in the community. It is happening to you.

I refer again to the Greek concepts of time: *chronus* and *kairos*—measured time and soulful time. Ken Wilber, a psychologist and author, defines the latter as "narrative time," the time that marks the history of one's own life story or self; the time that carries and re-creates hopes and ideals, plans and ambitions, goals and visions; the subtle time that can speed up or slow down, expand or collapse, transcend or concentrate, according to its interest. This time is marked, in a sense, by the experience of forgetting about measured time. It happens when you are with someone you love and don't realize that hours have passed. It means you are involved in some activity that reflects your true self—a hobby, an interest, and, for some people, their job. It means you are not living up to the expectations of anyone else but rather are simply being you, possessing a renewed awareness of your environment.

Archbishop Desmond Tutu, who won the 1984 Nobel Prize for his role in the antiapartheid movement in South Africa, spoke of his experience. "When you have a potentially terminal disease, it concentrates the mind wonderfully. It gives a new intensity to life. You discover how many things you have taken for granted—the love of your spouse, the Beethoven symphony, the dew on the rose, the laughter on the face of your grandchild."

When we try to live up to the expectations of others—our family of origin, our family of choice, our culture, our memberships, our employers—we compromise our authenticity. In fact, we may be estranged from who we really are and what we would really like to do. This results in anxiety. Perhaps it is the anxiety at the core of all anxiety, that is, the anxiety of *not living the life we would truly like to live.* Certainly, it contributes to death anxiety. In that sense, it would seem that death anxiety is related to life anxiety. *If I am living in a way that is true to myself, would I fear death? And if I fear death, am I really living as I would like to be living? If I lived my life without trying to meet the expectations of anyone else, who would I be, how would I live? If I knew my life were coming to an end within a specific amount of time, how would I live now?* To ask those questions—and to answer them—is to experience both components of time, *chronus* and *kairos.* Bob's life was consumed by such questions. He struggled for the answers. For him, that struggle resulted in ambivalence and anxiety.

Marjorie, a woman who had cancer for ten years and who joined a cancer support group during the latter stage of her illness, spoke of her experience:

When I'm in the support group and somebody new comes in and says, "I know this is going to sound crazy," I know what they're going to say, and that is: "I'm glad I have cancer." I've heard this at least thirty-five times over the years. The reason we say this is because it has turned our lives around, it has made us see what is worth while in life and what is a crock, what is not worth worrying about or being angry about. The first time somebody said this, I felt as though she had poured holy water on me.

In writing about death anxiety, Dr. Irvin Yalom, a psychiatrist working with people who have cancer, cites the work of James Diggory and Doreen Rothman. Those two researchers asked more than 550 people in the general population to place seven consequences of death in order of importance. The people who responded to the questionnaire reported that their number-one concern was the grief their death would cause relatives and friends. I have found that this deep anxiety about the effect of your own death on the people you love may keep you from speaking about that fear or speaking about your own fears regarding death. It may add to a sense of isolation and aloneness. For some people, the need to take care of others is greater than their desire to alleviate their own fears and anxiety by speaking about those emotions. According to Diggory, the respondents' greatest fear about death as it affected their own individual lives was that all their plans and projects would come to an end and that they could no longer have any experiences. They also mentioned fear of pain in the process of dying, an inability to care for dependents, and fear of what might happen to them if there is life after death.

Death anxiety has to do with the fear of "not being," of annihilation. Yalom also cites the work of Kierkegaard. Yalom explains that Kierkegaard was the first to distinguish between fear and anxiety, that is, fear and dread. Fear of something as opposed to a fear of "no thing," the latter being identified as dread. "One dreads (or is anxious about) losing oneself and becoming nothingness." This anxiety is not specific, it is a generalized sense of dread. A fear that is not specific and cannot be understood "becomes more terrible still: it begets a feeling of helplessness which invariably generates further anxiety." In this way, fear that is not specific becomes an anxiety.

How then can we address death anxiety? Again, as Yalom states, "If we can transform fear of nothing to a fear of something, we can mount some self-protective campaign—that is, we can either avoid

the thing we fear, seek allies against it, develop magical rituals to pla-
cate it, or plan a systematic campaign to detoxify it."

Although death cannot be avoided, most people consciously avoid
thoughts of death. Many live in denial of the reality of death. It is
more difficult to avoid or ignore death once you receive the diagnosis
of a terminal illness. Knowing that you have a limited amount of time
remaining, you are challenged to face death and embrace living. You
find yourself asking, *Have I lived the life I have always wanted to live?* The
degree to which you are able to answer in the positive will likely
affect the degree of anxiety you experience.

According to Yalom, the attributes of death anxiety include concern for others, fear of premortal (pain) and postmortal (life after
death) possibilities, and annihilation, that is, "not being." This is the
emotion we experience when we stop the clock to think and feel who
we are when the clock stops, when time as we know it ends. Who are
we then? We are no longer who we thought we were. Knowing that
we will cease to be becomes part of our new reality. That realization
results in a universal anxiety. It is an emotion without boundaries, like
floating in a limitless ocean, no horizon in sight.

As much as the swimmer requires assistance and new resources
when learning to swim in the deep end, anyone facing a terminal illness would do well to seek resources that address the fear and anxiety resulting from the diagnosis. We can speak to experts about pain
management; we can speak to those we love about our sadness in
leaving them and the grief they will experience after we have died;
we can make arrangements to address the financial, emotional, and
spiritual burdens or well-being of those who are dependent on us;
and perhaps we can gain perspective on questions of life after death
from religious leaders and from those who have had a near-death
experience. These are all important strategies that will reduce the
anxiety. However, there is still cause for significant anxiety, namely,
that no one returns from annihilation, from "not being." Can the anx-

iety be altered or reduced? Can the experience of dying be other-wise?

It can be so, but only by asking the questions directly that pertain to our anxiety. The anxiety must be translated into a fear, for fear can be met with courage. Begin by asking yourself, *What is it about this anxiety that can be identified as a fear?* Name the fears. The first step to getting rid of the fear is to say it aloud:

> *I am afraid. I am afraid of the disease within me. I am afraid of dying. I am afraid to tell you how fearful I am. I am afraid to let you know that I know I am very sick. I am afraid of speaking about my fears. I am afraid of how those around me will cope if I say out loud what I am experiencing on the inside. I am afraid that I won't have the courage to do and say what needs to be done and said. I don't want to die. I don't want to suffer. I need courage to face my dying. If I have all this fear, what does that say about my present existence? About my faith or my religious tradition? What does that say about who I am, who I have been, and who I want to be?*

In this context some people confront the fear by acknowledging that they are not living the life they would like to live, not being in relationships the way they would like to be, not experiencing spirituality in a way that is meaningful to them. On a profound level, these people ask themselves, *Who am I?* They speak their truth and listen to the truth of those who are dear to them. They seek and find meaning in the transcendent.

Euthanasia and Physician-Assisted Suicide

In the course of living with a terminal illness, some people eventually begin to long for life to end. Some people tire of waiting, tire of pain or fear of pain, tire of losing control, tire of suffering. They fear they won't be able to make choices pertaining to the way they live, where they live, how they receive care, who provides that care, and what is involved in the care. Most people don't want to die, but some explore to varying degrees what it might mean to end their suffering by committing suicide.

This was evident in the stories of those who participated in the research for the Project on Death in America. It made me wonder whether some of the people I had known in palliative care over the years might also have wanted to speak about suicide. Was their silence on the issue related to their anxiety about speaking openly with a doctor on this subject, or was it related to my not being ready to hear them speak to the issue? Are there many people who would raise the topic in a safe environment, or are there only a few? Perhaps the process of speaking about the desire for control in terms of one's own death is one way of coping with death anxiety.

I clearly remember the individuals who asked me to help them end their lives. One of those requests occurred on a sunny summer afternoon. I was on call, and because friends from out of town were spending time with us, we were at the beach. One of the nurses urgently paged me repeatedly until I got to a pay phone. Ken, a twenty-six-year-old with testicular cancer, was experiencing excruciating pain. I gave some orders by phone and hurried to the hospital. When I arrived, I found that his pain had not improved a great deal. He grabbed my arm and begged me to help him end it all. Suffering, he cried out, "David, please just kill me, kill me! I can't take it anymore." I struggled with his suffering—and my own anguish.

I am not an advocate of euthanasia. I don't believe it is the way to resolve suffering. At the same time, though, I feel great anguish when I witness the suffering of others. In moments of great suffering, I long for my patients to be relieved for their own sake, as well as that of their loved ones and those who are providing care to them. I feel strongly that euthanasia must be a topic that we can speak openly about. Otherwise, we risk adding a sense of abandonment to the suffering the person with the terminal illness is already experiencing. I knew that if we were unable to control Ken's pain, I would be in a dilemma—emotionally, ethically, and legally.

It has been the rare case, but I have experienced the dilemma of being the physician for someone whose pain cannot be controlled. It redefines suffering for all who are present. In those instances, the dilemma cannot be resolved. The patient's suffering ends at the time of death, but that suffering continues in the minds of the care providers, in their hearts and in their memories. The only resolution we can offer is to sit in the presence of the one who suffers and, as much as is possible, to suffer along as the patient does. I have welcomed death for the patient who could not be freed of physical pain or their emotional and spiritual anguish. In those instances, the arrival of death frees all who are present from at least some of the suffering. At those times I feel strongly that we need a deeper understanding of who we are as human beings—physically, emotionally, spiritually—and how all those components and their interrelatedness affect one's suffering. Is there something to be gained in suffering, in suffering alone, in suffering together?

I wanted to assure Ken that we could end the pain. Very often, there is a high probability that doctors can end or significantly alleviate the pain with medication. However, there is no guarantee that we can do so in every situation. Fortunately, in Ken's case we could. A day or two later, when his pain was controlled, I asked him if he had really wanted me to kill him. He said, "No, really I only wanted you to kill the pain." That response adds to the complexity of the dilemma. Our understanding of physical pain is not complete. Our understanding of psychological and spiritual pain is even less well understood. How do we learn more, understand more, so that we can effectively alter the pain and suffering that people experience at the end of life?

It's not only people with physical pain who speak of suicide. I recall another very successful forty-five-year-old businessman, Mark, who wanted to discuss his prognosis. For him, that included a discussion about suicide. He believed strongly that it was his right to take his own life and wanted to know about what assistance he could expect to receive. I spoke to Mark about the law in Canada, which states that assisting someone to commit suicide is illegal. Even counseling someone to do so is against the law in Canada. He said that for him it was not just a fear of pain but a deep concern that he would lose his freedom of choice. He expressed his fear of losing control. He stated that to exercise his right to suicide would be to maintain control. I informed him that I would not assist him in the act, but I assured him that the team would work hard to allow him to maintain control of all decisions regarding his care. I added that I would be pleased to discuss these issues with him (and/or his partner, if he so chose) as often as was desirable. We had several conversations over the course of the next few months.

About a week before he died, Mark called for a team meeting. Once we were all present, he thanked each of us for the work we had done, for helping him control his pain and manage his other symptoms. He then stated that the rest of his journey was a spiritual one, and that he would like to spend as much time as possible with friends who could guide him during that journey. He felt he would not require our services other than to maintain the level of care he was enjoying at the time of the meeting and informed us that he would call us as necessary. He died peacefully, pain-free, naturally, several days later, in a private room in the hospital, surrounded by family and friends.

In their deliberation, some people fear the consequences of suicide. Bob, the HIV-positive patient, considered taking his life:

I have thought of killing myself, but then I'm afraid that whatever I would try wouldn't work. I would never use a knife or anything like that, 'cause I can't stand that, but you know my thoughts were taking an overdose, but then I don't know how much or what pills would do me in. And then I just think, *Oh god, you're going crazy, thinking about that.* And then I think about the things that I would miss. But then sometimes it just seems like it's not worth it to keep living this way.

Frieda, a woman with cancer in her late sixties, was very frustrated with time.

I can't do anything. I can't get interested in anything. I can't travel; I can't go anywhere. I used to enjoy movies and bingo and things. I've lost all enjoyment in them. So it's just a matter of living from day to day, waiting to die, and that's no good. They can't tell me anything when I ask them, "How long do you think it'll be?" They have no idea. I know they can't tell to a certain point, but I mean, between six months and two weeks is a big difference! I have no idea whether I'm going to live a year or I'm going to live a month. That's very hard to take. Especially when I'm just living to live, that's what I'm doing. I live to take the puffers [inhaled medication that opens up the airways, which makes breathing easier] six times a day, to take the pills so many times a day, to fill the pills up every four days. . . . All I'm doing is working with pills and puffers. It absolutely controls my life.

Frieda experienced anxiety about the life she was living, about the possibility of pain, about being alone at night. She entertained the idea of ending her life but found that such thoughts only increased her anxiety and made her feel depressed:

I'm depressed, very much so, because I can't live. I can't live and I can't die, and that's depressing. I guess I could die, you know. I've certainly thought about it, but I think you pay for it, if you do. Whatever you do will come back on you, I think, and if you do that, something's going to come back on you that you're not going to like.

Frieda had known pain earlier in her illness and was anxious about it recurring. She felt paralyzed with regard to her normal activities in that she did not have a good sense of the length of time she had left. She considered suicide but felt anxious about the consequences, in the spiritual sense. This became the focus of her thoughts and conversations. She experienced intense anxiety while waiting for her life to end.

Thoughts and feeling about suicide seem to include a component of control. Kathryn, a woman in her mid-seventies, had worked as a lawyer until her seventieth birthday.

> I have ovarian cancer. I learned about it a year ago. It was a shock. We were traveling in Europe at the time, so it was only after I got back that I found out what was happening. Then I thought the chemotherapy and other therapies were going okay. And I thought I would have a remission, but in fact I didn't. About two months ago, the doctor told me that my symptoms were bad. I kind of knew it already; I could just tell. Right now mostly I want it to be over as quickly as possible. The lack of control, lack of success, lack of energy and completeness—it is intolerable.

Kathryn felt she did not have a lot more to say. She died a few weeks later.

Death Awareness

In Leo Tolstoy's short story "The Death of Ivan Ilych," there is the following passage in which Ivan experiences an awareness of death:

> "And now here it is!" he said to himself. "It can't be. It's impossible! But here it is. How is this? How is one to understand it?" He could not understand it, and tried to drive this false, incorrect, morbid thought away and to replace it by other proper and healthy

thoughts. But that thought, and not the thought only but the reality itself, seemed to come and confront him.

And to replace that thought he called up a succession of others, hoping to find in them some support. He tried to get back into the former current of thoughts that had once screened the thought of death from him. But strange to say, all that had formerly shut off, hidden, and destroyed, his consciousness of death, no longer had that effect. . . . His judicial labours could not as formerly hide from him what he wanted them to hide, and could not deliver him from *it*. And what was worst of all was that *it* drew his attention to itself not in order to make him take some action but only that he should look at *it*, look it straight in the face."

While writing this chapter, I received a call from a friend. Her father-in-law, Ben, was dying of lung cancer that had metastasized to his liver and bones. I get a lot of calls like this. According to the information she has been given, there is a 1 percent chance of a five-year survival with chemotherapy. Without the therapy, his life expectancy would be eight months. Because he witnessed the effects of chemotherapy when his mother took it, he was reluctant to go ahead with the treatment. But his children begged him to try at least one treatment. They also encouraged him to seek alternative treatments. He responded to their wishes. But what might his real wishes be?

According to Dr. Peter Singer, a bioethicist at the Joint Centre for Bioethics at the University of Toronto, the real wishes and perspectives on quality end-of-life care, for those who participated in a survey, consist of five domains: having adequate pain and symptom management; avoiding inappropriate prolongation of dying; achieving a sense of control; relieving burdens; and strengthening relationships with loved ones.

Ben's family's hope was that he would be in the 1 percent that enjoyed the five-year reprieve. It was the focus of the entire family.

Yet perhaps he doesn't want the treatment because he is prepared to die but is uncertain how to say that to his family without their feeling betrayed. What about the family's relationship with the father? What about his sense of self, his relationship to family and friends, his understanding of spirituality? These issues were not addressed. I have seen this happen all too often. The waiting has started—waiting for the diagnosis, waiting for the chemotherapy, waiting for the benefits and side-effects of the chemotherapy, waiting for the effects of alternative therapies to kick in. Time passes—days, then weeks, then months. The hope for cure is paramount. Efforts to enhance intimacy among family members pale in comparison.

I wanted to tell Ben and his family that the only time available to them is now. One thing that they do not need to wait for is the work that could be done with regard to their relationships, to speak the unspeakable, to really hear what they have to say to one another, to share their memories—the challenges and pains they experienced as a family. They could begin to review their life as a family and to tell their father what he means to them, who they are because of him, what they will take with them because they have known him. All of this can happen in the context of their hope for a miraculous cure. Like Ivan Ilych, too many people wait too long to begin the inward journey of learning who they are, what the meaning of life might be for them, the value of relationships and of spirituality.

Time is now. That was one of the major lessons I learned in spending time with people who knew they were dying. Time passes quickly. People wait for the optimal circumstances for intimate conversations. They wait for the courage to do what they have never done before. But then the illness progresses faster than anticipated. (Doctors predict three to twelve months of life remaining, but people only hear that they have twelve months.) Fatigue sets in. (*I'll do this tomorrow; I might have more energy then.*) Cancer affects thought processes (body chemistry, side effects of medication, metastases to the brain, low oxygen supply). People who may not have a specific diagnosis of a terminal illness but are aging wait for the doctor to inform them that they are dying before they take time seriously. They think difficult conversations can happen later. But will they? And will they be any easier once the terminal illness has been diagnosed? Will they be easier at age eighty-five than they are at age fifty-eight?

The following exercise is merely a simulation so readers can get a sense of *chronus* and *kairos*. This exercise can be done on your own, with a friend, or in a group. Consider a time line. On a sheet of unlined paper, draw a six-inch horizontal line. On the left side, write the word "Birth," on the right the word "Death":

Birth ———————————————————————— *Death*

Think of this line as representing your lifetime. Place an X on the line to indicate where you believe you are at present. That is, if you believe that you have lived half of your life, place the X midway between Birth and Death. If you believe that you have lived two-thirds of your life, place the X two-thirds along the line. Once you have placed the X on the line, take note of your feelings. Do you have a sense of relief? Of anxiety? Of fear? Or a realization that much of your life has passed?

Next think of six significant events in your life: examples would be meeting your spouse or partner, the birth of a child, the death of a friend, an exciting vacation, a failure, a good financial investment, graduation from university, the birth of a grandchild, a car accident. Number the events 1 through 6 and place the numbers on the line between your birth and the X. What emotions do you feel about each of those events? What about the emotion you feel about your life as a whole? Are you satisfied with the life you have lived? Do you wish that some things had been different? Are there events that ought to have been placed on the line but because of the pain they caused you omitted them?

Focus on the line between the X and Death. How might you best embrace life in the time that remains? If you didn't have to live up to the expectations of anyone else, how would you live, who would you be? Are there things you would like to do? Places you would like to visit? People you would like to spend more time with? Conversations you would like to have? Events you would like to attend—the baptism of a grandchild, the graduation of your eldest child, a birthday, a bar mitzvah, a wedding, an anniversary? Choose six events. Number the events beginning with the number 7 and place those numbers on the line between the X and Death. How do you feel about each of those events, the people involved in them, and your life as a whole?

Imagine the scenario in which your family physician informs you today that the symptoms you and he have been investigating are those of a terminal illness. Unfortunately, there are no known treatments that can reverse the disease process. Some of the medications available may slow the disease, but none of them are known to arrest it. Your life expectancy is six to twelve months. How do you feel?

Draw another timeline. This time, place an X one centimeter from the right end of the line:

Birth ————————————————————————— *X — Death*

If you knew that this was accurate, would you live differently? Starting when? Would you care as much what other people think about you or about what you do, how you live? How would you fill your time?

How does the new reality affect the answers to your questions in the previous time-line exercise? What effect does this have on your feelings? What about unfinished activities? Are they still important to you? Are there other activities that seem important now that you have only six to twelve months remaining in this world? And what about looking back over your life? Does the knowledge that you are living with a terminal illness change your feelings about your memories? Are there other relationships or events that come to mind as being significant? Are there things you wish you had done? Things you wish you had not done? And are there conversations that you wish had not happened or had been different? Do you wish you had said some things that you did not say?

You may become aware of events that you will miss. With that realization, there will likely be a sense of loss and grief. You may want to write a letter or dictate a message to someone to be opened or listened to in the future. For example, if you think that you might miss a birthday, a wedding, a graduation, or any other celebration, you could write a letter to the individual who is significant to you in that event. If you are a parent who will miss your child's graduation from high school or university, you might write a letter to be opened on graduation day. If you are a grandparent who will miss the birth of a grandchild, you could write a whole series of letters that could be opened periodically by your grandchild. The letters could include information about yourself, your childhood, and features of the family history that you feel are important for the next generation of family members. By participating in such activities, your grief and despair may turn to mourning and hope.

Anxiety can be reduced by introducing certainty. When facing the anxiety associated with a terminal illness, you can create a degree of certainty by developing a plan for your care and through the process of a life review, in which you consciously consider the meaning and the unfinished business of your life. A "life review" simply means living in the present while looking at the past. It enables the individual to reconsider life events, relationships, successes, failures. It may also remind the person of conversations and activities that might still be desirable. The process of developing a plan is described in chapter 4. A closer look at the life-review process is outlined in chapter 5.

I remember a lesson I learned some time ago from Zen Buddhism: A monk was being chased by a panther when he found himself at the edge of an embankment. His eyes rapidly scanned the bank. He saw a rope, which he believed would serve as his escape route. He quickly began his descent, but looking down he saw a second panther waiting below. He looked up again, this time to see a mouse gnawing on the rope. He stopped. In front of him and within arm's reach he saw a ripe strawberry. He picked and carefully placed it in his mouth. "What a most delicious piece of fruit," he said.

CHAPTER TWO

Bad News

Talking about death is difficult for a lot of us in the beginning.

Brent

The way in which the physician spoke to me caused me
more pain than I experienced from the disease itself.

Marjorie

The dying need the friendship of the heart— its qualities of
care, acceptance, vulnerability; but they also need the skills
of the mind—the most sophisticated treatment that medicine has to offer. On its own, neither is enough.

Dame Cicely Saunders

First, do no harm.

Hippocrates

Great Expectations

In ancient Greek mythology Thetis was the great goddess of the sea and ruled over all that moved in its depths. But it was time she married, and Zeus, king of the gods, had received a prophecy that if Thetis married a god she would bear a son who would be greater than Zeus himself. To prevent this, Zeus espoused the sea-goddess to Peleus, a mortal. The marriage was successful, although Peleus sometimes resented his wife's supernatural powers, and Thetis sometimes felt she had married beneath her station.

In time, Thetis bore a son, whom she called Achilles. Because he was fathered by a mortal he was a mortal child, allotted his time on earth. But Thetis was not content with that prospect. Being immortal herself, she did not wish to remain eternally young and watch as her son grew old and died. So she carried the newborn to the River Styx, in whose waters lay the gift of immortality. She held the child by one heel and dipped him in the waters, believing thereby that she had made him immortal. But the heel by which she held him remained untouched by the waters of the Styx, and therefore Achilles was vulnerable in this one place.

When Achilles reached adulthood and fought in the Trojan War, he was killed by an arrow that pierced his heel. Although Achilles achieved great glory and was remembered forever, Thetis could not cheat the Fates or turn that which was human into the stuff of the gods.

❁

Peggy, one of the participants in the research project, a fine-featured woman in her late sixties, lay quietly in her hospital bed. The December sun flooded through the window, warming the room. She was wondering what her doctor, Dr. Neilson, would say when he came to see her. Would he tell her that the cancer was spreading, or would he give her information about some other process in her body that was causing her shortness of breath? Whatever the message, she was confident that he would be honest, thorough, and compassionate. For now, the slight pain in her chest wall was a small price to pay for the ability to breathe more easily again. Six days had passed since she was admitted to the hospital—Room 7033 in the old south wing, which meant the windows could be opened and she could feel "real air" moving across her face. Peggy was no stranger to the hospital; this was her tenth admission. She was pleased to be in a private room this time so that she could enjoy the company of family and friends without disturbing roommates who might be trying to get some rest.

With her eyes closed, Peggy recalled how just a week before, after coming up the stairs from the basement, she found herself gasping for breath, alone in her kitchen, wishing she could die, believing she would die, when her daughter, Kathy, dropped by on her way home from work. Thank God Kathy got there when she did and called for an ambulance! Today, for the second time since her admission to the hospital, the draining of fluid from around her lungs had given Peggy "new breath." She remembered a time in her life when her physical activity had not been compromised by lack of energy or shortness of breath, when she was able to take long walks along Jericho Beach, her dog, Duke, beside her, the mountains in clear view across English Bay. Those walks seemed to give her a certain calmness, a deep sense that an inner strength would sustain her through anything.

Peggy was expecting Dr. Neilson to arrive any minute. He always came by to see her after a procedure. She was aware that he might be bringing bad news, which was not new to Peggy. She remembered her mastectomy that was done in 1970, and her lobectomy (removal of part of the lung) just three years ago, followed most recently by a wedge resection of her lung. And just a week earlier she had been told right after they tapped the fluid that had collected around her lungs that, like all the other surgeries, this too was due to the cancer. Peggy felt that Dr. Neilson knew her and her family very well. He didn't need to fiddle around. He simply had said, "Yes, it's also due to the cancer."

Peggy's memories and thoughts were interrupted by a gentle touch on her right arm. It was Dr. Neilson. He spoke with her about draining the fluid from her chest cavity, of injecting a substance to prevent the fluid from collecting again, and of what she might expect in the days and weeks ahead.

A few days later, Peggy welcomed me into her hospital room. A picture of her family was pinned to the corkboard on the wall at the foot of her bed. She had an IV in her right arm. From her room she had a view of Vancouver's downtown area. After dark, once the lights were on, it was a lovely view, especially at this time of year with Christmas only weeks away. At the time of my visit, the sky was gray, and a few raindrops were hitting the window of her room. It was a perfect day to be at home, reading a book, next to a fire.

I met with Peggy earlier that week to discuss the research project. One of her daughters had used a similar research method, and so Peggy was familiar with our approach. Now it was time for our first formal interview.

The first question I always asked my coresearchers was how they learned about their illness, either the initial diagnosis or the point at which they were told that it was not curable, that in fact it was a terminal illness, one that would likely be the cause of their death. All of them described the situation in considerable detail. Some of them remembered exactly how it had happened even though it had occurred years before.

Peggy replied:

I've been very, very fortunate with the medical care I've received. I guess the first thing to tell you is that I trust all my physicians.

They've been totally up front and answered questions in detail. I have a daughter who's very involved in the medical field, and she has sat in on all the important interviews and has asked questions that have clarified things in their minds, too. So in my case, I couldn't have asked for it to be handled better because everybody has been so up front with me, told me what it might be, what it might not be. I mean they just couldn't have been more honest, so it didn't come as a shock, a bolt out of the blue at all. It was just one of the case scenarios they described that they hoped it wouldn't be.

I asked Peggy to be specific about the interactions between her doctor and herself with her family. Her response:

What is particularly in my mind is the day my youngest flew in from Cleveland, Ohio. It was the first time Dr. Neilson had seen all three girls together. I asked him to go over my history with them because the way things happened was a little confusing to them. He did it very succinctly but with a lot of empathy, touching me from time to time while he was talking to them. My youngest lost her cool. She got up and left the room. He finished talking to the other two and left, and then one of my girls went to find their younger sister. They found her in the lounge. Dr. Neilson was there with her, his arm around her, comforting her. I feel an aura of spirituality around him. He would never lie to any of us or fudge the truth on anything. There have been occasions when he could have "soft-soaped" anything. He didn't, but then obviously he's got a clear sense of how much we could take.

I wish Peggy's experience was typical. I wish it were the norm. Unfortunately, that is not the case. In fact, if you have been told by a physician that you have a terminal illness, it is very possible that you felt hurt through that experience. Although I'm certain that it was the intent of the doctor to provide comprehensive care and not to add to the suffering, all too often that particular encounter causes suffering. People expect their doctors to be there for them through their illnesses, but it doesn't always happen. In fact, for some it's the opposite.

Max was a man in his late twenties, a graduate student who also worked in computer systems for a transport company. He knew that it was important to be disciplined, at work and in his studies, in order to complete his degree without accumulating debt. At times he wondered whether he could keep up the pace, especially when his friends complained that he never had time for them. Max was determined to complete his degree without a student loan and therefore kept his job; he valued his friends and was confident that they understood why he was so busy.

Max was one of the first people I interviewed. He welcomed me into his modest home. He was keen to tell his story and did so with great clarity. It was approximately eight years earlier that he had been diagnosed with diabetes. He understood the disease and knew how to manage it. Four years after the diagnosis, he began to experience some strange symptoms, which he described as "tension in the skin that began in the hips and moved down the buttocks and the back of the thighs."

It was almost as though somebody was stretching my skin, pulling it taut. I thought nothing of it at first, but gradually it grew in severity and I noticed a correlation with my diabetes. As soon as the blood sugars would rise, these symptoms would appear. I'd take some insulin and wait the requisite time for it to get into my system and start doing its thing. As soon as it brought my blood sugar down, the symptoms would disappear. So naturally I formed the conclusion that it was a diabetes complication. As soon as you're diagnosed with diabetes, you are absolutely bombarded with information about complications—shortened life span, kidney problems, eye problems, blood vessel problems, and stuff like that. I assumed this might be just another complication. When I met with my endocrinologist, he said, "It's not that big a deal."

The pain got more and more severe, and nothing seemed to relieve it. There was no position I could lie in or sit in that would relieve it. There was no analgesic or painkiller I could take that would alleviate it. It seemed to be related to my blood sugar, so I didn't look for another explanation. It got so bad that my sleep became fragmented, and this started to affect other areas of my life. This lack of sleep was affecting my studies and my ability to do my job. I got to the point where I couldn't go a night without it happening. I knew that if my blood sugars went an iota above 10, I'd be in pain; so I'm having to keep tighter control on my blood sugars, which is increasingly difficult. It's starting to invade other areas of my life—my friendships, my relationship with my girlfriend. I started to do strange things. Since I'm not able to sleep, I would sit huddled up, watching TV and waiting for the insulin to take effect, to drop my blood sugars so that the pain would go away. I started to take excessive amounts of Tylenol because now the pain had entered my lower abdomen.

Max spoke of getting a bit of sleep whenever he could during the day because often the pain was so great at night that he was unable to sleep at all. In an effort to alleviate the pain, he took "handfuls of Tylenol." He could not wait for the insulin to take effect, so he started jogging in the middle of the night to lower his blood sugars. "It's 2:00 or 3:00 in the morning and I'm getting dressed for a jog. Afterward, I'd check my pulse and make sure that my heart rate was up so that my blood sugars would drop and the pain would go away." Sheer determination combined with an equally strong desire for pain relief enabled Max to do what for most people would be very difficult, if not impossible: to jog with severe pain.

Max's dreams and ambitions began to waver. "My schoolwork was absolutely nose-diving at this point. I'd been a reasonable student up to then. I had good study habits even in high school, and university wasn't that hard for me, though it was a lot more work. But now I was so exhausted that I had to drop all my classes." All that was important to Max began to change. His relationships changed: "I started snubbing friends so much that they stopped asking me out." His performance at work changed: "I tried to continue to go to work, but at this point I was in such severe pain in the abdomen that I was walking hunched over." His ability to care for himself changed: "I got so exhausted that I literally couldn't take care of myself—breakfast, dinner whatever—I was so exhausted I wouldn't eat, plain and simple. If I had to get up and actually make food for myself, it just wouldn't get done."

Max lived in that vortex of pain, sleeplessness, exhaustion, and despair for six months.

> I didn't have a whole lot of confidence in the medical profession. So I let it slide until eventually it had such a hold on me that I knew I had to get help. For the first time in six months, I went to see a doctor. I told him about the weight loss and night sweats, and he just gave me a little speech about how everyone's thermostat is set at a different level. "You're just a naturally slender guy," he said, "and you're too stressed out. Relax a little and don't worry about it." Then he sent me on my way. Well, I was not happy with this. Later, I got my medical records and found that he'd written: "Patient is obviously unhappy. I could do nothing for him."

Sitting with Max in his living room was not easy. I had a sense that he was going to tell me something about my profession that I did not want to hear. But I knew I had to listen, had to bear witness, to what Max had to say. Many thoughts ran through my head. *Surely, he*

must be the exception. He must not be remembering clearly. It must be that he is
angry about the cancer he knows he has and is projecting all his anger about having
cancer onto the medical profession. It can't possibly have been the way he is describ-
ing it. Why doesn't he admit to his anger at the disease process, his limited ability to
function in the world, his severed relationships with his friends, his aborted studies,
his premature death? Every doctor knows that cancer must be considered when the
patient speaks of weight loss and night sweats—how could anyone tell him to relax
and not worry? Attributing Max's symptoms to stress and a slender body type is
obviously inadequate. What about his pain, his inability to sleep, his compromised
performance at work and at university? Max must be mistaken. No doctor would
have been so dismissive. But I have the advantage of hindsight. Maybe things weren't
so clear at the time.

It was my natural response to defend the doctor, to suspect that
Max might be overreacting, accusing the doctor falsely, or not
describing things the way they really happened. I didn't want to be a
witness to what he was saying or be incriminated by association. Like
Max, I, too, was feeling angry over what had happened to him, at the
fact that this doctor had dismissed him without understanding how
his symptoms were affecting his life. But at the same time I had this
strange loyalty to my profession. In the end, I reminded myself that I
wasn't there as a doctor. Max and I were coresearchers—that's what
I'd told him in my introduction, and that's what it said on the consent
form he had signed. It was my job to listen, to bear witness, to work
with every ounce of my being to understand Max—his pain, his suffering, his despair, his sense of abandonment and isolation. It was my
duty to appreciate his feelings of being trivialized, of anger and
resentment toward my profession. I could dismiss neither the facts
nor the emotions Max had experienced. The least I could do and perhaps the most that could be done at that time was to take Max seriously, to believe his story.

Max continued to describe the progression of the disease:

I had an attack after lunch one day at work. The attack was so bad I collapsed in the elevator. I thought I had food poisoning, so I had the nurse take a look at me. She didn't want to release me, but finally I managed to convince her to let me go home. I thought, *Well, I'll give the doctors another chance.* I went the next day, thinking that I'd stop in before work to see the doctor and then go to work and everything would be hunky-dory. This was a different doctor. He took my claims seriously. When I started talking about night sweats and not being able to sleep and having to take lots of Tylenol, it immediately sent bells off in his mind. He palpated my stomach and immediately said, "We want to admit you to the hospital. We need to run some ultrasound tests." "Whoa, slow down! Admit? Don't you only do that for people who are seriously ill?" He looked at me and said, "This is definitely not your imagination. There is something going on in there. It's involving at least your spleen and your liver."

This doctor took Max very seriously. He did not trivialize the information regarding Max's inability to function at work, the changes in his relationships with his friends, his loss of concentration that affected his academic performance.

So on the one hand, I was extremely freaked that this sort of diagnosis was dropped in my lap. On the other hand, I was relieved. It had been two years of going through bullshit, and now I was finally gonna get some answers. I spent about two weeks in the hospital. The entire time I was there, they sort of danced around the issue. You know . . . *what is it?* "It could be anything. What we know for sure is that there is a mass in your lower pelvic region and we'll know more once we do more tests." Well, more tests were done, and my condition deteriorated quite rapidly. Doctors are running around doing all kinds of tests that I've never heard of—needle biopsies and all kinds of things. And then a surgeon comes up and says that he wants to perform an open biopsy, a laparotomy. I was hesitant but decided to go ahead with it. After the open biopsy was performed, I waited and waited. Days are clicking by. This is very stressful, not only for me but for my whole family.

I got tired of waiting. I knew when the nurses would be on rounds and away from the nurses' station. I went to the nurses' station and pulled my chart, opened it up, looked under diagnosis, and there it was: metastatic carcinoma. That meant nothing to me, so I wrote it down on a little piece of paper. When the nurse came in to do the vitals, I said, "Do you have a medical dictionary? I'm curious to look up a few terms." She brought the dictionary, and I flipped right to "carcinoma," which it turns out means cancer. So then I looked up the word "metastatic," which means something that has spread. I wrote that down: "spread cancer." I finally had some idea of what was going on.

The next day the team of physicians—the one who first admitted me to the hospital, my endocrinologist, the one who did the open biopsy—all came by one by one and said that they'd be transferring me to a hospital where they could deal with this better. I said, "Oh, what hospital is that" They said, "The one that has more expertise in caring for people with cancer." Then it dawned on me: First, that they actually wrote down in my chart that I had cancer but didn't tell me, and second, that I'm being transferred to the cancer hospital. That didn't really hit me until I actually walked through those doors. The regular beds were taken, so they admitted me to the leukemia ward, the bone-marrow transplant ward where when you walk in, you have to wash your hands and turn the taps with your knees and stuff like that. This is all just sending me over the top. I didn't like it and made this fact known. The admitting nurse turned to me and said, "Well, what do you expect, this isn't the Westin Bayshore Hotel."

As I write this chapter I still hear the wincing in Max's voice, I see the anguish in his face. Even today, several years later, I want to change the story, for two reasons. First, I wish for Max's sake that someone had greeted him with compassion, empathy, and understanding; that someone had held him, touched his shoulder, or placed their hand on his hand; that someone had addressed the anxiety, the fear, the uncertainty he was experiencing. And second, I am shy and reticent to speak the truth. It's as if I would at some level prefer to ignore Max's experience, to protect the nurses and doctors from being exposed. At times I feel like a traitor, as if I have betrayed my colleagues by speaking the stories of the people who have been their patients. It would have been easier to exclude this theme from my study and from this book. But as much as I wanted Max's experience to be the exception, I now know that is not the case.

Max continued: "The oncologist came in and rattled off a big pathological name and told me that I was going to die in two to two and a half years. In the span of about two minutes he took away all my hopes and dreams. At that point, I felt like suicide was a viable option."

Despite all the good that is done in the context of medical practice, there is an important component that at times is neglected. Poor communication can render ineffective all the good in medicine, as it has the potential to increase suffering. Poor communication may therefore be regarded as the Achilles' heel of the medical profession. There are many physicians who have strong communication skills, making them very effective in the work they do. However, there are many more who—without being aware of it—cause people to suffer by not communicating in a compassionate manner. You may have a painful experience in your encounters with physicians or interactions with other health care providers. The fact that this is part of the experience of living with a terminal illness became very apparent through the course of my research. It was a disconcerting realization.

*

Marjorie was a pleasant, articulate, silver-haired woman in her mid-seventies. There were times when she appeared to be so healthy and active that I wondered whether she was really sick. She had been a bank manager by profession. She was also a natural teacher; Marjorie taught me a lot from the moment I met her until she died many months later.

During my first visit with her, I asked how she learned about her diagnosis. She told me about discovering the lump in her left groin and about the events that followed: the visit to her family doctor, the consultation with a specialist, then waiting for three months while the lump grew to the size deemed necessary for excision. She was assured that the growth was likely benign. This process of investigation, diagnosis, and treatment had happened ten years before Marjorie told me about it, but she remembered the details of the events as though they had happened within twenty-four hours.

She was keen to tell me about her experience of learning she had a terminal illness.

> I was still in the hospital. This part is the first trauma. Up to then I don't remember any great emotion. I was lying in my bed, still coming out of the anesthesia, and the doctor appeared at the door. Without coming into the room, he told me, "We were wrong. It's cancer." No, he didn't say cancer. He said, "It's metastatic carcinoma." Normally I would know what that was, but I was dazed and I said, "What's that mean?" He said, "It means you have cancer. Don't worry, I'll make an appointment for you at the cancer clinic." He never came in. He spoke to me from the door and then left.

She felt hurt and very angry.

Subsequently, Marjorie was told she could go home the next morning. She had spent the night weeping, not because she had learned that she had cancer but because of the way in which she learned about it. Although she didn't think of herself as a very assertive person, she decided she would not go home until she had spoken with her doctor. In the morning, he appeared at the door again, and she asked him to come in.

He said, "What's the matter? You can go home now." I said, "I have to tell you something." He said, "Well, what is it?" And I said, "It's the way you told me I have cancer. You've known me for more than three months. I thought that you considered me a person, not just a disease, but then you stood in the door and told me I had cancer and went away." He said, "What should I have done?" I said, "Well, you could have come in and put your hand on my shoulder and then told me I have cancer. It would have made a big difference to me. You don't have to say, 'Oh, you poor thing!' Just say, 'You've got cancer, and we're going to take care of it.'"

Looking back over the ten years since that diagnosis, Marjorie said that the emotional pain she experienced was greater than any of the physical pain she experienced.

The situation was further complicated because the doctor had informed her family of the cancer before speaking with her. "My daughter, an only child, came to see me. As we began to talk, she said, 'I understand you're going to be going to the cancer clinic. If you don't mind, I'd like to be with you when you go.' And I said, 'That would be fine.' It didn't occur to me to wonder how she would know. This was right after the doctor told me." Marjorie would have preferred to tell her daughter in her own way. She felt that she had not been treated with respect. In fact, she felt a sense of betrayal, a breech of confidentiality. She had trusted her doctor to inform her in a compassionate manner and to do so before he informed the family.

Most, if not all, doctors do not intend to do harm. On the contrary, doctors generally intend to do good. Why, then, do they cause suffering? The reasons include some old traditions of medical practice, lack of communication skills, the doctors' own emotional and psychological issues, time pressures, and other factors. These rub up against the emotions patients experience when receiving bad news. If your own experience of receiving your diagnosis has caused you to suffer, perhaps an explanation will help you understand how it happened and why you might be feeling the way you do. These are some of my ideas after giving this a great deal of thought. I hope these ideas, or the fact that I include them here, do not add to your hurt, anger, or frustration. I am not including this explanation in order to excuse doctors or to justify their actions.

As recently as the early 1960s, most doctors who trained in North America kept information about serious illnesses to themselves. Reticence was the norm, in keeping with cultural values and expectations. Doctors—and society at large—felt back then that telling people about a terminal illness would only add to their suffering. There was no appreciation for the desire that individuals might have to prepare for dying and death. There was no sense that the end of life might be the most meaningful time in a person's life. People had to rely on their own sense of what might be happening with regard to the progression of the disease.

Twenty years later, values had changed. Most doctors began informing patients about their illness and prognosis. But such openness—which seems so patently necessary today—is still a relatively new phenomenon. Your doctor may have come of age in a different era or been trained by doctors who did. Medical schools still by and large do not provide adequate training in the communication skills necessary to sensitively convey difficult news. As stated previously, talking about dying is difficult for most human beings in our culture, and doctors are human beings, with all the anxieties and shortcomings common to the species.

Today, patients, families, and friends generally want to know the diagnosis and what it might mean to their well-being. In some cultures, however, it is still the norm to avoid any conversation about terminal illness. The responsibility of making decisions pertaining to health and well-being is passed on to a spouse, a son, a daughter. And even when it is the cultural norm to be given medical information, there are patients who prefer not to know. Each patient must decide for herself, in the context of who she is, how she wants to make decisions pertaining to her illness.

Informing a patient of a terminal illness is difficult for any doctor. As a physician, it is one of the most difficult tasks that I face. All my training in medical school focused on curing, on restoring full physical health; in medicine, anything less is often regarded as unacceptable, and many physicians regard death as a failure on their part. Whether I am talking to a new patient or one I've treated for years, it is difficult to inform anyone about terminal illness. It means I have to deal with mortality—theirs and, in a way, my own.

At times my whole being resists difficult discussions with patients. I do not want to inform any patient that she has a terminal illness, that the disease is progressing; I prefer to talk about successful treatments. I chose to study medicine because I wanted to treat illness, to cure it if possible. But here I become the one who informs a patient that he or she will die, that is, I become the messenger of death. There is a constant and powerful temptation to deny the reality of death. Instead of speaking about its likelihood, it is easier to introduce a new protocol, something I may have recently read about. And even though the odds are against a cure, I'm tempted to emphasize even the slimmest of chances as a measure of hope.

What is the alternative to that hopeful message? In this case, it seems that the alternative is a message of gloom. But is the slim possibility of a cure—whether it be 5 percent or 25 percent—really a message of hope? Is there any other component of hope that might make sense at the moment? How will the patient feel when she learns that the cure is not for her? How does that affect her sense of hope? Is there a way to relay the information in such a way so as to minimize the shock while imparting the reality of the message?

Stewart had been a patient of mine for several years. He was considerably older than I, and in a sense he applied his skills as a renowned local soccer coach to our relationship. Stewart had been such a vibrant coach and had given so much to the soccer players of our city. He never lost that life-loving spirit despite his inability to get around as he had in the past. There was a fondness between us that I can attribute only to personal chemistry.

Stewart had a terminal respiratory condition. His reasons for visiting my office usually pertained to a decrease in physical function coupled with shortness of breath. Over time he moved more slowly, at times gasping for air. Then he could no longer drive and was brought to the office by his wife. Next he came with a portable oxygen tank.

I had been working with a respirologist, Dr. Reid, to keep Stewart as active as possible. But now I had received a letter from her, basically informing me that no further medical intervention was possible; that the disease progression was such that in essence Stewart was now in a palliative situation. In other words, the best we could do was to help Stewart feel as comfortable as possible while he was dying. Stewart came to my office to hear the results from his most recent tests and the report about those tests from the respirologist. I thought I was relatively calm, and I believed in my own communication skills. However, when I was sitting across from Stewart, I couldn't say the words; they stuck in my throat. In fact, I choked up and felt anxious about losing it right there in front of him. I did not want to be the one to tell him the truth about his lungs; I wanted to inform him that there were other options. I wanted Stewart to live, and so I couldn't bring myself to tell him that he was dying.

Ever the teacher, Stewart said, "David, I have something to tell you. I know there is nothing that can be done to reverse what is going on in my lungs. I know I am going to die. I have started the process of finishing my unfinished business. I am going to be all right." What a gift! He said it, he spoke his truth, he talked of dying more easily than I ever could. He spoke the D-word so casually; he didn't pause, stutter, or choke on it. Then he went on to speak comfortably of his work, his family, and his wife. He was sorry not to live long enough to meet his grandchildren and to see them play soccer. I had little to say, other than to tell him how much I valued him as a person, that I would miss him all the more because of what he had just taught me. I continued to provide care to Stewart for several months, until he died. I went to his funeral, which was a true celebration of who he was in the community. The church was full of soccer players of all ages, and the music reflected his taste and personality.

In any doctor-patient relationship, there are several levels at which the two want and need to understand one another. The key is to remember that both are experts. The doctor's role is to identify the disease, to reverse or minimize its impact, and to understand the patient. The doctor holds the knowledge and skills to make the assessment, the authority to order investigations, and the responsibility to prescribe the appropriate treatment. Throughout the process the doctor must provide information so as to enable the patient to understand what is happening. The patient's role is to give the doctor the information necessary to make the most accurate assessment and diagnosis. For her part, the patient must also feel free to express concerns and preferences as to treatment options. If there is a real understanding on her part—the kind that grows out of good communication and mutual respect—then she is able to fully participate in choosing the optimal treatment plan as prescribed by the doctor. The doctor has the information; the patient holds the power to choose. The doctor-patient relationship is thus defined by two people working together to reverse a disease process, decrease pain and other symptoms, optimize the ability to function independently, and work toward healing.

My patient and friend Stewart knew the reality of his destiny better than I did. He had confronted death, whereas I had not. Stewart knew he had choices. He knew what to say and what to ask in order to get the information he needed to make those choices wisely.

To speak to anyone about terminal illness without adding to their suffering is an art that requires communication skills and self-knowledge. As a doctor, it took me a long time to realize that the way I speak with people might actually add to their suffering: the tone of my voice, the amount of time I spend, whether I touch them, the content of what I say—all communicate my ability (or inability) to see the patient as a person rather than as a disease.

I remember working as a resident in the emergency department of a children's hospital. The hours were long, sleep was elusive, and my energy was low. When on a twenty-four-hour shift, I always hoped for a quiet night so I could catch up on sleep. On one such shift I dozed off in the early-morning hours following a particularly busy evening. About twenty minutes into my slumber, I was summoned to the emergency room. A young mother, a single parent, had come by taxi with her baby. Her concern for the baby was based solely, it seemed, on the baby's bad breath. During the physical examination, I found nothing abnormal. Just before I sent her home in the middle of the night, I told her that if she continued to have concerns, she should see her family doctor.

Several days later, I recounted this episode to a senior physician, Dr. Bient, complaining about being woken from my very brief sleep, about the cost of a visit to the emergency department, about the inconvenience—all because of a baby's bad breath. I had practiced what I thought to be medically and scientifically appropriate given the baby's symptoms (or, to my mind, the lack thereof). Dr. Bient wondered what was going on in that woman's life that she should feel the urgency to bring her child to the emergency department in the middle of the night. "While you attended to the baby, how might you have heard the mother?" he asked me. In fact, I had done little to calm her fears. I had not spoken harshly to her, I had listened carefully, and I had examined the baby appropriately and assured her that her daughter was all right. However, I had not understood that she might be very worried about her ability to care for the child. She might have felt isolated, wondering at times what to do for her child as well as for herself. I had responded to the specific symptom, the possible disease, whereas Dr. Bient would have responded to the person.

As a resident, I was not able to distinguish between the two, actually believing that I had fulfilled my responsibility to the woman and her baby, unaware that I might have increased her dis-ease. I needed Dr. Bient to teach me the art of medicine. The science, the routine, the process of taking a history and doing a physical exam, had served me well; once the task was completed, I might steal another few minutes or perhaps an hour of sleep. But the mother, and therefore the baby, had not been treated with compassion. In fact, my dismissive attitude may have added to her lack of confidence and her sense of isolation as a single parent. Had she come during the day, I would have been too busy to provide care any differently than I had provided that night. Limitations of time and energy are often such that the burden of addressing patients' suffering sometimes seems too great.

Communication is complex. First, as the doctor I must speak so that you can understand what I'm talking about. Equally important, I must listen to your feedback in such a way that I know what you actually heard. In fact, I can know what you heard only when you repeat the message back to me. I have come to realize that once people hear words such as "cancer," "AIDS," "no more treatment options," or "ALS" (amyotrophic lateral sclerosis, or Lou Gehrig's disease), they do not hear anything else. Many people have told me that they were unable to hear what they were being told about having a terminal illness. They suggested that the message about the disease be given to them again and again, in different ways and at different times. You may need to ask your doctor to explain the disease process, investigation, and treatment options several times before you understand what each entails. Hearing the message is a process. Some people are able and want to hear it as soon as possible; others are able to hear it only after several visits; a few do not want to hear it at all.

When Thetis immersed her son in the River Styx, she believed she had assured his immortality. She did not realize her slip-up—that holding him by the heel left him vulnerable. If doctors do not recognize their ability to wound people through words, then even the best of intentions will be compromised. When Marjorie confronted her doctor about her emotional pain after his rather evasive demeanor, he said, "Because of the work I do regarding women with breast cancer, I have to tell so many women this. That's the only way I can do it." He did not know his Achilles' heel; he had no intention of hurting her and seemed not to realize that he could have spared her much suffering if only he had spoken with compassion.

One of the most difficult times in the doctor-patient relationship is the moment when the doctor breaks the news that the disease process will likely result in death. Both suffer, and each has his own coping mechanisms. Both must work to make sense of the disease process, of a new reality. One is left to make sense of a profession that cannot cure everyone, and the other is left to make sense of a lifetime that is now coming to an end. For the patient, it is a single event; for the doctor, the same event is repeated time and again. Both will likely experience frustration, grief, and a sense of despair.

The moment at which the doctor breaks the news is pivotal. It often occurs when the emotional and spiritual needs of the patient are the greatest, whereas the doctor's training to address those needs is minimal. It is a time when the patient longs for a message from the heart, whereas the doctor is trained to communicate the facts. An emotional need is met with a cognitive response. The doctor, most likely, is a specialist, highly trained in a special area of medicine, with knowledge and skills for a set of diseases or disease processes. As long as the disease and its consequences are present, then there is a reason for the relationship. If the disease is cured, the relationship is no longer necessary. And if the disease is terminal, the focus of the physician changes. Who provides medical care at that point? Is it the specialist, the primary care physician, or both? Or is it a physician with additional training in palliative care?

It is my sense that people visit physicians expecting to be heard, taken seriously, and understood. Martin Buber speaks of the essence of relationship in his book *I and Thou*. He states that an I-Thou relationship is one in which both people meet and experience one another in the context of their wholeness, their personhood. Only then do the two become equals with regard to dignity, integrity, and power. Aldo Carotenuto, a professor at the University of Rome, says this with regard to relationship: "One must realize that in any relationship, along with the possibility of having a Thou with whom to dialogue, one always runs the risk of losing oneself, of becoming an It."

We experience objects as It; our relationship with them as I-It. When the doctor regards the patient only as a disease, without appreciation for the impact the disease has on the life, the relationship is at risk of becoming the I-It variety. That is also true if the patient regards the doctor only as a body of knowledge, disregarding the impact the doctor-patient interaction might have on the doctor. Hence, the relationship may be reduced from I-Thou, to I-It, perhaps even to It-It. The relationship is at risk of becoming "a disease speaking to a body of knowledge, a body of knowledge speaking to a disease."

In some instances, both physician and patient are satisfied with the interaction, especially if the patient simply wants the doctor's knowledge and authority regarding a particular disease process. Say, for example, that a patient has a bacterial pneumonia that is appropriately treated with antibiotics. The patient seeks medical help because of a cough, fever, and fatigue. The physician makes the assessment, orders a chest X-ray, prescribes the antibiotic, explains the side-effects, and suggests that the patient return if symptoms worsen or don't begin to improve over the next two or three days. The patient who improves is pleased, satisfied with the interaction as well as the outcome. But say the same person does not respond to the antibiotic. He returns to see the physician and over a course of several days learns that there is an underlying cancer for which there is no cure. Now, knowledge and authority are not enough. The patient will expect empathy and compassion. An I-Thou relationship seems to be particularly valued once dying and death become a reality. At that time, if the relationship is other than the I-Thou variety, then suffering is likely to occur.

This pain and suffering—inflicted by another unintentionally—is what I call "iatrogenic suffering." According to *Dorland's Medical Dictionary*, "iatrogenic" means "resulting from the activity of physicians; said of any adverse condition in a patient resulting from treatment by a physician or surgeon." The adverse condition is the emotional suffering experienced by patients; the treatment in this instance is the way in which doctors speak to patients.

In my experience, iatrogenic suffering occurs when patients bear the burden of a doctor's own unresolved psychological and emotional issues about death, suffering, pain, and relationship. Whatever the personal issues may be for the doctor, if not addressed or unresolved these will likely affect the patient. If I as a physician have not asked myself questions like *What would my life be like if I were told today that I had a terminal illness?* or *What would I feel about who I am and about my relationships to those I love?* or *What would I feel if I knew that the usual course of the disease I just learned I had is rapid and includes considerable pain or discomfort?* then I might talk without empathy or sensitivity. My tone and manner might convey disregard for their very humanity—for their grief, fear, and anxiety. I might be keeping a physical and emotional distance because I resist the grief, fear, and anxiety of my own feelings. If I still possess unresolved feelings following the death or suffering of a family member or friend, I might be all the more unprepared to get close to death, that is by getting too close to my patient. I'm afraid that if I get too close, then I might have to experience aspects of *his* life that are very sad, unjust, complicated, and unfixable. I'll be helpless in the face of tragedy, far too aware of the limitations of the science of medicine and my personal inability to cure, fix, or repair his suffering and death. I'll feel like a failure. I'll experience grief—an emotion I would rather avoid. Besides, there is no place or time in my schedule for processing emotions, and outside the workplace other commitments and issues occupy my time. To explore emotions requires time and energy, two precious commodities in my busy life.

But if I want to be a compassionate physician and not cause harm, then I must address my feelings. Any emotion that I have not recognized or expressed is likely to be projected onto my patient, potentially adding to his suffering. The patient will experience my avoidance, fear, guilt, sense of failure, and other denied emotions as a deliberate failure to engage them as a human being, a deliberate decision to disregard the meaning and importance of their life. They will feel that I abandoned them at the very moment they needed me most.

So how do people want to hear the bad news? Put simply, they don't—nobody wants to hear bad news. And if the desire is to shoot the messenger, then the "heartless" breaker of bad news merely reinforces that anger. People visit physicians with hope and belief that the physician will do something to cure them, or at least help them feel better. They don't go to hear the message that cure is not possible, that death is inevitable. This idea is explored in the following myth:

> King Acrisius of Argos pondered his daughter's future: "My daughter, Danae, grows tall and ripe," he said to himself. "Her eyes fog over

when I speak to her. She is ready for a husband, but am I ready for a son-in-law? I dislike the idea and always have. A son-in-law will be a younger man waiting for me to die so he can take the throne. Perhaps he will even try to hasten that sad event. Such things are not unknown. I loathe the idea of a son-in-law. But she is ready for a husband, and princesses must not be spinsters ... a grave decision ... I shall consult the oracle."

He sent to the oracle at Delphi, and the messenger returned with this prophecy: "Your daughter will bear a son who will one day kill you." Acrisius was shocked by the bad news. He had expected to hear a prophecy about how his daughter's future husband might someday seek to overthrow him. He did not expect to hear that he would be killed by his grandson. Acrisius had the messenger beheaded for bringing him this bad news. Then he retired to his throne room to continue his brooding. He decided that in order to avoid this prophecy, he would imprison his daughter in an underground chamber. But Zeus, the greatest of the gods, desired Danae, and by transforming himself he entered the chamber through an opening in the roof of the chamber. Subsequently Danae bore a son, Perseus, whose cries reached the ears of Acrisius.

In his terror, Acrisius shut Danae and Perseus in a great chest and set them afloat on the sea. As they floated away, Danae wept as she sang to her son who lay sleeping upon her breast. In time they were rescued by a fisherman, Dictys, whose brother was Polydectes, the king of the island of Seriphus.

Perseus grew to be strong and handsome, a fearless young man who was talented in running, swimming, climbing and fighting. He eventually returned to Argos and competed in athletic games in which he threw the discus, which accidentally struck and killed Acrisius.

Acrisius had assumed that envy and malice would motivate someone to kill him, whereas his death was the result of an accident. The truth of the message that he would die prevailed.

Hearing bad news often results in anger—at change, at information, at life, illness, mortality, and, finally, the messenger. How the message is given can effect the emotional response. Thus one must ask, *What is the best way of giving and receiving information that is difficult to hear?*

Remember the stories of Max and Marjorie. It was Max who said, "When the staff doctor gave me my diagnosis, suicide became a viable option." One patient on the palliative care unit told me that he was left alone in his room for two hours after being told he would die from his illness. Subsequently, he attempted to kill himself. You may have your own examples of when a doctor, nurse, or other health care provider spoke to you or your loved one, or was silent, in a way that added to your suffering, despair, frustration, and anger. Those who describe the experience usually do so with a degree of anger and disbelief, a real sense of betrayal.

In my research, a portion of the suffering that people experienced resulted from the way in which doctors communicated with them. It also resulted from their interactions with other health care providers. Although the doctor makes the diagnosis and breaks the news to the patient, many other health care professionals are involved in a hospital stay. For some of my coresearchers, interactions with these professionals added to their suffering; for others, they engendered a sense of trust and safety.

Isabel was a soft-spoken woman with a strong will and a great interest in her community. She lived a simple life in a small one-bedroom apartment near the hospital. Although she cherished the visits from her children, her true delight was in her grandchildren. She had a wonderfully warm smile. When in the hospital, Isabel regarded her room and the area around her bed as her personal private space. When a health care provider entered without speaking to her, she felt as though there was an intruder in the house. "I was lying in my bed, talking on the phone, and suddenly she was working on my arm while standing behind me. I just about turned around and slugged whoever it was touching me, and then I realized it was the nurse. She never told me what she was doing or why. I would like to have known." She was embarrassed to speak about her emotions, and she worried that if she complained it might jeopardize her relationship with the caregiver.

Isabel wanted to be treated with respect rather than as a disease. "I want them to think of me as a human being. I might be going to die, which they wouldn't have known then anyway, but they should still treat me with respect." She worried about her IV. "I just wonder about this thing. I've had it in for a long time. I'm wondering if it could get covered with skin? And would it be hard to take it out?" Isabel had questions to ask but didn't feel that there was anyone she could speak to about her concerns.

One approach Isabel might have taken: Say to the nurse, "I have some concerns about my care, when might I speak to someone about them?" Or "I don't understand why I am getting the medication through an IV. Is there someone who could discuss this with me?" People working in health care are familiar with their environment, their jobs, and their responsibilities. Some forget that your admission to the hospital might be your first and therefore assume you are as familiar with things as they are. Express concerns, ask questions, work to participate in the decisionmaking regarding your care. I know this is difficult when you are tired, experiencing discomfort or pain, and feeling vulnerable due to your dependence on others. Ask family and friends for support in getting the information and the interaction you need.

Brent, a man in his mid-thirties who had several hospital experiences, told me what he wanted health care providers to know about being a patient. I include his story because it might provide you with a frame of reference for interacting with health care providers during your own illness. Brent says, "You have to be able to deal with patients as people and be able to relate to them on some level in order to provide the care that they need. I'm not just a name or a chart. I'm a human being, I'm an individual. . . . There's a person underneath all of those mechanical things."

Brent described some of his experiences with caregivers when he was hospitalized for pneumonia. "I was tired of being told that I was pulling the oxygen mask off at night. No one in their right mind who needs oxygen is taking the mask off. It's falling off. I'd wake up and I'd be gasping for air, terrified. They'd come in and say, 'Well, you almost died, you gotta stop pulling the mask off.' Well, I'm not pulling it off! Someone's supposed to be coming in here to check that it's on. It was terrible. That's what I will never forget, that they were blaming me. I felt very vulnerable and realized I needed someone there to help; I needed a protector." Brent felt strongly that the attitudes of health care providers toward their patients were evident in the ways they spoke to and treated patients. "The way a person turns someone over tells you how they treat them." He felt that there was discrimination against some patients. "'You know, he's so heavy, let's just leave him in the room and close the door.' That's exactly what they do."

Brent found that some nurses knew what it meant to listen, to be compassionate and understand him. He felt that being understood in this way enhanced his understanding of himself. "I found that nurses did listen to you. Very often they heard things you didn't know you were saying. They often helped me understand myself." It seems that most people who have been patients experience both beneficial and hurtful encounters with care providers. If that has been your experience, you are certainly not alone.

Max also had a positive experience with some nurses, but others added to his suffering. "Some nurses were absolute dolls. Others, well, maybe I'm asking, 'Please don't use that vein.' They come back with something like 'I've been doing this for seventeen years, and who do you think you are trying to order me around.' And they just go ahead.

Nobody deserves to be treated like that. It's not fair to the patient or to the patient's family."

Ron was a fifty-year-old with dark hair, brown eyes, and a tentative smile. Ron had a similar experience in a different hospital. "I had a daily IV that had to run its course. I told the nurse it was bad. It hurt. It turned a rashy red. I complained again. I said something is wrong here, I'm in a lot of pain. Turns out, when she changed the IV, she'd missed the vein. The stuff was going into my arm and it was swelling up. She said, 'I'll come back in five minutes if it still hurts.' I'm ready to rip the thing out and climb out the window." Ron felt that he was not heard or taken very seriously.

Some doctors may feel that the moment they break the bad news about a terminal illness is the point at which they have nothing more to offer. On the contrary, they can commit to being there for the patient regardless of the outcome of treatment, to control pain and manage other symptoms, to support family and friends. This may be the time of greatest need for the patient. It is when the focus shifts to prolongation of life, quality of life, pain control, symptom management, and issues that contribute to suffering—physically, psychologically, and spiritually. Suffering is diminished when those who suffer are understood. For your own benefit, ask your attending physician what you might expect from him during the course of your illness.

Experiencing pain because of a bad interaction with a health care provider isn't uncommon. Don't be afraid to do what you think is right: Marjorie, who heard the bad news from a physician who nonchalantly stood in the doorway, did the self-respecting thing and let him know how his way of communicating was hurtful. She was able to communicate person-to-person, but she might also have written a letter or phoned him from home. This is something you might want to consider: Explain your point of view, identify your preferred outcome, and relay your preferences for the future. This is your experience, your illness, your life—not his. If the pain is too great and you have lost your sense of trust in the doctor, then it might be time to find another doctor. This is *your* life, *your* experience, so don't let someone treat you otherwise.

Regardless of your previous interactions with health care providers thus far in your illness, it is likely that you will have more. I often receive phone calls from friends and acquaintances asking how to communicate with physicians, how to get the information they need and want. In this section I offer general advice for patients; advice and guidelines regarding doctor–patient communications are provided for physicians in the appendix, "Talking to Terminally Ill Patients: Guidelines for Physicians."

What if you are visiting a doctor because of a symptom that is causing you concern, a symptom that has disrupted your life? The doctor thinks of that symptom in terms of a disease process and seeks to understand it more fully through clinical observations and by running tests (blood work, urine samples, X–rays, etc.).

If you have more than one concern to discuss, write them down in order of priority before you visit the office. Mention at the beginning that you have several concerns and would like to discuss the top two or three if time permits. Ask how much time you have. If only two concerns are addressed, inform the doctor of the third so that she can assess its urgency and make another appointment if necessary. But keep in mind that if your doctor spends an extra ten minutes on every patient, the waiting room would soon fill up with "im-patients." If you work within the system, the patient-doctor relationship will benefit.

Give as much specific information as you can for each symptom. Describe the experience of the symptom—when it started, how it has changed over time, what makes it better or worse (see chapter 3). If you feel a burning sensation in your stomach during a nap, don't just say, "I think I have an ulcer" (but feel free to add your personal "diagnosis" after describing the symptoms, especially if you've been treated for similar symptoms before). In your description, include any treatment you tried at home (including alternative treatments—don't be apprehensive about that); name any and all the medications you used; and by all means, inform her whether you've seen another health care professional about this. If you feel awkward about something you did, then say it: "I feel awkward saying this, but I want you to know that...."

Once the doctor makes her decision about the disease process, she will speak to you about the diagnosis and treatment. The doctor may also recommend tests. Be sure you understand their purpose, the process, and the diagnosis. If you're anxious, fearful, or upset in any way, tell the doctor. She may be able to clarify things in a way that reduces your fear. Knowing what to expect at the outset means you won't let your imagination run wild.

Some doctors, especially those who know their patients well, give information in small doses knowing that the patient will get the bigger picture in due course. Other doctors hold back for fear they will increase their patient's anxiety. Asking for information or stating that you would like to know as much as possible will help the doctor to overcome her own concerns. Ask questions until you understand the disease process, the treatment options, and the expected outcomes. You could say things like, "If I understand you correctly, what is happening is...."

If the treatment includes medication, ask when you might expect it to start working, the presence and severity of its side effects, and how long you will likely have to stay on it. Make certain that the doctor knows about other medications you are taking and whether you have prescriptions for them or not. Birth-control pills, medication for indigestion, and over-the-counter sleeping pills are often forgotten. Take notes if necessary. Friends and family members will ask you a thousand questions if they know that you have been to see a doctor.

A few notes may be valuable in answering those questions, not to mention keeping a record for yourself.

The key words to remember are "truth," "touch," and "time." Ideally, your physician is able to speak the *truth*, *touch* you with compassion, and give the *time* that is necessary to bring you to a frank understanding of your situation while minimizing distress.

If you sense that you're facing a life-threatening illness, or news that a disease has progressed, bring along a friend or family member. Some people value the company, even for more mundane visits. Most people, even veteran health care professionals, feel some anxiety when visiting a doctor. An extra set of ears could make a big difference. But if you do invite someone to join you (or you yourself accompany a patient during a visit), consider the following suggestions.

Go to the doctor's office together. Ask the doctor's permission in advance, takes notes on the key information, and write out some questions before the visit. Some people actually tape the meeting. Perhaps this is not necessary when hearing the bad news for the first time, but it might be helpful on subsequent visits when decisions are being made about treatment plans.

Make a follow-up appointment for test results, anticipating when they'll become available. Making a follow-up appointment at the time of the initial visit can reduce waiting time and the consequent anxiety.

Ask the doctor how much time she has for the visit (usually ten to fifteen minutes). Listen carefully. Ask questions. Have terms and concepts defined and clarified. Request copies of reports. Offer to pay for photocopying. Have the reports explained in layman's terms. Ask more questions. Advise the doctor that you'll want all the information that is known about the disease process (known as the "natural history of the disease"). Ask what you can expect in following a particular course of treatment (the "protocol") and what you can expect if you choose not to have the treatment. How many patients has the doctor cared for using this particular treatment? What was their experience?

What was the outcome? If surgery is recommended, how long will the recovery period be? How tired will you be through the recovery period? Will you have the energy to do the things you want to do? How much is the recovery period compromised because of the underlying disease process? If you decide not to take a particular medication or have a recommended surgery, does that mean such options will forever be foreclosed? And if you choose not to have them, who will provide medical care as your disease progresses?

Tell the doctor this information is valuable to you as well as your family; you want as much control of your life as possible. There are things you still want to do, people you want to see, some inner preparation you may need to make. Ask permission to call back with other questions or requests. (But remember that doctors don't generally get paid for telephone conversations. For that reason, some might prefer that you make another appointment. It's not that the doctor is only interested in money; she practices medicine, and seeing patients is how she earns a living.)

There are many decisions once someone is told he has a terminal illness. It is crucial to remember that the choices belong to the patient, whether they pertain to the disease process, treatment, or the life you want to live with the time and energy you have remaining. In fact, the unfinished business, your sense of self, and your relationship with others may be as important (even more important) than focusing all your attention on the disease process.

Karen was a woman in her early thirties. She had seen much of the world as she worked for a travel company in Maple Ridge. She loved her job. In it she was able to combine working with people and travel. She developed close friendships outside of work centered on shared interests like tennis, badminton, and music. She played the piano for personal enjoyment as well as for her church. She had a close relationship with her parents and with Andrew, one of her three brothers who was a year younger than she was. Although Karen was not as close to the other two siblings, twin boys eight years younger, she was very fond of them.

Dr. James had been Karen's doctor for several years. She had confidence in him and trusted that he was thorough in his assessment and appropriate in his treatment plans. She appreciated his manner and his honesty when he spoke with her. Karen especially enjoyed talking about her travels with him, as he always seemed to be interested in her as a person.

Karen had been feeling some discomfort in her lower back for several weeks before she went to see Dr. James. She attributed the pain to a tennis injury; she had not played for several months and then played in a two-day tournament, after which she began to suffer. She had experienced similar pain several years prior to this following a car accident. It cleared in a matter of months with some physiotherapy and an exercise program. Now, bothered by lower back pain again, she resumed those exercises. The pain subsided but didn't clear. Thus she went to see Dr. James. After his assessment, he suggested a return visit to the physiotherapist and advised her to come back to see him if there was no significant improvement in ten to fourteen days.

Karen returned in a week because of a tingling sensation in her right leg. This time, as a result of his physical examination, Dr. James had a sense that there might be something more than just a soft-tissue injury. He set up a consultation with a neurologist. Karen was seen within twenty-four hours. The neurologist ordered magnetic resonance imaging, which indicated a mass in her lower back—a tumor, hopefully benign, but likely malignant. Surgery was the treatment of choice, and within days she had undergone the operation. The pathology report on the tumor indicated that it was in an advanced state, meaning it could not be cured. Karen would at best be treated with palliative care. Karen would likely die as a result of this mass, this foreign tissue that would continue to grow, to spread, to consume. Even before the surgery, Karen had a sense that something sinister was going on in her body.

As her family physician, Dr. James, in consultation with the neurologist and neurosurgeon, decided it was most appropriate for him to give Karen the results of the pathology report. He went to her bedside with information and compassion. He also approached her with a considerable amount of self-doubt. Had the tumor been present at the time of the car accident several years earlier and been missed by him? Had he acted quickly enough this time? Perhaps if he had sent her to see the specialist instead of the physiotherapist, it would have been detected two weeks earlier. Would that have made a difference to the outcome?

Walking through the hospital ward toward Karen's room, his shoes felt like cement blocks. His natural inclination was to turn away from this responsibility, but it was his and could not be delayed. Karen was resting quietly. The music from her tape deck was a Beethoven piano concerto. Dr. James recognized the piece. He wished they could discuss music, tennis, maybe Karen's travel plans. He sat down, took her hand, and asked her, "If I needed to speak to you about some difficult health issues, would you want a friend or family member present?" Karen thought for a moment and then replied, "Yes, I would like my brother, Andrew, to be here." "When might he be available?" "I'm certain he could be here sometime tomorrow." The time was set for noon the next day.

Twenty-four hours later, Dr. James returned to Karen's bedside. Andrew and one of the twins, Jake, were present. Jake was sitting on the end of the bed, Andrew on the windowsill. Dr. James sat next to Karen. Like the day before, he took her hand. This time he turned off the music. He paused for a time, looking down. The period of silence seemed like an eternity. Dr. James looked up at Karen, who had her eyes closed. He began: "Karen, I have something to say to you that is very difficult for me to say. I want to make certain you and your brothers understand what I am about to tell you so I will be checking with you and with them as I talk with you. Your eyes are closed, and I want to make sure you are awake."

"I am awake." Her words were clipped.

"I am sorry to tell you that the results of the pathology report indicate that the mass in your lower back is malignant." Dr. James knew he was hiding behind the word. He didn't want Karen to have to ask for definitions, so he added, "That means it's cancer, and unfortunately it is the type of cancer for which there is no cure." Again he paused. This time the silence was deafening.

Then Karen spoke. "Does no cure mean I'm going to die?"

"That's right, the cancer will likely be the cause of your death, and as I said I am very, very sorry to have to tell you this, but I do."

Andrew was angry, "Why did you wait, why didn't you send her to the specialist rather than the physiotherapist? Is this a diagnosis you missed four years ago?"

Dr. James responded, "I think I can appreciate how you feel, Andrew. Those are exactly the questions I have been asking myself for the past twenty-four hours. In fact, I have been asking them for the past week, ever since Karen came back with tingling in her leg. In hindsight I wish I had sent her to the neurologist rather than to the physiotherapist, and I wish I had ordered more investigations five years ago when she first came to see me after the car accident. But it made sense that the low back pain resulted from the accident, and it improved with the treatment. This time, that was not the case. Still, I wish I had sent her to the neurologist after that earlier visit."

Andrew asked a few other questions and, in time seemed, to appreciate that his sister had been given appropriate care. Dr. James stayed with them until all their questions were answered. Then he let them know that he would be pleased to return at the end of the day, and he would certainly come back the next day to discuss the cancer and what they might expect. They set a time for a second visit. That visit occurred, as did a third, after which Karen made her wishes known. One of those wishes was that Dr. James not speak to her about the disease again but that they manage the symptoms, working to keep her comfortable and functioning independently for as long as possible. He agreed, with one condition: If there were any significant changes in her condition, he could inform her or her brother of those changes. He reassured Karen and her brothers that Karen would not be abandoned but that she would continue to receive the best care possible. Dr. James felt that it would be important for someone to know what he was noting about the disease's progression. Karen, Andrew, and Jake agreed. Dr. James offered to speak with Karen's parents.

Through his compassion, in this case Dr. James demonstrates how to inform someone of a terminal illness without increasing their suffering, without destroying their hope. He supported Karen and her family by understanding and acknowledging their emotional experiences.

The strongest relationships we can have are those in which we feel safe and are able to trust one another, where expectations and needs are expressed and individuals are explicit about which of those expectations and needs can realistically be met. Even in relationships where that occurs, being hurt is a possibility, but the probability is diminished. Your doctor may not be perfect, and he may have already made mistakes that have hurt you. But you can work to create a better relationship with the doctor—one that will help minimize your anxiety and suffering. If your efforts to do so are not met with equal effort in return, you have the choice to move on and to create that relationship with another doctor. The suffering you have experienced in that regard need not continue.

CHAPTER THREE

Physical Pain

I'm only afraid of pain. I'm not afraid of death, I'm not afraid of dying, I'm afraid of pain. I'm terrified of pain, bad pain, cause I've gone through so much of it, you know.

Frieda

We all must die. But if I can save him from days of torture, that is what I feel is my great and ever new privilege. Pain is a more terrible lord of mankind than even death himself.

Albert Schweitzer

I'm very tired. You can get tired of pain. And everything that comes with it, and all the upset to people who love you. . . . They tell you pain is a teacher. I question that.

Tracey

Chiron, the Wounded Healer

In very ancient times, Cronus, an Olympian god, was known for devouring his young. For that reason his wife, Rhea, hid their baby Zeus from Cronus. Cronus wandered the countryside in search of his newborn son. In his wanderings he was attracted to Philyra, an earthly nymph, who changed herself into a mare in order to hide from Cronus. However, she was not able to escape from him, for he changed himself into a horse and in that disguise mated with her. The child born to them was Chiron, a centaur, with the body and legs of a horse and the torso, arms, and head of a man. Philyra found the very sight of Chiron to be repulsive, the thought of him suckling at her breast unbearable. She believed that she had given birth to a strange species. Because of her great loathing toward him, she asked the gods to change her into anything other than what she was. On her request, the gods turned her into a linden tree. Cronus also abandoned Chiron, which left Chiron an orphan.

Apollo, the sun god, master of healing, music, poetry, and prophecy, adopted Chiron. Under the teaching of Apollo, Chiron became known as a wise man and, like his foster father, was also known as a musician, physician, prophet, and teacher. Chiron was responsible for teaching the other centaurs and for teaching in various small kingdoms in northern Greece. Although centaurs were notorious for rowdy living, unruliness, their violence when intoxicated, and general incivility, Chiron was an exception. In fact, kings sent him their sons to be initiated into manhood and educated in the arts of leadership. He taught heroes such as Achilles, Heracles, and Asklepios that which Apollo had taught him.

In one account, Heracles (Hercules), the greatest of all Greek heroes, one day came to the cave of Pholus, a centaur, who welcomed Heracles and served him a meal. Heracles requested some wine, and although Pholus was reluctant to open the wine as it belonged to all the centaurs, he opened it to serve his guest. The scent was such that it attracted the other centaurs, who arrived armed and ready to fight. A battle ensued. Heracles was well prepared for an altercation such as this and was able to repel many of the centaurs. In their retreat, one of them took refuge with Chiron. At that time, Heracles shot an arrow that missed its target, striking Chiron in his knees. Heracles' arrows had been dipped in the blood of the Hydra, making them poisonous, a tactic that Chiron himself had taught the hero. Because Chiron, as a demigod, was immortal, the poisoned arrow could not kill him. Heracles, in remorse, repented of his action to his former teacher and drew out the arrow. Chiron applied herbs in an effort to treat the wound. To no avail. He was left with a painful and incurable wound.

After the injury Chiron withdrew from the company of others, into his cave, howling in pain so excruciating that he wished to die. However, the wound would never heal, and because he was immortal he could never die. He suffered unceasing agony from the wound and spent his days searching for a cure. As he wandered the countryside around his home, he became knowledgeable in the healing powers of plants and herbs. He also began to meet the mortals around him who told of their pain and suffering. Because he could now understand and appreciate what it meant to live with constant pain, his empathy toward the sufferings of others grew with his knowledge of the herbal remedies of the day. With that combination he was very helpful to others and became known as the "wounded healer." Even as a healer of others, Chiron longed for his own pain and suffering to end.

In his travels, Heracles came upon Prometheus, who had been chained to a rock by Zeus as a punishment for stealing fire from Mount Olympus. In that imprisonment Prometheus was exposed to the heat of the daytime sun and to the cold of the nighttime sky. Every day a griffin, that is, a vulture-like bird, came and tore out Prometheus's liver, which regrew at night, cursing him to a cycle of eternal torment. By Zeus's decree Prometheus could be released if an immortal being would relinquish his immortality. Heracles pleaded for Chiron to be that immortal being. Zeus agreed to the exchange, meaning Chiron could die, ending his pain and giving freedom to Prometheus. Nine days after Chiron's death, Zeus intervened and immortalized him as the constellation Centaurus, which is present to this day in the night sky.

❁

Just as Chiron experienced pain as the result of an emotional wounding at birth and a physical wounding as an adult, so pain belongs to each of us. It is part of our entry into the world, of existing in the world and of departing from it. Pain has many faces. An athlete appreciates that pain is a likely part of training and competing; a pregnant woman can anticipate the pain that precedes the birth of her child with the realization that it will end with a baby in her arms; the patient welcomes the surgical removal of an inflamed appendix that has declared its presence with excruciating and nauseating pain; and the teenager with a broken arm knows that once the bone is set healing will begin and pain will eventually subside and disappear. Though some people experience a terminal illness without physical pain, it is, for many, part of living with such an illness. For some it is a constant, with no apparent pain-free end in site. For others it is an intermittent reality, perhaps a fear and anxiety that pain is yet to come or will return. Pain is complex. It always has an emotional or psychological component.

Every day in our world, millions of people experience pain as part of illness. The pain can result from disease, treatment (surgery, chemotherapy, radiation), or unrelated factors. Many can have more than one type of pain, each with a different cause and thus treatment. Whatever the cause, however, the initial fear and anxiety experienced with an increase in their pain or a new pain may be that the disease has progressed or recurred. Pain may or may not increase or change as the disease progresses, that is, the degree of pain does not necessarily correlate to progression of the disease. In fact, some people never experience pain, others experience a great deal of pain even though they may not have "a lot of disease." Many people with a terminal illness often receive the necessary care to control their pain and other symptoms, such that they are able to enjoy some quality of life. For most, pain can be controlled. Unfortunately, in many cases pain that can be controlled is not.

*

It was a late Friday afternoon, starting my weekend rotation of being on-call. A colleague reviewing the patient roster suggested I meet Tom because of his escalating pain and the complexity of issues regarding his care; she sensed he might present a challenge during the weekend. Tom was a thirty-one-year-old man with AIDS, with a prior history of intravenous drug use; he was admitted to the palliative care unit for pain control and symptom management. His pain was located primarily in his abdomen, due to the effects of the disease, and in his back, due to a preexisting injury.

Tom had difficulty describing his pain beyond saying there was more and more of it. I asked Tom about the pain—when it started, how it changed, if there was anything that made it better or worse. The questions focused on determining the physical aspects of the pain. While answering the questions, Tom blurted out, "I haven't had a very happy past, you know." He was speaking about his childhood and the many foster homes he had lived in. Interestingly, like Chiron, Tom's mother could not keep him as an infant and had given him to someone else to parent. Of those foster homes, he said, "I went back two, three, sometimes even four times, ... around thirty foster homes. . . . The things that some of these foster people got away with is unreal. . . . I saw a lot of mean things happen there." He tearfully spoke of isolation, His foster mother "locked me in my room. . . . Her sons got out but I'm not let out." He also spoke of the punishment and abuse he experienced. "Like the punishment that they had—you had to kneel on a brick wall with your hands behind your head. You try that for ten hours, your knees get so sore from kneeling on the brick. . . . If you were bad and if you ran away, [when] they caught up to you, you had to go back there—they would tie you down and put a rope around your ankles and tie you up." With regard to a foster mother who adopted Tom when he was six, he said, "I was always being punished. . . . I used to pee the bed and because I used to pee the bed she'd put me in a tub of cold ice water with the pissy sheets."

As Tom spoke, his pain increased rapidly. Was that because of the story he was telling or was it a purely physical pain? He couldn't sit still, he began to cry, and continued speaking, faster and faster. He spoke of being a model, of feeling betrayed by the partner who had AIDS and didn't inform him of the fact, of close friends in other cities, of his biological mother, of foster mothers, of the drug addiction that had been under control for a year—and his wish that all this suffering would come to an end.

Because other methods of managing the pain had not been effective and the pain was increasing rapidly, Tom was given narcotic analgesics intravenously. The strength of this medication exceeded the requirement of any other patient cared for in the ten-year history of the palliative care program. I was amazed that Tom was still able to communicate despite such a large dose of pain medication. Tom was not a large man, but his suffering was great. The room was filled with his despair, his anguish, his deep yearning to be free of pain—for his life as he knew it, right then, to end.

His pain was all-consuming. Emily Dickinson spoke to the issue in her poem "The Mystery of Pain":

> Pain—has an Element of Blank—
> It cannot recollect
> When it began—or if there were
> A time when it was not—
>
> It has no Future—but itself—
> Its Infinite realms contain
> Its Past—enlightened to perceive
> New Periods—of Pain.

How much of Tom's pain was physical? How much was emotional, mental, or spiritual? Was Tom's desperate assertion of unending pain, despite the narcotics, a manipulative effort to get more drugs? I remember thinking that it was time to go back to two of the basic rules of pain management: First, pain is what Tom says it is and not what I or others think it ought to be; and second, the right dose of pain medication for Tom is the dose that eliminates the pain.

Patients tell me of their pain, and sometimes I recall that others with a similar diagnosis did not articulate their suffering like this. And if I use my own pain threshold as a reference point, I might dismiss or trivialize whatever the person is saying. This has become very apparent not so much as a physician but as a parent. There are times when my children complain of pain that in my opinion simply doesn't seem to fit the injury they suffered. Thus I might try to toughen them up in the belief this is all much ado about nothing, that they are seeking attention rather than responding appropriately. In any event, the child begins to learn that her pain will not be taken seriously. In fact, she may feel ashamed of having pain or feel blamed for getting injured. (Pain is a natural response to injury; pain is not the fault of the person experiencing it). Soon she learns to live with the pain rather than to cry or express other feelings. Who benefits from that? Have my own judgments about the "appropriate" level of pain interfered with my ability to fully understand my patients' experiences? Children who feel disrespected and helpless when a parent diminishes their experience might exaggerate the next episode or fail to report it at all. Likewise, the physician who minimizes or doubts the patient's report jeopardizes that patient's trust and therefore the possibility of controlling the pain. And like the hurt child, this patient might also feel trivialized and learn to live with the pain: "What's the use in telling the doctor about my pain, since he doesn't take me seriously, anyway?" they might ask. Or perhaps the patient, again like the hurt child, will exaggerate the pain to get attention. In either case, when the physician trivializes the pain, both the pain and mistrust are likely to increase. Tom needed me to believe him as the first step in reducing his pain.

I was somewhat anxious about the dosage of narcotic Tom was receiving. But I reminded myself—Tom's pain is what he says it is, and the right dose is the amount necessary to alleviate the pain. As the narcotic began to take effect, Tom began to relax. Within twenty-four hours we were able to control the pain with a combination of medications.

Tom's pain was both physical and psychological (related, in part, to his childhood experiences). Pain is always that way; one component affects the other. Pain can affect the ability to eat, sleep, work, and enjoy time with others. Tom's pain was so great that he no longer found pleasure in life. He welcomed death. His pain had become the focus of his existence; it interfered with his relationships, prohibited activity, and deterred his ability to relax and sleep. That is what happens with pain: One experiences a changed sense of self. Recall an old toothache or a migraine: It is virtually impossible to think of anything else but the sheer agony. Eventually, untreated pain will sap the joy out of life.

So if you are experiencing pain, it is important to express to your health care providers as honestly and thoroughly as possible the nature of that pain and the way in which it intrudes on other valued aspects of your life.

Pain begins with a physical stimulus (damage to tissue or nerves) which is modified in the brain. It results in an awareness that something harmful or noxious is happening somewhere in the body. This results in an emotional response, a behavior that is associated with intense feelings of displeasure. Pain has a protective purpose. It is a warning sign of wounding or damage.

With the growth of hospice and palliative care programs, many people do not need to be admitted to the hospital for pain management. Teams working in the community are often able to effectively manage the pain, the symptoms (nausea, vomiting, constipation, etc.), and the care (bathing, meal preparation, hygiene). But in order to manage the pain, health care providers must understand a variety of features about it. That is why they ask many questions about the pain. The details about your pain are helpful. For that reason I have included, in somewhat of a textbook format, information that a doctor or nurse might need in order to accurately evaluate your pain. Because it is difficult to concentrate or remember details when you are having pain, it might be important to jot down some notes about your experience before visiting your doctor.

Where is the pain?

- Did the pain start in that location?
- Is it always there?
- Does it spread to other places in the body?
- Do you feel like every part of your body is uncomfortable, aching, or painful? Pain that feels like it's everywhere can mean that the source is difficult to identify. If the source is difficult to identify, or if your body really does hurt everywhere, describe the sensation as best as possible—"there are times when my whole body hurts"; "I get this aching throughout my body and there is nothing I can do to make it go away"; "every part of me hurts"; "I've never experienced anything like this before."
- Is the pain present in several areas of the body at the same time?

When did the pain start?

- How long have you had the pain? Pain is distinguished as being *acute*, meaning new or of recent onset, that is, present for a few hours or days; or *chronic*, meaning it has been present for many weeks, months, or even years. People with chronic pain have often learned to live with pain and may not even describe the experience as painful. Rather they have "discomfort" or "depression"; they are "feeling blue" or they "used to feel different." If this sounds like you, it would help if you tried to remember when you last felt well, free of discomfort, and were able to do whatever you wanted without the ache or awareness of a particular muscle, joint, or other body part.

- Does the pain come and go (is it intermittent?), or is it always there (is it constant)?
- Is it constant pain with episodes of more severity?
- Since the pain started, have you ever been pain-free? What have you tried—medication, treatments, exercise—to control the pain? Did anything work? How was the pain best controlled? While the pain was controlled, did you ever have pain for brief periods (so-called breakthrough pain)? What have you tried that didn't control the pain?

What is the nature of the pain?

- What makes the pain worse?
- What makes the pain better?
- Has it changed? If so, how?
- Does it change with activity?
- Does it waken you from your sleep?
- Does it interfere with your work, daily activities, or relationships with friends and family?

How severe is the pain?

- Looking at a scale (known as a "visual analogue scale") of 0–10, 0 being no pain and 10 being the worst pain you have ever had, how would you score the pain you have at present? Other scales might include descriptions like no pain, mild, moderate, severe, very severe, or worst possible pain; or perhaps none, annoying, uncomfortable, dreadful, horrible, or agonizing.

- Some professionals will ask whether the pain is aching, nagging, gnawing, sharp like a knife, burning, tingling, uncomfortable, steady, severe, stabbing, shooting, worst pain ever, like a toothache, like a headache, excruciating. Can you describe your pain using any of these words?
- Have you ever had pain like this before? What was the cause of the pain at that time? How was it controlled?

Your doctor ought to ask you questions like these, but if she doesn't, think about them and compose answers that accurately express your experience; and offer them to the doctor. Write out your answers, or ask a friend or family member to do so. Your doctor should then do a physical exam, order some investigations, and prescribe pain-control medication. In many instances, especially in the home or hospice, a doctor will complete the assessment without ordering additional tests or investigations, as the trip to another facility can be problem-filled and even add to pain and discomfort.

Max, who I introduced in chapter 2, experienced severe pain as a result of cancer:

I'm not sleeping at all and it's getting to the point where in the middle of the night four or five o'clock in the morning rolls around I'm tossing and turning from the pain and from the discomfort. And I'm just so exhausted, you know this has gone on for weeks on end and I fall asleep simply from sheer exhaustion not from actually being able to fall asleep or anything like that. I was falling asleep with the pain and I was just thankful if I got forty minutes, fifty minutes whatever the case might be.

He spoke of the effect on him, his ability to work, his relationship with friends, and his appetite. Max experienced pain for months. It affected his whole sense of being. Chronic pain commonly results in social isolation and withdrawal, depression, changes in ability to function, and sleep disturbances. At times Max was hesitant to speak to his parents about his pain because he did not want to burden them. This resulted in a greater sense of isolation and contributed to the anxiety he experienced. Like Chiron, he went howling in pain into his cave.

Is it possible to live with a terminal illness yet experience no pain at all? Yes, it is possible. The medical literature has focused on people with cancer and AIDS, and doctors agree that for most people—85–95 percent—pain can be controlled. So, why is it that so many people with these illnesses do experience pain? Some physicians lack adequate knowledge about pain medication (analgesics) and their side effects. Some may fear losing their license to practice medicine if they prescribe narcotics. They might also fear that use of narcotics will lead to addiction. Patients can also be apprehensive about reporting pain or feel that seeking out relief is a sign of weakness; they have internalized the message to tough it out. Sometimes people avoid pain medication for religious or cultural reasons or fear the stigma of taking a narcotic, even for legitimate reasons. Some lack access to adequate services.

There are many ways or routes by which to take pain medication: by mouth (oral) in forms of liquid, tablet, or sustained-release capsules; by rectum; across the skin by wearing a patch (transdermal); under the skin by a small needle (subcutaneous); through the veins (intravenous); patient-controlled pumps; and small tubes (catheters) implanted in specific areas (the spine, known as an epidural, the brain, or places that affect specific nerves or pathways). For its cost-effectiveness and convenience, the oral route is preferred. It means people can stay at home, move around, and travel. But the other routes are important, as each patient has a unique disease experience and benefits from different medications and routes. There is always a method to deliver pain medication.

The first medications used are not necessarily narcotics (also known as "opioids"). If the pain is mild, the doctor will likely recommend over-the-counter medications, no prescription necessary: aspirin, acetaminophen, ibuprofen, and nonsteroidal anti-inflammatory agents. It is always important to read the instructions and descriptions that come with the medication and to ask the pharmacist or doctor to identify the possible side effects. This becomes even more important when you are taking more than one medication (whether prescribed or over-the-counter) and when you have a history of liver disease, kidney disease, internal bleeding, allergies, stomach ulcers, substance abuse, or other problems that can affect the way in which the medication is processed (metabolized) in the body. Apart from the side effects, there can be interactions specific to the combination of medications. Some of these can be beneficial, others harmful. Some people don't think of nonprescription medications as medicine and will forget to mention them to their doctor. Don't make this mistake! When you visit a doctor to manage pain, be sure to bring along a list of all the medications you are taking (prescription and over-the-counter), noting the dosage of each. Always discuss the entire range of medication issues with your doctor to gain a clear understanding of the expected outcome and possible side effects. It is also valuable to understand how long before the medication takes effect; the same goes for side effects. Always be aware of possible interactions when taking more than one medication.

Over-the-counter medications have ceiling effects, that is, a dose at which maximum benefit is achieved. If someone takes more than the maximum dose, that individual risks serious side effects. If the maximum dose is not effective, don't take more, and tell your doctor. In fact, inform your doctor whenever you near the maximum dose. When nonprescription medications are no longer effective, the doctor will likely consider an opioid, such as codeine, morphine, hydromorphone (Dilaudid), oxycodone, fentanyl, or methadone. Morphine, an opioid, is effective and available, typically the first one that a doctor will prescribe when an opioid is necessary.

It is generally more difficult to chase pain than it is to stay on top of it. What does that mean? If you wait until the pain surfaces before taking medication, you will experience unnecessary discomfort; it is better to take medication on a regular basis to prevent the pain in the first place. When a doctor prescribes analgesics, it will be on a regular basis, not on an as-needed basis. That means you will take medication every four, eight, or twelve hours (instructions are given when the medications are dispensed). Long-acting forms of medication are generally taken every eight or twelve hours. This means you don't have to interrupt your sleep to take it. For immediate-release medication, taken every four hours, you must wake from your sleep. This can be frustrating, but remember that it is easier to go back to sleep without pain; if pain wakens you, you will likely stay awake until the medication takes effect.

Even when pain is controlled, people can experience episodes of pain—breakthrough pain, also known as "incident pain" occurs due to physical activity; sometimes it is unpredictable; and sometimes it occurs just prior to the next regular dose of analgesic. Breakthrough pain requires a breakthrough dose of medication. Apart from the regular dose, then, it is important that your doctor also prescribe an as-needed dose to eliminate breakthrough pain. When someone is on regular medication, the breakthrough dose is usually taken an hour or two after the regular dose if the person experiences pain at that time. A breakthrough dose may be necessary for anyone taking regular pain medication regardless of whether you are on immediate-release or sustained-release analgesics. Keep a record of the number of breakthrough doses that you take; mark a calendar or appointment book; record the effects. And remember that some pain might not be related to the disease process. Maybe you had headaches before the disease, just as you might after the diagnosis. And though it's probably okay to take standard headache medication as you did before, be sure to check with your doctor.

Sometimes an activity (walking, bathing, sitting up for a visit) will cause pain. For Tom, merely walking from his room to the smoking area of the palliative care unit was a painful activity. He enjoyed smoking and enjoyed the company of other patients he met in the smoking area. In those instances, his pain could be prevented with a breakthrough dose taken twenty to thirty minutes beforehand. (If your own breakthrough dose controls such pain, use the same dose the next time. If this makes you drowsy, consult with your nurse or physician about decreasing the dose the next time; if you still have pain, discuss increasing the dose.)

Understanding the concepts of pain management and working with your health care providers will give you personal control and a better sense of well-being. Try to find a professional who will work with you. Contact a local hospice or palliative care association, ask family members and friends, or consult health services in your area.

The appropriate dose of opioid, again, is the amount that relieves the pain, provided side effects are minimal or at least tolerable. As doses increase, side effects are more likely. However, each person is unique and will experience side effects differently. If the side effects are intolerable, ask your doctor to treat them. That way the dose of opioid can be increased if necessary. When side effects become intolerable, it might be valuable to introduce another medication or treatment (in addition to or in substitution).

Common side effects from opioids are constipation, nausea, vomiting, and drowsiness. Some people also experience confusion and, on high doses, muscle twitching (myoclonus). Opioids generally act on the gastrointestinal tract (movement is slowed and secretions are diminished). That, combined with decreased physical activity, less fluid intake, and diet, contribute to constipation. A rule of thumb: At a minimum, people need a bowel movement every three days. Constipation can be difficult to resolve—stool softeners or laxatives may be needed. It helps to drink fluids, especially fruit juices; also, you can eat fruit, bran, and any other foods that have been beneficial in the past. As opioid doses are increased, the dose of softeners and laxatives are usually increased as well. For most people, constipation is uncomfortable. As with pain, it is better to prevent constipation beforehand than to treat it after the fact. We routinely prescribe constipation medication at the same time that an opioid is prescribed.

When people first start on an opioid, they may experience nausea and vomiting. Opioid-associated nausea occurs for several reasons: physiological response, the taste of the drug, fears and concerns about opioids, or anxiety that the opioid is a sure sign that the disease is progressing. Nausea and vomiting can generally be treated with an antiemetic medication, usually taken before the opioid. As with constipation, anticipate your strategy for nausea and vomiting. If your doctor doesn't prescribe an antiemetic or laxative when first prescribing opioids, raise the subject yourself. "I've heard that people who take medications for pain often get constipated and some feel nauseated when they take them. What might I do if that happens to me?" Having instructions about over-the-counter medications or a prescription in hand for constipation and nausea could serve you well. This may actually reduce your anxiety. For most people the nausea and vomiting will decrease or clear in a week or two, meaning the medication for those symptoms can be reduced or eliminated.

Many people experience drowsiness when they first take an opioid. Essentially this happens for two reasons. First, the drug affects the central nervous system; and second, people who have lived with pain are usually exhausted from that experience. When they get to be pain-free, they relax and with the relief comes the overwhelming need to sleep. The drowsiness usually clears in a day or two, but it can take longer. If drowsiness persists for more than seventy-two hours, check with your doctor. He may need to decrease the dose or switch to an alternate medication. Your doctor should tell you what to expect, and you in turn should inform friends and family about things such as side effects, treatment, benefits of the medication, the time-frame, and changing medication. Without this information, they may be surprised and concerned that you actually seem sicker after taking an opioid. They will also benefit from a reminder that pain can occur at any time during a terminal illness regardless of your outward appearance and that drowsiness will likely clear in a few days.

In some instances, people who take opioids become confused or experience delirium. Some may have hallucinations. Such symptoms can also be caused by the spread of the cancer to the brain, compromised function of the liver, kidneys, or lungs, and changes in metabolism that occur as a result of the disease. If it is determined that confusion or delirium is a result of the opioid, the dose can be reduced or an alternate opioid can be tried. Symptoms caused by one opioid might not occur with another. The older you are, the more likely you are to experience confusion and delirium. Therefore dosages might be increased more gradually. However, if the pain is severe or has been present for a long time, you might welcome the relief despite the side effects. For most people side effects can be managed, leading to better overall quality of life.

Very high doses of opioids can lead to muscle-twitching (myoclonus), not unlike the muscle twitching that occurs just prior to falling asleep. For some, the twitching interferes with their activities, so it may be of value for your doctor to add a muscle relaxant. If the twitching is severe and cannot be controlled with a muscle relaxant, discuss this with your doctor who may consider switching to an alternative opioid. Often the twitching is more problematic for friends and family sitting at the bedside than it is for the person experiencing the twitching.

One of the greatest concerns people have with opioids is addiction. Some people are initially reticent and refuse them simply on that basis. If you are taking an opioid as prescribed, you will rarely become an addict. Addiction is a psychological disorder. It is based on the craving of and the compulsive use of a substance that has mind-altering or psychic effects. Often, the addict seeks an altered state of consciousness with the hope of escaping into euphoria.

If you have ever experienced pain in your lifetime, you know that people with pain seek to be pain-free. The opioid is intended to achieve that outcome. As long as pain is present, the effects of the opioid will work and an altered euphoric state will not occur. The point is not to alter your state of consciousness but to manage your pain. Thus the likelihood of addiction is minimized. Addicts also deserve to be pain-free. Methods for managing their pain are similar, and specific medications might be used.

Tolerance and physical dependence can be mistaken for addiction. "Tolerance" means that the dose of pain medication will need to be increased over time in order to keep the effects of analgesia. This is actually a useful feature of opioids in that tolerance results in clearing the side effects. "Physical dependence" occurs to all people who take opioids. It means only that the body gets used to having the medication present and that the medication must never be stopped suddenly. If opioids are stopped suddenly, the person is more likely to experience symptoms of withdrawal—nausea, diarrhea, muscle aches and pains, and general discomfort. The person is not left with a craving for euphoria or the need to have the medication. For recovering addicts, their addiction must be taken into account when reducing opioids. If you are a recovering addict, make sure your physician understands your history in this regard.

Some people may be reluctant to take opioids for religious reasons. Dr. Janet Abrahm is an associate professor of medicine at the University of Pennsylvania School of Medicine and is the medical director of Wissahickon Hospice. In her book *A Physician's Guide to Pain and Symptom Management in Cancer Patients* she outlines the position of the Roman Catholic Church with regard to painkillers to alleviate pain in people who are dying. According to Abrahm, the church's position was first stated by Pius XII in 1957 and reiterated in the Catechism of the Catholic Church (1994, subheading I, Euthanasia, 2279):

> Even if death is thought imminent, the ordinary care owed to a sick person cannot be legitimately interrupted. The use of painkillers to alleviate the sufferings of the dying, even at the risk of shortening their days, can be morally in conformity with human dignity if death is not willed as either an end or a means, but only foreseen and tolerated as inevitable.

This is known as the "doctrine of double effect," meaning that provided the medication is given to relieve pain, and not to end life, an unintended shortening of life is acceptable. People providing medication in this context are not viewed as euthanasiasts, and the patients are not regarded as suicidal. According to Abrahm, the doctrine of double effect is also supported by most Orthodox Jewish and Islamic opinion. In the context of another religion, Buddhism, some people who are searching for enlightenment and awareness choose not to take analgesics if they feel that the medication will interfere with their ability to meditate.

Apart from opioids, there are many other medications that are used to manage and control pain. The pain experienced when a nerve has been affected by the disease process is known as "neuropathic pain." It is often described as burning, searing, and the like. Neuro-pathic pain is effectively treated with medications usually used for depression (antidepressants) and seizures (anticonvulsants); steroids are also helpful.

Doctors practice medicine with the intent of curing disease, elimi-nating pain and suffering, and working toward an optimal quality of life for the patient. Every medication and treatment, although intended to do good, can also have a harmful side effect. It is difficult to anticipate every side effect, but it is helpful to have a general sense of what to expect.

Once their physical pain is controlled, people can shift their focus to other concerns and issues in their lives, whether emotional, mental, or spiritual. Anne had been on the palliative care unit for some time when I went in to see her. Although her home was Grand Forks, North Dakota, she had been admitted to the St. Paul's Hospital Pallia-tive Care Unit for pain management while visiting her family in British Columbia. As I entered Anne's room, her daughter Kathy was sitting at the foot of the bed. Anne and I spoke about her pain. She was pleased and relieved to finally be free of the discomfort. While talking about the relief, she began to cry. I was surprised and, for a second, felt some anxiety about asking Anne about her tears. Would she say something I couldn't respond to properly? Would I be quali-fied to address the issues or concerns she might wish to speak about? Was she dissatisfied with the care she had received while in the hos-pital? Would this require a great deal of time and therefore slow me down with regard to the other patients I still needed to see?

I said, "I see your tears, is there something you would like to say?" Looking at me, she said, "I want to say that I have not been a very good mother." What a painful and yet courageous thing to say! Silence. Did Anne have more to say? I looked at Anne. She was cry-ing as was Kathy. She had tears streaming down her face. What was I to do? At that moment I felt an overwhelming desire to escape from the despair I felt in the room. However, to ignore or walk away from that despair would likely increase what Anne was already feeling. I asked Anne to tell Kathy what she had just told me. Kathy seemed not to want to hear what her mother had to say—it was painful for both of them.

Anne looked at Kathy and said,

You know when you were five years old, you begged to take ballet lessons. We couldn't afford those lessons—it would have meant a long drive into town which would have taken me away from the work on the farm, and we just didn't have the money to be able to let you take those lessons. But all our neighbors who had little girls made the effort and provided that for their daughters. I have great regrets about not making that happen for you and I feel like I was not a good mother.

Here it was: the burden she had carried for twenty-nine years. Kathy looked at her mother and without missing a beat stated, "I might not know how to dance as a ballerina, but how many of my childhood friends or adult colleagues know how to lasso a calf?" The tears changed to a smile and then a chuckle. I stepped out of the room. They continued to speak for several hours. Shortly after her conversation with Kathy, Anne invited her son Tony to come from North Dakota. She had things to say to him as well.

Once Anne was free of physical pain, she was able to address her emotional pain. In a sense, you might say, she stepped into it. She made the choice to speak of her despair. This resulted in changing what seemed to be a failure into a celebration. She could have chosen to keep silent, to contain her despair, but in expressing the despair her pain took on a new meaning—not only for her but also for Kathy. As is true of anyone with a terminal illness, Anne might have felt that the real opportunities in life had passed her by. But dying created new opportunities. Twenty-nine years after the fact, Anne was finally able to describe the scenario and speak her truth. Her truth consisted of the facts as she remembered them, the feelings as she had experienced them, and her judgment of being a woman who had not been good enough as a mother. Her truth carried with it a sense of failure. It was spoken to Kathy, one of two people who could say whether Anne's truth was her truth as well. Finally, Anne was free of the isolation, the sense of failure, the self-judgment. The part of her that died twenty-nine years earlier was restored and reintegrated into her being. She would die with less despair and greater integrity. She would die pain-free, both physically and emotionally.

Back to Tom. His pain was reasonably well controlled. He did experience considerable drowsiness due to the pain relief and the opioid he was taking. Another medication was started to clear his thinking, decrease his anxiety, and further control his pain. Other methods of pain control were included in his care plan: therapeutic touch, transcutaneous electrical nerve stimulation, visual imagery, massage, physiotherapy, and music therapy. We might also have included relaxation therapy, hypnosis, meditation, and a support group.

Tom, like Anne, could address his emotional pain once the physical pain was under control. He spent time with a counseling psychologist who was able to facilitate a therapeutic life review. Through that process, Tom gained some valuable insights. He was able to speak his truth, to ask that his story be recorded and transcribed with the hope that he would be able to send it to his foster parents. He also hoped, once he felt better, to begin working with the government agency that supervised the placement of children in foster homes. His greatest hope lay in the insight that in telling his story he might be able to prevent the abuse and suffering of other children in foster care. This insight gave him a new sense of meaning. It diminished his despair, giving him compassion for children in situations similar to his own. He told his story to the counseling psychologist and to the woman providing pastoral care to patients in the palliative care unit. It was recorded and transcribed. He was given a copy of the transcription. Tom asked that his story be told as often as possible as a means of communicating with other people who might be or have been foster children, those who were foster parents, and agencies that could positively influence the needed changes in the system to prevent an experience like Tom's.

After Tom saw the counseling psychologist, his pain medication was reduced by half. He was able to get out of his bed to go to the smoking lounge. Eventually he was discharged, and he died at home several months later. His pain was under control from the time of his discharge until his death. He had come to a new understanding of who he was and that he could be an instrument of change despite his circumstances. Therein was Tom's hope.

In summary, pain is part of living with a terminal illness. For some, like Tom and Anne, pain can be a constant reality, however well controlled. For others it occurs occasionally. And for some it is only the fear or dread of what might happen. In any case, pain cannot be ignored. If pain is present, it can usually be alleviated. In those few instances when that is not possible, it can be addressed and at least diminished. In the rare cases where even that is not possible, there are ways to increase pain medications and add sedatives so that people are not conscious of their pain experience. These cases are the most difficult for me personally. The occurrence of uncontrollable pain is one of the uncomfortable realities that lead me to explore the spiritual and psychological issues of living with terminal illness. It is difficult to sit in the presence of a person with uncontrolled pain. At times the anguish is unbearable. At that point, asking for help from any and all sources is imperative. No one with pain ought to be left to experience it alone.

Remember that pain is always a combination of physical and psychological features, and for some it has a spiritual component as well.

Pain must be assessed from the perspective of wholeness. Only then can the pain be eliminated and the suffering reduced such that one can achieve an optimal quality of life.

Brent acknowledged that pain is a part of life:

> Well you know, that's part of life, pain is part of life. The only way you can feel absolute joy is to feel pain. You don't know what joy is until you've felt pain, and you can't feel happy for someone for being at peace unless you know how much they've suffered.

When Brent was asked whether he experienced greater physical pain because of his psychological pain, he answered,

> Affect my physical pain? What an interesting question. To a point it would because part of the pain I was feeling at the very beginning was fear of being alone, and I was so scared. I remember being terrified. The one comforting thing was having my sister there. [I was afraid of] not having done enough, not having resolved all this stuff that had been going on for years and not having real answers to any of these things. When I finally accepted the fact that maybe I really was going to die, I said a prayer. I said well, if you're gonna take me, make it quick, and if you're not, please don't make me suffer too long.

There were days when my coresearchers could not participate in the study due to their discomfort and pain. I came to understand that when physical pain is present, it is virtually impossible to address spiritual and psychological concerns. Frieda described her experience of pain:

> I'm only afraid of pain. I'm not afraid of death, I'm not afraid of dying, I'm afraid of pain. I'm terrified of pain, bad pain, cause I've

gone through so much of it you know. I've had a rough time, the last year, the last two years, a real rough time and I've gone through a lot of excruciating pain.

Tracey described how she was "very tired. You can get tired of pain. And everything that comes with it, and all the upset to people who love you. . . . They tell you pain is a teacher. I question that."

Chiron suffered two significant wounds in his life. The first occurred at birth when his parents abandoned him—his mother because of the great loathing she experienced when she saw him, his father because he did not want to assume responsibility for the child. It was a deeply emotional wound. Similarly, Tom experienced a wound in his childhood, for he, too, was abandoned. The abandonment was significant in the story he told at the end of his life. He longed to understand how his biological mother could leave him to be raised by foster parents who abused him. That experience very likely affected his physical pain at the end of his life.

Like Tom's second pain—his physical illness—Chiron's second wound occurred during his adult years, when he was shot by Heracles. That was a deeply physical wound for which he spent his lifetime seeking a healing herb. Through the experience of the second wound, he began to understand himself, the suffering of others, and methods of healing that could benefit people around him. However, he could be free of pain only by giving up his immortality. He chose to do exactly that. In the context of Chiron becoming the wounded healer, perhaps there is always value in asking what there is to learn from the pain we experience. What lesson is there to learn? How might I better understand myself and others through this experience? Brent would say those questions are important. Tracey would be less certain. Those are difficult questions at the best of times and perhaps even more difficult at the end of one's life.

CHAPTER FOUR

Being Touched, Being in Touch

Our whole conception of what exists outside us is based on the sense of touch.

Bertrand Russell

Whatever else we are, we are bodies and that as bodies we need to touch and be touched by each other as much as we need to laugh and cry and play and talk and work with each other.

Frederick Buechner

All I cared about was that someone was touching me; and I knew that I wasn't alone. It's so important.

Brent

To Touch, to Heal

A great multitude was following Him and pressing in on Him.

And a woman who had had a hemorrhage for twelve years, and had endured much at the hands of many physicians, and had spent all that she had and was not helped at all, but rather had grown worse, after hearing about Jesus, came up in the crowd behind Him and touched His cloak. For she thought, "If I just touch His garments, I shall get well." And immediately the flow of her blood was dried up; and she felt in her body that she was healed of her affliction. And immediately Jesus, perceiving in Himself that the power proceeding from Him had gone forth, turned around in the crowd and said, "Who touched My garments?" And His disciples said to Him, "You see the multitude pressing in on You, and You say, 'Who touched Me?'" And He looked around to see the woman who had done this. But the woman fearing and trembling, aware of what had happened to her, came and fell down before Him, and told Him the whole truth. And He said to her, "Daughter, your faith has made you well; go in peace, and be healed of your affliction."

Gerasim smiled again and turned to leave the room. But Ivan Ilych felt his presence such a comfort that he did not want to let him go.

"One thing more, please move up that chair. No, the other one—under my feet. It is easier for me when my feet are raised."

Gerasim brought the chair, set it down gently in place, and raised Ivan Ilych's legs on to it. It seemed to Ivan Ilych that he felt better while Gerasim was holding up his legs.

"It's better when my legs are higher," he said. "Place that cushion under them."

Gerasim did so. He again lifted the legs and placed them, and again Ivan Ilych felt better while Gerasim held his legs. When he set them down Ivan Ilych fancied he felt worse.

"Gerasim," he said. "Are you busy now?"

"Not at all, sir," said Gerasim, who had learnt from the townsfolk how to speak to gentlefolk.

"What have you still to do?"

"What have I to do? I've done everything except chopping the logs for tomorrow."

"Then hold my legs up a bit higher, can you?"

"Of course I can. Why not?" And Gerasim raised his master's legs higher and Ivan Ilych thought that in that position he did not feel any pain at all.

"And how about the logs?"

"Don't trouble about that, sir. There's plenty of time."

Ivan Ilych told Gerasim to sit down and hold his legs, and began to talk to him. And strange to say it seemed to him that he felt better while Gerasim held his legs up.

After that Ivan Ilych would sometimes call Gerasim and get him to hold his legs on his shoulders, and he liked talking to him. Gerasim did it all easily, willingly, simply, and with a good nature that touched Ivan Ilych.

❋

"Touch" means to have contact with another person; it means there is a connection between people. Through touch—both touching and being touched—a healing process begins. Suffering is reduced, pain altered. One person touching another affects both people. This healing can include a strong sense of connection and even, for some, a new way of seeing things. For many people who live with a terminal illness, social roles have been lost and relationships irrevocably altered. For them, perhaps even more so than at other times of life, touch plays an important role in reconnecting with others and in creating new connections. A new connection is what happened when Gerasim held Ivan Ilych's legs on his shoulders, and they talked; they were in touch—and feeling connected.

People who are dying often feel "out of touch" physically and emotionally. They feel that no one knows their experience. They feel isolated. They crave physical contact, not merely as a means of physical comfort or pain relief, but more significantly as a way to counteract the feeling of being untouchable and separate. I have learned that the primary importance of touch is as an antidote to isolation and despair. "Being in touch" means that I know that another person knows my experience of living with a terminal illness. Being touched and being in touch are experiences of the present, experiences of now.

In this chapter I discuss the value of being physically touched by another person and of being emotionally in touch, that is, emotionally connected with people who care for you and who are going to be involved in your care, people who work to know and understand you as a person living with a terminal illness.

Being Touched

Anna Lyne, a fifty-five-year-old, lived with her mother in a two-bedroom townhouse on the outskirts of the city. At the time of my visit, someone had just mowed the lawn—the smell of fresh grass lingered in the air. The last of the season's tulips were still in bloom in the window box, the red and yellow flowers complementing the deep-blue trim of the building.

Anna and her mother lived together following the death of Anna's husband two years earlier. He died of cancer. "I had a very ill husband so I had to look after him, which meant I could not look after me. I was in the background for a number of years." Her son, divorced after a relatively brief marriage and working on a degree in education, didn't visit her often. He would occasionally drop off his young daughter, Liza, to spend time with her Oma, as they called her. On one such visit, just before Christmas and shortly before her husband died, Anna was lifting Liza to carry her from the couch to her crib in the den. "I lifted my granddaughter and twisted when I felt a sharp pain as if I had broken a rib. Of course, the kid fell back on the couch. I just stood there, bent over [in pain], and I thought, *Oh my god, a rib!* I cracked a rib. So I went to see my doctor and told her what had happened. The doctor ordered an X-ray."

We were sitting in Anna's dining room. It was impeccably clean. The house was quiet until her mother entered, carrying bags of groceries. Anna's voice softened. Once her mother was home, Anna seemed to be self-conscious. As the groceries were unpacked, I had to ask Anna to repeat a part of her story. Consequently, Anna called out to her mother, "*Mutti, du machst Krach! Es ist zu laut!*" (Mom, you're making a racket! It's too loud!).

At age nineteen, Anna had immigrated to Canada from Germany with her mother and her stepfather. She was married at twenty-nine. Her husband, Albert, was a high school principal; Anna worked in a fabric store. Both of them enjoyed their work, and both took great pride in remodeling and decorating their home. Their son, Wayne, was born on their fourth wedding anniversary. He was their only child.

Anna first learned that she had cancer ten years before I met her.

I was very naive. I had no idea what was happening to me, why I was sore when I was sitting down. I was reluctant to see a doctor for about a year. When I did go, I was told that I had a sizable growth between my spine and large intestine. I was sent to the hospital, where they removed the growth. When they removed the tumor, they cut into the rectal muscle so I had no more control of my bowel. I had to have a colostomy. I was told that the tumor was the size of a golf ball and that the area around the tumor was "clean," that I was cancer-free, that there was nothing in there any more. Low and behold, eight years later, here I am, learning that the cancer has returned, metastasized to the bone. I had a hairline fracture of one of my ribs.

When I was told the cancer had returned, at first I wasn't quite sure whether to be angry, to shout, to ask why me, what did I do to deserve it? And I thought, *My gosh, this is it, you won't see next Christmas!* I was getting sicker and sicker. It was really an odd thing that first year. I was so sure I wasn't going to see Christmas; my doctor was sure I wasn't going to see Christmas. I just let myself go. *This is it,* I said to myself—*my husband is sick and I can't look after him anymore, so what's the difference? If I die, at least I can get back at him.* Really, it was getting back at him for something that he didn't do. It's just that he was sick and he needed help. And I needed help, but I didn't get it. I was angry at the fact that I had to play nurse to him, yet I was just as sick. Who was going to help me? Nobody. I was very alone, so very alone.

She didn't die by Christmas—or for years thereafter.

Anna felt alone in her marriage. Loneliness set in when she returned home after she learned that she had cancer. She expected her husband to be supportive, to understand her because he also had a terminal illness, and yet she felt she was alone, "so very alone." He wasn't there for her. She longed to feel close to him, but she didn't. She also felt alone in her illness. "I always wanted to have somebody to converse with who had the same type of cancer. I asked, 'Is there anyone in Vancouver?' No. 'Is there anyone in Canada?' No. 'Is there anyone in the United States?' Maybe. What do you do then?"

Anna spoke of her husband's death:

When he died two years ago, I could start thinking about me. I was a little bit angry at the world cause I thought, *I've had a good life, yes, but nothing big, nothing fancy, no big trips and stuff.* Here I am, I could do things now, but now I'm sick. I said, "It's in God's hands." Why should I worry what God's will is? It's His ball game, not mine. I haven't done anything to get sick, I didn't do anything to deserve it, so I'll let Him worry. I cried a little bit here and there.

When I had the colostomy, I was told they had "colostomy clubs" [support groups]. When I went there, I thought I was nuts because most people that were there were in their seventies and in their late sixties. I had just turned forty-five. I felt, *What's happening here? I don't belong.* When they asked me why I had the colostomy, I couldn't tell them the whole story because I felt that something had gone wrong with the surgery.

Anna couldn't bring herself to speak openly and honestly about her anger at the surgeon for making an error. She also felt some anger toward the group members, as she was forty-five and they were twenty to thirty years older. They were there because of a disease process; she was there because of an error the surgeon made.

So what do you say? You say "oh well" and just make idle conversation, but it doesn't mean anything. You're alone. That's the only thing that I feel very strongly about—the aloneness in the illness. It would be nice if there was one person you could converse with, someone you could exchange ideas with—what works for that person, what works for me. But that's not there.

Anna wanted to be understood by someone who had the same diagnosis as she did. She wanted to connect with someone who knew her experience. "People who have breast cancer have breast cancer; those with bone cancer have bone cancer. Mine isn't just the bone, yet it goes into the bone; it's gone through the rib. They can't do any more radiation in this rib cage because it's already as brittle as it can be. It's the aloneness that makes this harder. It is the aloneness in itself."

At times Anna also felt as if she was contaminated, which contributed to her sense of aloneness. She felt that there had been something within her since the time of her birth that had resulted in the cancer.

I realized I had cancer after I fell down the stairs on my rear. It was summer when I fell. I fell down seven steps on my tailbone. My tailbone got it on every step. That's where the cancer set in. Is that where it was all the time, and just needed the injury to make itself known? When I broke my rib, the cancer came. Now that makes me think. I'm starting to wonder about a possible correlation? Is it something that is still within me, is it something that came to me, or did I have it from day one? There are a lot of unanswered questions. I'm very critical of myself. Everything has to be a certain way, everything has to be straight. I don't believe in unfinished business, but this is unfinished, this is very unfinished.

Some people who know they have a terminal illness feel out of touch—out of touch with who they were before, out of touch with people they care about and who care about them, out of touch with normal life, out of touch with their God. It is a sense of estrangement from the familiar, the beginning of a process of increasing isolation. The physical touch of another counteracts that sense of aloneness, that sense of being out of touch and of being untouchable. Physical contact—touch—eliminates the space between two people. Aldo Caroteneuto, a professor in the theory of personality at the University of Rome, says that

[t]he experience of body contact is even deeper and more necessary than nourishment. Touching and caressing represent basic essential ways of knowing and loving. . . . Physical proximity is the most direct and intense form of nonverbal communication. It is renewed in the moment of danger or fear or tenderness, akin to the time when the

mother pressed her child to her breast. Such moments are re-evoked and relived in adult life and grant us the possibility of communicating silently.

What is the loneliness of knowing you have a terminal illness? If you have a terminal illness and are reading this book, you know the answer to that question. You know it includes feelings of being untouchable, an awareness that those you love fear that if they touch you they might get sick as well, tears of sadness, grief, and nostalgia for the past, for the way that life was and will never be again. You have likely experienced an intermittent panic and sense of guilt because of the finite amount of time you have left to accomplish what seems like an infinite number of tasks. And there is the despair and isolation of realizing that you must say goodbye not to just one person but to all the family members and friends who have been significant over the course of your lifetime. Fear associated with being alone, with the loss of intimacy, with a sense of abandonment, may keep you awake at night. Being touched and being in touch counter act all that.

For those who want to understand the loneliness, imagine what it would be like to give up the things you enjoy doing the most—playing a sport, going for a walk with a close friend, reading books, holding your child, carrying your grandchild, listening to music. Imagine not being able to complete any of the tasks you are now working on or would like to work on in the next three to six months. Imagine visiting each one of your friends and family members who are important to you, holding conversations as if you would never see them again. Imagine lying awake at night staring into the darkness with a new and painful sense of awareness that you are not immortal, that neither love nor science can stop the disease process within you. Imagine feeling the apprehension other people have about being in your presence or touching you. Imagine feeling alone and lonely.

The fear of abandonment or of being misunderstood stems in part from the emotions that emerge whenever the topic of death is introduced into a conversation. The topic of death calls forth some very deep feelings—feelings that may not have been known to us or expressed to others before the diagnosis was made, feelings that define, more accurately than words, who we are. Do I dare to experience those now? Do I risk sharing them with another person? If I let them know how I feel, will I be rejected by those I love? How do I move from this place of aloneness to a place of intimacy? Where do I begin? Ultimately, no one can protect us from the reality of death, our own death. On an existential level, we are indeed alone. Only in the womb are all our needs met by another. We are born with a longing to recover that same sense of connection, first with our parents, and then perhaps in relationship to others.

Audrey was in her early sixties. She lived alone in a cozy one-bedroom apartment. She had a beautiful view of the mountains from her bedroom window. Audrey maintained contact with friends by meeting them for lunch, going to movies, or enjoying a card game followed by a cup of tea. She learned that her friends could easily talk about the movies, books they were reading, their children, and their activities. But they were resistant to speaking about death and dying. Audrey wanted to talk about death. "Why do people get upset when you talk about it? It's going to happen, so why not talk about it? I think it should be as open as any other subject that you want to discuss. But it seems to be a taboo subject. I would think by now, in this day and age, that we should be able to talk about death easily and openly."

In part, it is because friends and family members avoid the topic of death that people who have a terminal illness feel alone and out of touch. Health care providers also avoid the topic of death. I remember a family meeting that took place on the palliative care unit at St. Paul's Hospital, where I was the program coordinator. In fact, I was facilitating that particular family meeting. (The process is described at the end of this chapter.) The purpose of the meeting was for Sam to discuss with his family and the palliative care team his future wishes, his options, his unfinished business. Sam had been a patient on the unit intermittently for several months. We thought we knew him and that he knew us, that he felt safe and comfortable talking about himself with us. We started the discussion with the usual introductions and then proceeded to talk about Sam's options with regard to medical care, what he could receive in the hospital and what could be provided at home. Once that was done, I suggested we also speak about Sam's personal wishes with regard to any nonmedical issues or concerns he might have.

Sam started by saying, "Most important to me is to be able to speak the D-word. I've been on this unit about four times, spending a week to ten days here each time. Nobody ever talks to me about dying or about death. I want to talk about it—with my brother, my father, and the staff here. I thought that's what would happen on a palliative care unit." He was right. The palliative care unit was meant to be a place where patients, families, friends, and staff could speak openly about death and dying. But sometimes even for us, it had been easier to avoid it. I was relieved to hear Sam speak about what he wanted. Apart from wanting to talk about death, Sam also wanted to spend as much time at home as possible, to ride in his red sports car with the top down, and preferably with his cat on his lap. (The cat enjoyed car rides.)

The sense of aloneness that people who have a terminal illness experience, and the desire they have to speak about dying, became apparent through a study done in the early 1980s by Dr. David Spiegel of Stanford Medical School in California. He conducted a study with a group of women who had breast cancer. From his extensive clinical work, Dr. Spiegel informed us that, like Anna, Audrey, and Sam, people with cancer can experience a feeling of isolation, among other feelings such as grief and pain. Family members and friends withdraw from people with cancer because they are afraid that it may be contagious, that they can catch the cancer. They may feel awkward and inept in dealing with a situation that demands confrontation with difficult emotions or challenging physical realities. They may also feel a high level of anxiety about the impending death of someone close to them.

People with AIDS have the same experience. In fact, the isolation experienced by people who have AIDS is often more extreme because of the higher level of anxiety the disease creates in others. (Imagine what it feels like when you sense that those you love and who love you avoid hugging or holding you, giving you a kiss, shaking your hand, caressing or massaging your body.) I remember our early experiences providing care to persons with AIDS and how family members would stand at the foot of the bed or sit in a chair at a considerable distance. Some preferred to stay outside the room entirely. In 1989, Amanda Heggs, a woman with AIDS, was quoted in the London *Guardian*: "Sometimes I have a terrible feeling that I am dying not from the virus, but from being untouchable."

Dr. Spiegel invited women with metastatic breast cancer (spread beyond the primary site) to participate in a psychological support group that would meet weekly for ninety minutes. Each group consisted of seven to ten women and had two leaders, one a psychiatrist or social worker, the other a counselor who had breast cancer in remission at the time. The purpose of the support group was to focus on discussions of death and dying, related-family problems, difficulties in obtaining treatment, issues of communication with physicians, and living as fully as possible with the knowledge that they had a terminal illness. They worked together to explore their relationships to family members, to admit to and discuss their fears, to learn from each other about life lessons encountered as a result of having a terminal illness, and to face their own death. They shared their grief as members of the group grew sicker or died. Knowing they had a terminal illness, and having leaders that were helpful and comfortable in confronting death and dying, enabled the group members to keep on task.

Dr. Spiegel and his colleagues worked to create an atmosphere in which the women could talk about the hard stuff, the issues and feelings that seemed to be unspeakable in their homes and with friends. They watched carefully for signs of emotion, for someone who looked as though they might start crying, for someone who looked worried, unable to speak about the cause. It was these women who were encouraged to speak, these issues that the leaders focused on—the very issues that the participants had not been able to discuss with anyone.

In evaluating his work, Dr. Spiegel found that the women who participated in the weekly group sessions, "working together in facing common problems, became less anxious, confused, fatigued, and fearful."

Speaking of the experience of having a terminal illness changes the anxiety and fear; it diminishes loneliness and isolation. Many of the people who participated in my study would say, "I've never spoken about this to anyone." Another response was, "I feel better after talking to you today." Once people knew they had a terminal illness, they wanted to speak about it—to be in touch, emotionally and physically, with at least one other person. In some peculiar way, it seemed that the loneliness served a purpose for some people. These people began to identify what was really important to them. They started a process of being in touch with their inner self.

Philanthropist George Soros contributed millions of dollars to create the Project on Death in America, an organization that seeks to promote a better understanding of the experiences of dying and bereavement and, by doing so, help to transform the culture surrounding death. In a 1994 speech entitled "Reflections on Death in America," Soros contrasted his experience of the death of his father with that of the death of his mother. Of his father's dying experience he said,

My father died at home in 1963. He was terminally ill. Although he agreed to an operation, he didn't particularly want to survive it because he was afraid that the combination of the illness and the operation would invade and destroy his autonomy as a human being. Unfortunately, that in fact is what happened. After the operation he had very little time left. I'm afraid I kind of wrote him off at that point. I was there when he died, yet I let him die alone. I could see him, but I wasn't at his bedside. The day after he died I went into the office. I didn't talk about my father's death. So I kind of denied his dying; I certainly didn't participate in it. Afterwards, I read Kübler-Ross and learned that I might have maintained contact with him if I [had] tried. Had I read Kübler-Ross earlier I would have probably held his hand, because I did love him. I just didn't know that it might make a difference. I forgave myself because I did not know any better.

Albert Schweitzer once said, "We are all so much together and yet we are dying of loneliness." Although that may describe the experience of George Soros and his father, such was not the case with his mother:

My mother's death was more recent. She had joined the Hemlock Society and had at hand a means of doing away with herself. I asked her if she needed my help; I offered it, although I wasn't particularly keen to do it. But I would have helped her because I felt that I owed it to her. At the point of decision, however, she did not want to take her own life, and I'm glad she didn't. Her decision gave the family a chance to rally around and be there as she prepared to die. And this time we did maintain good contact right to the end.

What is the significance of human contact, of touch? In an interview with Bill Moyers in 1993, Rachel Remen, a doctor who has been working for more than twenty years with people who have terminal illnesses, and the author of *Kitchen Table Wisdom* and *My Grandfather's Blessings*, begins to answer that question. She speaks of touching as a way of healing. She acknowledges that we don't touch each other a lot and, when we do, that it's often misunderstood or sexualized. Physicians are taught that they should touch people only to make a diagnosis: If they touch their patients in any other way, even as a means of comforting them, it might be misunderstood. As Bill Moyers writes, "Touch is deeply reassuring and nurturing. It's the first way a mother and child connect with each other ... what a mother is saying to her child with that touch is 'Live ... your life matters to me.' Remen also describes how people with cancer often feel when they're touched by health care providers. They say they feel as though they are merely a 'piece of meat.' She reports that one woman said, 'Sometimes when I go for my chemotherapy, they touch me as if they don't know anybody's inside the body.'"

Remen now works with adults who have cancer. Earlier in her career she was the associate director of pediatric clinics at Stanford Medical School. During her time there, one of her colleagues, Marshall Klaus, chief of the intensive care nursery, conducted a study to explore the effect of touch on infants so small they could be held in one hand. Half the infants were touched (gently rubbing the baby's back with a pinkie finger) for fifteen minutes every few hours. Those babies were more likely to survive than the ones who were not touched. Remen surmises that isolation can weaken us and touching can strengthen the will to live.

We experience touch through our skin, the largest sensory organ

of the human body. The human embryo develops from three cell layers: the endoderm, the mesoderm, and the ectoderm, the latter being
the outer layer. This layer gives rise to the nervous system and to the
general surface covering the body—hair, nails, teeth, skin—and to
the sense organs of smell, taste, hearing, vision, and touch. One of
the primary functions of the central nervous system is to keep the
organism informed about what is going on outside the organism. The
nerve endings in the skin send signals or messages via the spinal cord
to the brain. The brain analyzes the information, interpreting the
effect of the touch. The brain then informs the rest of the body about
the response it will have to the touch. Interestingly, the skin also
informs the world outside the organism about what is going on within
the organism. As a physician, the color, temperature, texture, moist-
ness and dryness, thickness, and elasticity give me information about
what is going on under the skin and within the body.

The outer layer of skin, the epidermis, contains the nerve endings
that respond to touch. Dr. Ashley Montagu, an anatomy expert, has
written extensively about the tactile system. He states that

the surface area of the skin has an enormous number of sensory
receptors receiving stimuli of heat, cold, touch, pressure, and pain. A
piece of skin the size of a quarter contains more than 3 million cells,
100 to 340 sweat glands, 50 nerve endings, and 3 feet of blood ves-
sels. It is estimated that there are some 50 receptors per 100 square
millimeters, a total of 640,000 sensory receptors. Tactile points vary
from 7 to 135 per square centimeter. The number of sensory fibers
from the skin entering the spinal cord by the posterior roots is well
over half a million . . . in the adult male, in whom [the skin] weighs
about 8 pounds, containing some 5 million sensory cells.

The functions of the skin include temperature control, protection,
metabolic functions, and sensation.

Touch is essential not only for the newborns but also for children, adolescents, and adults. Dr. Montagu speaks of contact between mother and child as being the first contact we experience with the world. It provides comfort, security, warmth, and food. He quotes Dr. James L. Halliday, a psychiatrist who wrote about psychosocial issues in medicine, as saying that "infants deprived of their accustomed maternal body contact may develop a profound depression with lack of appetite, wasting, and even marasmus [wasting away] leading to death." In the nineteenth century and through about 1920, the death rate for babies abandoned to institutions was nearly 100 percent. After 1915 doctors made rules requiring that babies be picked up and carried around several times a day. Handling, carrying, caressing, caregiving, and cuddling became known as basic experiences necessary to the infant's ability to survive.

Self-esteem is based on bodily relationship and connectedness, beginning in infancy and continuing through childhood and adolescence. Montagu's book *Touching* includes a second report by Dr. Jimmie Holland, who early in her career worked with leukemia patients at the University of Buffalo School of Medicine. In order to prevent all skin contact between patients and others, the patients were isolated in germ-free rooms as part of their treatment. They could look out of the rooms and be seen from without. They used verbal communication facilities to interact with people outside their rooms. Seventy-five percent of the patients "experienced an acute sense of isolation, chiefly related to the inability to touch or be touched directly. The loss of human physical contact generated feelings of loneliness, frustration, a sense of coldness, and a lack of emotional warmth." Physical contact—that is, touch—is an essential ingredient to a sense of emotional connectedness.

Terminally ill people also need to be touched. For some people, connection begins with touch, physical touch. Marjorie, who was in her early seventies, attended support groups at the cancer center. She also attended weeklong retreats for persons with life-threatening ill-nesses. She said that "touch is a necessity of life. We need to be touched. When you attend one of the group meetings, prepare your-self, because there's a lot of touching going on there, and I think it's magical. I really do feel that if it isn't physically healing, it is certainly emotionally and psychologically healing."

Her experience in the support group was very different from when she was admitted to the hospital for a medical procedure. "There was nobody to be with me, to hold my hand and tell jokes or anything. It was the most horrifying experience, and I was angry. I was really angry."

Throughout that initial hospital experience she felt absolutely alone, not connected to the physician performing the procedure, in pain and horrified. She realized that for subsequent procedures in the hospital there might be value in inviting a friend or a member of her support group to join her. "I felt that I would be fine if there was someone from my support group sitting beside me and holding my hand and talking—I didn't care what they were saying, just a voice going through me while I was doing it. The result was painless, two absolutely painless biopsies."

Marjorie felt that through the touch of another person, a sense of togetherness was created and healing could occur. During her medical procedures in the hospital, her friend's voice also contributed to a pain-free experience even though she couldn't remember what her friend had been speaking about; the content of what her friend said was not important. She also recommended that doctors touch patients in a reassuring way as part of providing care for the patient.

Dr. Lewis Thomas, former president of Memorial Sloan-Kettering Cancer Center in New York City, wrote in the early 1980s that touching is a real professional secret, an essential skill, and "the most effective act of doctors."

Some people don't like being handled by others, but not, or almost never, sick people. They need being touched, and part of the dismay in being very sick is the lack of close human contact. Ordinary people, even close friends, even family members, tend to stay away from the very sick, touching them as infrequently as possible for fear of interfering, or catching the illness, or just for fear of bad luck. The doctor's oldest skill in trade was to place his hands on the patient.

Touch is the strongest nonverbal message that one person can give another. But how does touch occur when it's not already a part of an existing relationship, when it hasn't happened prior to knowing that someone has a terminal illness? One way that it begins is by asking to be touched or for permission to touch, as in: "'Can I hold your hand as we speak?" "Do you mind if I put my arm around you?" "May I hold you?"

In the past, when I read bedtime stories to my daughters, the youngest would become impatient for a hug. I had roughly three seconds to put my arm around her after we had snuggled into our reading position. Any longer, and she would grab my hand and swing my arm over her head and around her shoulders. The oldest one would say, "I need a hug." Both of them knew what they wanted (and needed). They knew they wanted to be touched as well, when they woke from a scary dream, had to walk in the dark, or were taking an unknown path. For them, touch, connection, and holding reduced their fears and anxiety. Security came from putting their hand into mine and knowing I was with them, physically present. In many instances that security did not require words. Assurance came from touch itself.

Family members left behind have often said to me, "No one told me to touch my mother" (or father, brother, sister, friend). "No one told me it was all right to lie beside the person and hold them. It's what I really wanted to do, but it felt awkward, so I didn't do it. But after the person died I was very sorry and regret not having followed my own instinct." One told me:

> I stayed with Bill, my husband, as he lay dying. I feel so bad now that I didn't lie beside him on the bed and hold him in my arms! I'm reading about this now, the need to touch. But worse than that was, I sent the children away. They came to say goodbye to their father. They stood there and talked with him and said what they had to say, which was very stoic. They didn't touch him, they didn't sit on the bed. I would have liked some direction. I wish I'd been told that it's okay to lie on the bed and put my arms around him and hold him while he's dying instead of sitting on a chair. I wish someone had told me that my children should stay with their father and sit beside him, sit on the edge of the bed, touch him, hold his hand, talk to him, and stay until he dies. But there was no one. I wish someone had been there to tell me how to do it right—which I now know but didn't know then.

Would that have been what the loved one wanted? In response, I ask another question: "Is that what I would want, is that what you would want?" If so or if not, its important to let others know about your wishes now. Touch is of value to the person touching and to the person being touched.

Being touched or held can be something you want and something you fear or feel awkward about. This might arise from your personality or be due to the setting, such as a hospital. If you long for touch (or more of it), I encourage you to speak to someone you trust, someone likely to understand. Ask someone you care about to hold your hand the next time you are together. It might also mean a hug when greeting or parting company. For some people this is natural, for others uncomfortable. Discomfort can stem from lack of touching experience in your past, but it is never too late to start anew. Touch is essential to one's sense of well-being. "Nurturing," "touch," and "connection" are synonymous.

Start simply: Sit across the table and hold hands as you speak. This may seem foreign, and perhaps only one or two people will make you comfortable. But if you try this, tell the other person how you feel: "I feel close to you and would like to hold your hand or sit next to you, but I want to respect you and not impose myself upon you. I would like to hold your hand as we speak." Next, do the same thing, but without the table; sit facing each other, knees touching, holding hands, and begin a conversation. Eventually you may feel comfortable without even speaking. Perhaps you can relate a story from your past describing how touch was important to your sense of well-being. In that connection, both feel reassured.

Marjorie spoke of her experience with her mother:

> I hugged and touched my mother, which made me feel good. And I think I told you, my mother was never a physical woman, never a demonstrative woman with her children, but by then I had learned. I was well into my experience with cancer and she used to say, "I'm a brittle little lady of a hundred years." I would hold her in my arms and give her a good hug. I thought, if I break something, well, what the hell, that doesn't matter!
>
> Touch is important. Even for the very few people who don't want to be touched, I take a chance on touching rather than being afraid to touch. Now I touch everybody.

I imagine Marjorie at the bedside of her mother like one of the final scenes in *Wit*, a play by Margaret Edson (and now a film) about the experience of dying. Marjorie sits, holding her mother's hand, stroking the transparent, wrinkled skin, realizing that her mother will never speak again. Slowly, without losing contact, she removes her own shoes, lifts the comforter that belonged to her mother for decades, and slips in beside her. She exchanges the hand for an embrace. She simply holds her mother in her arms, strokes her hair, and says through her touch and her words, "As you held me at the beginning of my life, I now hold you as your life ends. I want you to know and to feel the love I have for you."

Being in Touch

Some time ago Maggie, a good friend of mine, called to say that she needed help but that she didn't know how to go about asking for it. She had cancer. She had gone through conventional therapies with a diminishing hope of cure or remission. She had been a health care provider for many years and knew the health care system very well. I knew she had helped hundreds of people through the course of her professional responsibilities. Yet by her description the system did not seem to be serving her well. She was exhausted and felt stymied. She didn't know what to do next. She had been very private about her illness; she felt that few people really understood what impact the disease process was having on her life. In that regard Maggie felt out of touch. Until that point in her life, Maggie had always been the one to listen, to act as an advocate, to solve problems for others, and to influence change in the system. In that regard, she was well connected. This was different. She was too tired to continue on her own. The "system" seemed so big, cold, unapproachable, so unwilling to hear her. Being a patient was very different from being a provider. After hearing her story and discussing it, I suggested that she invite her closest friends and family members to her home for a meeting.

The Family Meeting

There are many decisions to make once someone is told they have a terminal illness. Often people feel overwhelmed and alone in making those decisions, wondering how to involve those they care about, fearful of asking for help from others or participating in the decisionmaking process. These decisions and choices pertain to more than just the disease and the treatment that might reverse, stop, or slow down the process; they also pertain to the life you want to lead with the amount of time and energy remaining. In fact, the unfinished business, your sense of self, and your relationship with others may be just as important, even more so, than focusing all your attention on the disease process. It is crucial to remember that the choices belong to you, the person with the illness. And living is a dynamic process, so you can always make new decisions and can change your mind about past ones.

If you have a life-threatening or terminal illness, or if you are getting on in years and would like to have a meeting with significant people to discuss your future, the five-step process outlined below can benefit you. I have used it with many families in the hospital, in my own family, and with friends like Maggie. In many instances, dying requires a community of support. It could be years, months, weeks, or days before you die. Depending on the prognosis, you might meet regularly—every month or two or even longer between meetings.

You might feel awkward or uncomfortable, perhaps because you do not want to inconvenience people. However, my experience is that people are generally relieved when someone invites them into a meaningful conversation. It usually benefits all who participate, often strengthening friendships and family relationships. The process keeps people connected and informed about what is happening, about your wishes, and about how they can be a part of your care plan.

Family members might not be accustomed to speaking openly and honestly about wishes for health care and dying, which means others will be left to guess. So when you invite people over, make certain they understand the purpose: to have an open discussion about living with dying, about making decisions that will affect how you lead the remainder of your life. The end of life usually involves friends and family members, and your relationship with people before you die will effect the grieving process for them. I encourage you to participate in a process like this. You could also tape (audio or video) a message for your family and friends.

If this is something you do not want or cannot do, it would still be of value to think about the discussion topics and write down what you would like to happen in a variety of circumstances. The process I present is based on work that was taught and written about by three Americans—Albert Jonsen, Mark Siegler, and William Winslade. These three developed a decisionmaking process designed to help ethics committees in hospitals to resolve ethical dilemmas. Their work has been adapted at St. Paul's Hospital in Vancouver to include families and professionals in the decisionmaking process. Initially it was used to resolve ethical dilemmas. It has also been useful in the complex decisionmaking process at the end of life. We invite patients and those who are important to them to join the health care team in developing a plan for the patient.

Maggie made a list of all the people she would like to invite to her home. A close friend of hers phoned everyone, explaining the purpose of the meeting, and asked them to bring some food so the group could share a meal together after the meeting. All those who were invited attended. They were honored to be invited, pleased to attend.

Organizing the Meeting

In order to conduct a decisionmaking meeting, invite the people who are important to you—close family members and friends. Invite professionals who know you and are involved in providing care for you (the meeting will have value even if they are not able to attend). The meeting can be organized by you, a family member, or a friend. Set the time, date, and place. The process usually requires two to three hours. Because facilitating a meeting requires a lot of energy, it is wise to ask someone in advance to act as facilitator. (If you know of someone with experience and skills in facilitation, invite that person to act on your behalf.) That way your energy can be spent on the decisions that need to be made rather than on keeping a group of people focused and on topic. Everyone involved must understand that the purpose of the meeting is to develop a health care plan for you.

It is important for the facilitator to keep the discussion moving in a respectful manner and to make certain that everyone present is given the opportunity to express opinions and raise concerns. The goal is to develop a comprehensive plan, with those present making a commitment to the plan and therefore making a commitment to you. Once everyone is gathered, make sure they are comfortable and within easy speaking range. Sitting in a circle helps. Introduce the facilitator, explain that you invited this person, and, if you like, why you chose that person. Next, ask everyone to introduce themselves and their relationship to you.

This is a very intense process. If at any time you are too tired to proceed, ask that the meeting end and set another time. If you are too tired to concentrate, you will have trouble knowing what you really want.

The facilitator begins by describing the process and the purpose of the meeting, identifying any decisions that need to be made. It is helpful for the facilitator to set a few guidelines for the conversation:

- Be sure everyone knows that he/she can participate and will have an opportunity to speak or ask questions. Be sure they understand that you welcome and value their opinions.
- Explain that it is important to speak respectfully.
- Remind participants to be aware that communication is verbal and nonverbal; people are invited to speak clearly and simply so that all those in attendance can understand; gestures like rolled eyes, raised eyebrows, grunts of disapproval, and the like are not welcome.
- Ensure that everyone has made a commitment to stay until the

end of the meeting. If someone is called away for an emergency, ask if they have anything to add before they leave.

- If at all possible, pagers and portable phones should be turned off; you want people's undivided attention.

Record everything discussed on a large flip chart so that everyone can see the information. It is also important to keep a to-do list; add to it throughout the process. One possibility is to conduct the meeting over the Internet via a chat room or e-mail. For some people, the first meeting is followed by e-mail communication.

We met in Maggie's living room in the late afternoon. The place was crowded, but everyone was comfortable and the eighteen people present could see and hear one another. Maggie introduced me to the group (her family and friends), asking me to explain how it was that we had come together. The usually take-charge Maggie was too tired to speak. She was also short of breath. She still sounded anxious but less so than she had been when we spoke on the phone two weeks earlier. After introducing myself and explaining the purpose and process of the meeting, I asked everyone to introduce themselves and explain to the other members of the group how they were connected to Maggie.

Imagine this in your living room: You are surrounded by family members and friends who care about you, who are willing to do some work on your behalf, and who want to keep in touch through the course of your illness, your remaining lifetime. You cannot predict what your needs will be or the exact course your illness will take. No one is able to do that. Unfortunately, for some the health care system will not be user-friendly. In fact, it can show indifference and even antagonism despite your circumstances. Therefore, some will need a strong advocate to speak and intervene on your behalf. The people around you are the people who will understand you, who will know what you want and how you prefer to live. Some of them will make a commitment to work with you in meeting needs, accomplishing goals, and speaking for you. Although this may be a difficult meeting, it is important.

Medical Information

You should speak first if possible. Inform the group about your health. Perhaps a close friend or family member has accompanied you to doctor's appointments; ask him or her to speak on your behalf or add to your comments. Go over the facts of your medical history and explain what has happened to you to require a meeting like this. Report on all the symptoms, the tests, and the results.

- What is the diagnosis (the name of the disease) and the prognosis (the future course of the disease)?
- Which treatments have you had to date? If you're talking about cancer, options would include surgery, chemotherapy, and radiation therapy. Inform the group about any alternative therapies you have tried. If your health care providers are present they would likely assist you in providing and explaining the information of your medical condition and history to the group. Invite them to do so.

The facilitator asks the questions. The recorder jots notes on the flip chart so everyone can see and understand the topic of discussion. Often, speaking about these issues clarifies what is important to you.

- Which therapies are you considering? What are the risks? What will your life be like if you have the therapy you are considering? What will it be like if you don't?
- If surgery is an option, how long will the recovery be? Do you want to spend that amount of time recovering, given the best estimate of your life expectancy at this point? How might your daily life improve if you have the most desirable outcome?
- If chemotherapy or radiation therapy is an option, or if there is

some medication that might have an effect on the illness, what is the time frame in which the treatment would take effect? What is the earliest point at which you might benefit? How long would you have to be on the medication until you would know whether it was working? What are the side effects of treatment? How are they managed? How long do they usually last? How soon would treatments have to begin in order to have some effect on the disease process? How long can you wait and still take them with benefit?

- Has your doctor spoken about your life expectancy? If so, be brave enough to include that.
- Is there any aspect of your illness that is reversible?
- If you are in pain, how is it being managed? What are other options? (See chapter 3.)
- And what about other symptoms, such as shortness of breath (dyspnea), constipation, nausea, vomiting, fatigue, or insomnia? What might you expect as the disease progresses? How are these symptoms being treated right now? Are there other possibilities? Every alternative you consider important should be included: physiotherapy, acupuncture, therapeutic touch, meditation, homeopathy, and so on.
- What has been your experience with the health care system? Do you usually have to wait a long time to see your physician, to have tests conducted, to receive results? Do you get information by phone, or do you have to visit your doctor for every question?
- If you are frustrated with the care you have been receiving or lack of information, what changes need to be made? How might that happen?
- Do you need someone to act as an advocate? Are you getting the information you need, and is it presented in a way that is easily understood? Do you believe that you understand all your

options? How much time and energy is being spent obtaining the information you want and need with regard to your health and treatment options?

- How well are you able to live a normal life? Are you self-sufficient? Do you need help with grocery shopping, preparing meals, personal hygiene like bathing or washing your hair, getting dressed? Are you able to go out as often as you'd like? Does it require too much energy? Do you need someone to go with you? Have you noticed any changes in this regard over the past months, weeks, or days? If not now, do you think you will need assistance in the near or distant future if things progress at the same rate? Would an assessment by an occupational therapist be of value?

- What features of this experience contribute to your suffering? The changes, the sense of loss, becoming dependent on others, fears about the future? What is affecting/changing your sense of self and/or relationship with people who are important to you?

You may not have all the answers to these questions. You may have additional questions. But if these questions have sparked a desire for more information from your doctor, who may not be present, invite someone along to your next visit with your doctor. Make a list of the questions you would like to ask (see the discussion in chapter 2 about visits to the doctor). Make sure the facilitator invites people to contribute or ask questions at specific points, especially if some people are shy.

Maggie spoke of how the diagnosis was made, how she had gone for radiation and for chemotherapy, and how the symptoms were recurring. It was a rare form of cancer. She admitted to a sense of desperation—she didn't want her doctors to give up on her; surely there must be something else that could be done. She felt that her doctor was giving her the information he had, but it seemed that there ought to be something else. Surely there was something someone could do somewhere. Her doctor was now on a leave, and she was uncertain about where to go with the questions she had. She didn't have the energy to go through it all again—meeting a new doctor, telling her story, waiting for appointments and for another opinion, another treatment plan. Why was the system so poorly organized? Maggie didn't want to wait; she felt she didn't have enough time. She talked of her increasing shortness of breath and her inability to do anything other than basic activities around her home. A friend of Maggie's spoke, as she had accompanied Maggie on a few visits to the clinic.

Maggie's biggest concern was her three children, none of whom were living at home. And though she wanted them to know the truth, she found it hard to speak to them about how sick she felt, her fatigue, and her fear that she was dying. She couldn't bear to speak about those concerns at this point in the meeting. She was also concerned about her youngest brother who had recently been ill. She knew her mother would have a particularly difficult time with the truth.

Your Preferences

The first part of the process focused on presenting the medical information. In the second part, review the choices you need to make and the actions you need to take with regard to the options discussed.

- Do you want to go ahead with the treatment plan your doctor has outlined? Would you like a second opinion?
- Will the treatment really make a difference? What are your goals with regard to the treatment?
- How will you know that the disease has progressed? What are the features of the natural history of the disease?
- Are there treatment options that are known to have a very low success rate that you would like to learn more about or that you would like to consider seriously? What would be necessary to persuade you to have a certain treatment or to dismiss it as an option? Do you need to try all treatments regardless of their

success, simply because you are someone who doesn't quit? How might that affect those who care about you with regard to your physical, emotional, and spiritual energy?

Most people begin with the wish for a cure, even when they know that the disease is incurable. Working toward a cure can include one more effort with a particular therapy. Some people place a lot of hope in that magic cure, the one with a 5 percent chance of reversing the disease process.

- Are you focused on that magical cure because that's what you want or because that's what your partner/spouse/children want you to do? Is your focus on the magic cure distracting you from other important issues that require your time and attention right now?

It is of value to dream out loud about what you would like to do in the time you have left. Although this can be a rewarding process, it is usually an emotionally painful process. Your preferences in this regard will reflect who you are as an individual (activities you would like to enjoy one more time; something new you have not tried before), your relationships with others (special events such as birthdays, graduations, and weddings; conversations that you need to have; time with favorite people), and your sense of spirituality (meaning, forgiveness, meditation, self-reflection, worship). And while you are expressing your dreams and desires, you may also experience a sense of grief because you recognize some potential losses.

- What are some of your other goals? Are there things you really want to do or see? Some people want to travel to a particular place because of certain memories. Some want to travel to visit family members or friends. Sometimes there are conversations people want to have while they have enough energy to do so. You might want to divide these goals into personal goals, goals that relate to family and friends, and goals that pertain to the spiritual domain.

- How might your health care team help you achieve these goals? If they are not present at the meeting, tell everyone about your entire health care team—all those that provide physical, spiritual, and psychological care and support—family members, friends, volunteers, and professionals. In a way, you are introducing them to the people who will likely meet through the course of your illness.

- Have you considered palliative or hospice care? Do you want those services, and are they available in your community? How might you get information about the hospice/palliative care program in your community? Is there anyone who does home visits from that organization?

- What about advance directives (documents outlining your wishes for health care decisions if you are incapacitated)? The intent is to give you control over decisions in the future.

- Do you have a health care proxy or a durable power of attorney (a document that names someone to make decisions in the event you are unable to do so) or a living will (which states what type of treatment you would like to have or refuse to have given various health situations)? Someday someone may need to speak for you or to make decisions on your behalf. Who is most able to act as your advocate? Who is most able to think like you do and take action accordingly? Who is most able to give voice to your wishes about end-of-life care? This might be a friend more than a family member. Some people choose a family member as a matter of loyalty, but a friend might be better. Advance directives are legal in every state, though laws in each state can vary. They are also legal in most provinces in

Canada. Do you know the laws in your state or province pertaining to advance directives, health care proxies, and living wills? Who might help you get this information?

This whole process might be very new for you. If it is, there is value in discussing how you make these decisions. Who do you include in the decisionmaking process? Again, at the end of this discussion, the facilitator goes around the circle, asking each person whether they have anything to add.

Maggie needed more information about treatment options before deciding what she would do. She asked whether one or two people might accompany her to all her visits to her new physician. She also said that she would feel more comfortable if she had a copy of her records; she would ask for a photocopy of her medical records, knowing that she would have to cover the cost of photocopying. She did say that she would like to go on a family vacation as well as to spend time individually with each of her three children. She hoped to have more energy so that she might be able to take each of them away for a weekend. Her wildest dream was to take all of them on a trip to England. Maggie did not speak about a living will or an advance directive. She had mentioned before the meeting that she was not ready to discuss those topics in a large group. In fact, she acknowledged that she was hardly prepared to approach those topics on her own or with her children.

Describing What Quality of Life Means to You

At this juncture, consider your quality of life—physical, emotional, mental, spiritual, financial, and social. This is often the most difficult and challenging part of the process. Frankness and honesty are especially important. Only you can define or describe what "quality of life" means to you. Your definition might be very different, not only from those in the room but also from your own in the not-too-distant past. That is one of the reasons this process is important. It gives you the opportunity to let other people know your wishes.

- What is important to you at this time in your life? What would "quality of life" mean if you had five years of life left? (Five years seems to be forever for most people. To imagine that you only have two years to six months of life remaining is more difficult.) What does quality of life mean to you if your life expectancy is two years? Six months or less? A few weeks?
- How are you living now compared to before this illness? Your answer might help others understand the changes in your life and might also provide a reference point as to how quickly changes are happening.

In my experience, this is where the group can differ in perspective. In some instances, the patient has begun a process of confronting mortality even while friends and family members still hope for a cure and don't want to address end-of-life issues. Therefore, at least one or two people need to know your decisionmaking background and be willing to back you up. So encourage discussion, invite people to ask questions, and express what they can do to help you achieve your goals—but make sure this is what *you* want.

Up to this point, we have been reviewing your past, your choices for medical treatment, and your wishes for the time you have left. Now, the discussion moves toward the actuality of your life.

- What is realistic? What is desirable? What is possible?
- How has your definition of "quality of life" changed with the knowledge that you have a terminal illness? What brings meaning to your life?
- Consider physical, social, psychological, and spiritual issues. What has sustained you emotionally and spiritually in the past? What sustains you at present?
- Are there circumstances under which you would consider stopping all medication or treatment? Given the preferences you

have expressed, which of the above are feasible, and how might they best be achieved?

As this part of the meeting draws to a close, the facilitator asks if anyone has anything to add before moving on to the next section.

It was difficult for Maggie to speak about all the possibilities that might result from her illness, especially the likelihood she might die as a result of the cancer. She felt overwhelming grief at the thought of saying goodbye to her three adult children, whom she dearly loved. As the facilitator, it was my responsibility to introduce the topic.

"While we have looked at all the favorable outcomes, we have thus far avoided one possibility. It is the most difficult of all to talk about, but we have decided that we must also talk about what will happen if all the remaining options are unsuccessful. We are told that if the cancer does not respond to treatment, it will likely cause Maggie's death." There was a silent pause. Then her eldest son blurted out, "What a relief, now we can be honest with each other! There's a lot to say and we want to say it." The other two children agreed—it seemed to be the moment they had been waiting for. We needed the previous hour and a half to get to that point. That was the beginning of greater intimacy within the family. Maggie's breathing improved as her stress decreased. She seemed to sense that her children wanted to share her pain, her aloneness, her anxiety. Her journey was less lonely than it had been once she was able to speak the unspeakable and begin to express some of her inner feelings.

Assessing Practical Considerations

The facilitator continues to raise issues and ask questions: Do you have one health care provider who acts as an advocate for you? Do you have someone who understands you and works with you? If not, is there anyone in the group who knows of such a person? If so, how might you be linked to that health care provider? If not, are there other people you could ask in order to find someone like that? The greater the ambiguity about the disease process, the more stressful the end of life will be.

Maggie felt there was a lot of ambiguity about her illness. She felt that she did not have a clear understanding about the natural history of the disease. Neither did she know what treatment options remained for her and how she might get the information she needed and her children wanted. Someone in the group knew of a physician in another city who had already provided some information about the disease to Maggie. He offered to make another contact; another person offered to accompany Maggie on her next visit to her cancer doctor to ask questions about the disease and treatment options; a third person was eager to surf the Internet for information.

- Where might you receive care during the course of your illness—at home, in a hospital, in an extended care facility, in a hospice? Although care at home is often a first choice, it can be taxing on you as well as your care provider(s). The good moments are certainly good, but the bad times can be very bad. It is great to be around for the intimate moments, the meaningful conversations, the time of shared quiet. It is more difficult during times when pain is poorly controlled, when diarrhea means frequent diaper changes, when wretching doesn't end.
- What are the financial costs? Are the costs of treatment covered by insurance? If not, what does insurance cover? What about medication through the course of your illness? What are other options for payment? In the United States, it is important to ask how Medicare, Medicaid, and private insurance differ. Because terms of coverage can change, it is imperative to ask your social worker, nurse, doctor, or case manager to assist you in determining what the costs will be and who will cover them. Can someone at the meeting agree to act as a financial advocate, research the options, and then deal with insurers should that become necessary?

- How important is the treatment to you? Is it based on a "last hope" because dying is simply something you're not ready for, or is there a likelihood that the treatment will reverse the disease process or prolong your life? Where would you have to travel in order to get treatment? Who might be affected by your choices? How convenient is the location? Do you know of anyone who has received care at that facility? What was their experience? Are there other facilities to be considered? Who in the group can help you gather information about them?

What are the resources available for optimal care? This includes, first, financial resources:

- Is there money available for equipment (e.g., rental of a bed, commode, wheelchair, etc.), for assistance (e.g., homemaking, nursing care, assistance with activities of daily living, etc.), or for care in a particular facility?
- What is the response of your health insurance company to your needs, to your desires? Who might help you with the mountains of paperwork your insurance company requests from you, or with the interaction that needs to take place between you and the insurance company?
- As you get sicker you will have less energy for all of this, and your family will want to be with you rather than fighting with an insurance company. Who might help your with the work?

Second, there are emotional resources. The emotional energy of the people providing physical, emotional, and spiritual support is a limited resource. It is important for them to be honest and to make commitments only if they are realistic. Some may want to give the idea more thought, and that's okay. Others might want to commit for a shorter period, after which you meet again and review how everyone is doing. At that time, some people may ask for a break to recharge their own batteries. Ask them to speak honestly about their commitments and limitations, and respond in kind. Some people have a tendency to overcommit, and everyone at some point will likely experience a degree of anger, frustration, guilt, or fatigue. Some people will remain stoic in the face of tragedy, unwilling to express their true emotions. But if stress is building, it's important to express it. Speaking openly helps everyone come through the experience healthier, stronger, and with a better understanding of themselves and one another. The burdens—and the rewards—are being shared.

Third, consider societal resources. In my experience, individuals often worry that someone else, a sicker person, might need the facilities more they do. That worry increases if financial resources are being drained. Be honest about your own needs and the needs of those who are supporting you.

What does the law say about your wishes? This is especially important with regard to euthanasia and physician-assisted suicide. It might be valuable to have a discussion about the topic. Many people want to talk about it, even if it's not an option for them. Physician-assisted suicide and euthanasia are against the law in Canada and in most U.S. states (Oregon is the exception). In Canada, it is against the law to counsel anyone toward either euthanasia or physician-assisted suicide. It is not against the law to discuss the topic.

That ends the series of questions. There may be other topics of interest or concern. The facilitator then invites everyone to make comments. The to-do list becomes the plan of action.

Once all the topics are discussed and recorded, look at what needs to be done—review the to-do list. This might include a visit to another specialist for a second opinion, assistance with regard to an activity (to go skiing one more time, to visit a friend in another city, to explore alternative therapies), a visit to a potential hospice, or the drafting of a living will. It is important for the facilitator (or, even better, you) to acknowledge the varied emotions triggered by the process. Be honest; talk about your loss of independence, about your appreciation for everyone's efforts. The plan will work better if people don't overcommit. Review each item and ask who will assume responsibility. Write down that person's name next to the item. Set a deadline for each task. Once the list is complete, set up a second meeting. There is often merit in setting priorities or checking the burdens and benefits of each item on the list. Is everyone who might be affected by this overall plan comfortable with it and able to contribute? If not, why not? What needs to change to enable everyone to put the plan into effect? Some may have to agree to disagree. How much effort (e.g., time, energy, money) will need to be invested to make the specific event happen? What happens if it cannot happen? What is the desired outcome? How will the person's life be enhanced if the item can be achieved?

Maggie's shortness of breath was evident through the meeting. We went through the issues and concerns. People were eager to help her find the information that she wanted and needed, to accompany her to physician visits, and to provide emotional support. There was a significant sense of relief in the room. Conversations continued after the meeting was ended. Everyone stayed to enjoy a meal together. It was the beginning of a community of caring established specifically for Maggie, a community of people who would keep in touch with her and with each other in order to make certain that she would receive the best possible care.

CHAPTER FIVE

Life Review

The unexamined life is not worth living.

Socrates

To thine own self be true.

Shakespeare

You really do wake up. All of a sudden all these things that were hidden are front and center; there is no hiding them anymore.

Brent

The Garden of Eden

Out of the ground made the Lord God to grow every tree that is pleasant to the sight, and good for food; the tree of life also in the midst of the garden, and the tree of the knowledge of good and evil.... And the Lord God took the man, and put him into the garden of Eden to dress it and to keep it. And the Lord God commanded the man, saying: "Of every tree of the garden thou mayest freely eat; but of the tree of the knowledge of good and evil, thou shalt not eat of it; for in the day that thou eatest thereof thou shalt surely die."

And when the woman saw that the tree was good for food, and that it was a delight to the eyes, and that the tree was to be desired to make one wise, she took of the fruit thereof, and did eat; and she gave also unto her husband with her, and he did eat. And the eyes of them both were opened, and they knew that they were naked; and they sewed fig-leaves together, and made themselves girdles.

And they heard the voice of the Lord God walking in the garden toward the cool of the day; and the man and his wife hid themselves from the presence of the Lord God amongst the trees of the garden. And the Lord God called unto the man, and said unto him: "Where art thou?" And he said: "I heard Thy voice in the garden, and I was afraid, because I was naked; and I hid myself." And He said: "Who told thee that thou wast naked? Hast thou eaten of the tree, whereof I commanded thee that thou shouldest not eat?" And the man said: "The woman whom Thou gavest to be with me, she gave me of the tree, and I did eat." And the Lord God said unto the woman: "What is this thou hast done?" And the woman said: "The serpent beguiled me, and I did eat."

And the Lord God made for Adam and for his wife garments of skins, and clothed them.... And the Lord God said: "Behold, the man is become as one of us, to know good and evil; and now, lest he put forth his hand, and take also of the tree of life, and eat, and live for ever." Therefore the Lord God sent him forth from the garden of Eden, to till the ground from whence he was taken.

❋

The fact that the story of the Garden of Eden is included here may come as a surprise. For many, it is a familiar story. Some of you will know it as a story about judgment; some will recognize it as part of the story of creation; and others will know it as a story about becoming mortal. It might also be about self-discovery, transition, and transformation. Adam and Eve left the Garden to start a new life, a new way of being. Their idyllic life was over, and a new work was to begin. They could never return.

But this story also speaks about loss—of a dream, of innocence, of relationship. The losses began when Eve tasted of the fruit of the Tree of Knowledge of good and evil and then gave Adam some to eat as well. They wanted the knowledge that the fruit would grant. By eating of the fruit, the two became aware of their own nakedness as well as their relationship to one another, the world around them, and to their God. They were told they would die. Death became part of their new reality. Therein begins one of the most familiar stories, one of the most familiar teaching texts. Adam and Eve move from a carefree world of innocence to a world of conflict, suffering, pain, and death. They paid a great price for their new knowledge. However, their lives didn't end; their lives changed. Imagine their response of feeling lost and bewildered, of looking back, of wondering what they might have done differently.

Our lives are full of transitions and changes—leaving home, discovering and developing our own values, relocating, having children, seeing children leave home—our stories are familiar. Part of us dies through each one of those transitions. Then one day we learn about having a terminal illness and our naïveté about life as we know it ends. Dying becomes part of our reality. We can't go back. We move through those transitions and changes to a new way of being, a new understanding of ourselves, of our community, and perhaps even of the world.

This chapter marks the transition between discussing your experience of knowing you have a terminal illness to exploring the effect of that experience on your life. In this respect, Kierkegaard said that "life can only be understood backwards; but it must be lived forwards."

There is a benefit to looking in the rearview mirror as you drive: You see where you have been and what is approaching from behind—all while you're driving forward. Perhaps one of the best ways to know where we are headed is to make sense of the past, of that which lies behind us. Reviewing one's life is a spontaneous process that begins once people *know* they are dying, once they *know* they have a terminal illness. It seems to be inevitable. Of that process, Frieda said, "I do a lot more thinking now, about my life, how it was and is, what I've done. . . . It's all coming up, which is very strange." The process is that of reflecting on one's life, on personal history. It begins from within, and it bursts into our thoughts and dreams. Some people blurt out their life story in conversation. They want their story, their legacy, to be heard. It is more than merely remembering or reminiscing. It is a process by which they make sense of their past with the desire to understand who they are, find meaning in who they have been, and hope for the future. This chapter will focus on the process of life review. It will serve as the basis for subsequent chapters: Speaking the Truth, Longing to Belong, Who Am I?

As gerontologists Gary Kenyon and William Randall wrote in *Restorying Our Lives*, "Ultimately, the richest resource for meaning and healing is one we already possess. It rests (mostly untapped) in the material of our own lifestory, in the sprawling, many-layered 'text' that has been accumulating within us across the years, weaving itself in the depths of, and as, our life." It seems that for most people a life story, or life review, includes a component of grief. It also contains love, joy, gratitude, pride, laughter, and hope. For some, it includes guilt and shame, emotional experiences that will be discussed in the following chapters. How do you conduct a life review? For those with a terminal illness, the process may already have begun, as it seems like a natural outgrowth. Two other gerontologists, James Birren and Donna Deutchman, authors of *Guiding Autobiography Groups for Older Adults*, have developed a useful structure for the process of life review. It also provides guidance for others who do not have a terminal illness but are trying to make sense of their lives or to find meaning in their past.

In this chapter I take you through a life review using the framework of Birren and Deutchman. You might take pencil and paper in hand to reflect about your own life. You may also choose to record your story on a tape. I present and incorporate the nine themes they developed for the "guided autobiography." As an example of someone who was in the process of reviewing her life when I met her, I tell the story of Florence. Over the course of many months, Florence shared the story of her life with me—times of quiet and silence, shedding of tears, chuckles and laughter, anguish, joy, anger, warmth, grief. She spoke of her family of origin, her chosen family, her work, her friends, her dreams, her memories, her losses. We didn't follow the exact format in this chapter, so I have integrated her story into the themes that I present.

Who was Florence? She was a delightful, dark-haired woman in her mid-eighties, a coresearcher in the study. She used our time together to review her history, to make sense of her life. On every visit she would greet me with a cheerful "Hello!," a fresh cup of herbal tea, and a date square or some other treat she had prepared for the occasion. It was always something different, just out of the oven, and always served with a cup of hot tea. She had a determination about her, reflected in the fact that she continued to bake even as her vision began to fail.

The first theme of the life review is major branching points. Each of the themes will include a statement and a set of questions that serve to stimulate thought and self-reflection. You might want to think about each of these before you read the corresponding section about Florence.

Major Branching Points

Life might be regarded as a branching tree, a flowing river, or a trailing plant that puts down roots in various places as it grows. "Branching points" are the events and inner processes that shape our lives in a significant way. These might be major events such as marriage, relocation, and retirement, or minor events such as reading a book, having a conversation, or going on a vacation. Learning that one has a serious or a terminal illness is certainly a major branching point. What were the branching points in your life? When did they occur? Do you feel they happened too soon? Too late? Who were the significant people involved in these junctures in your life? What were the emotions that you experienced at the time of each branching point? What emotions do you experience now? Did you feel that you had a personal choice in the matter? What were the consequences? What might your life be like if this event had not occurred? How does that event compare to learning about having a terminal illness? How specifically has your life changed since you learned about your illness?

Florence spoke to me of the most significant branching point in her life: "I lost an eighteen-year-old daughter. I'm just dealing with my daughter's death now, for the first time with a therapist, for I feel that if you don't learn, then it was for nothing, you know, and it's terrible to think that something so horrible could be for nothing—it's got to be for something. Doris died thirty years ago. If you had told me then that anything good could come of it, I would have tried to kill you." Strong words; strong emotions. That loss affected much of Florence's life.

Family of Origin and Adult (or Chosen) Families

Who is your family? Who is in your family of origin (grandparents, parents, siblings, aunts, and uncles)? Who is in your adult family (your family of choice)? Which family members played a role in shaping your life—in a positive way, in a negative way? What would I need to know about your family of origin to understand who you are? Who held the power in your family? Who made the decisions, and how were decisions made? How was affection expressed in your family? What were the areas of conflict? How was conflict resolved? What were the family rules? Who loved you in your family? How did you experience that love? What were the strengths and weaknesses of your family? What are some of your favorite family memories? What are some of your painful family memories? What events have torn your family apart or strengthened the family? What was your relationship to your parents? Who are the significant family members in your life at present, especially in the context of your illness? Who would you like to have present at the time of your death and why?

Florence spoke of her family of origin: "I'm Jewish. My mother and father were immigrants. I'm a first-generation Canadian. My mother was born in Warsaw. My father came from France. They met here in Canada, in Ottawa." She continued:

My mother was Polish. She was only fourteen years old when she left Poland, so she saw some horrifying things. She was a wonderful woman. When I think of what her childhood was like, I think of this fourteen-year-old girl who, because she was Jewish, hid in cellars with her mother and baby brother and sister. What she saw as a girl of fourteen you wouldn't wish on Satan himself. She came to America in 1905 and had to go to work in a factory without any English, not a word. She learned English and French. She made flowers for hats; women used to wear fancy dresses and large floral hats. She had a beautiful voice and developed that to become an opera singer. She also married and brought up four well-educated children.

My father was a very loving man who was emotionally crippled as a child because he did not come from a loving family. But he was proud of us. His pride in us was open. It was his desire to give us good lives and prepare us for a good life.

My father had a lot of grief in his life. When Doris died, my mother told me that he had said, "At a time like this, a mother's place is with her child, a father's place is in the synagogue praying." He seemed to know that men and women grieve differently. My father was not a man who was able to show his love or his emotions. But his children always felt, in spite of the fact that there was no hugging and kissing or anything like that, we always felt secure in the fact that he loved us without showing it.

I was brought up to say my prayers at night. I was guided by the teaching I got, and the example I saw of my mother being all things to her family. My father never went in the kitchen, he never lifted a hand to do anything. He might have wanted to, but my mother would never allow it.

Florence told me about the early years of her adult family:

I left home at twenty. I never lived at home again, just visited. My fiancé was overseas for five years. He came back an emotional basket case, a bit unstable from his wartime experiences. We married one week after he came home. I married a stranger, then moved from one end of the country to the other, away from family. My husband was a social drinker, like 95 percent of the men. Others call it social drinking, but I call it alcoholism. These men who come home from work and the first thing they do is have a drink. I call that alcoholism. God forbid there's no alcohol in the house! They'd go out and get it, you know. They go to parties and everyone calls it anything but "drunk," you call it by other euphemisms—you know, "sauced," whatever you want to call it—and it's acceptable.

My husband would come home from work and go into the living room, sit down with the newspaper. I came home from work, too, but

I went into the kitchen. I would take care of the whole meal, feed the children, read to them, and then get them ready for bed. I did everything. I remember getting up in the morning and taking the children downstairs so my husband could sleep. I had to keep them quiet.

We were a family of six—father, mother, and four children—just like everybody else. We had a reasonably normal life, no better and no worse than any other. I devoted myself to my children. We gave them the things that children are supposed to have. The children went to camp. They had a father who coached soccer on the playground, took them fishing and taught them how to make flies, showed them how to ski. Our summers were spent with our two boys and two girls, camping, fishing in lakes throughout the province.

After her daughter and husband died, many years before I met her, Florence had nothing left to give her three remaining children. She realized as she spoke with me that as adults they were strangers to one another. In some sense, she had "lost" them as well. In her grief, she became isolated from each of her surviving children, and they were in turn isolated from each other.

I sat my two sons and my daughter down after Doris died and after their father died and I said to them that I didn't feel capable of being a father figure for them. I also said that whatever their father and I had done that was wrong in their eyes, or unsuitable, or that they didn't like, they were old enough to damn well change it themselves because we had done the best we knew how to do at the time. I thought a long time before I said that to them.

Florence spoke of her relationship to her children in most of the interviews.

I have a feeling of aloneness where family is concerned. I have two sons and a daughter now. I have very limited contact with one of them. I often say to my other children, I haven't the vaguest idea how you feel about me. And it's true. I don't. I know that on the surface there is respect, and I think there's even a bit of admiration. They have seen me struggle and learn how to run my own life.

Often, one's life story is divided between love and work. Love pertains to the personal part of life, the relationships with family members and friends. Work pertains to one's job, one's profession, one's productivity.

Career or Major Life's Work

A career *is* a major life's work. It takes up your time and energy. Often we think of it as the work we do outside the home for pay. It might also include what we do in a relationship, for example, in being a husband or wife; a special interest such as art, music, or education; or work as a volunteer in community service. What is—or was—your career? How did you come to choose that career? As a child, what did you want to be when you grew up? What have been the benefits, hurdles, and surprises within that career? Do you wish you had made a different choice? Did you have more than one career over your lifetime? How did that happen? What do you consider the successes and failures in your work? What were the most enjoyable and least enjoyable aspects of your work? Which feature of your career do you most celebrate? If you did it all again, what would you do differently? What would you do the same? Depending on the age at which you became ill, do you experience a sense of loss with regard to your career? Are there things you would still like to do or to have done before you stop working?

With regard to her profession, Florence said, "I had a good life. I was a nursing instructor, and I felt that I was a big success in my cho-sen field." This gave her a strong sense of self-worth. "It's strange, you know. I got that from my nursing students; there are just so many of them who are attached to me. That meant a lot to me, but I never was able to admit that it was something good and wonderful. We were taught not to brag. But now, I'm not afraid to say that my presence has added to their lives. That's good, because I'm admitting that I'm a whole person and valuable. I'm very fortunate that my relationship with some of my former students turned out to be much more than I would ever have expected."

Florence took real delight in her former students. Decades after being their teacher, some of them continued to be in a relationship with her, phoning, meeting for lunch, or dropping in for a visit. She seemed to long for relationships with her children similar to those she had with her students.

The Role of Money

Money is an important theme in life. It affects many aspects of our lives: family, education, career, relationships, activities, and self-esteem. Attitudes toward money are affected by a variety of positive and negative influences. Who taught you about money and how? What role did money have in your family of origin? Were you poor or financially secure, and what impact did that have on you as a child and as an adult? How important has money been to you as an adult? What was the biggest financial mistake you made, and what was the greatest financial success? Are you generous or stingy with money? Have you managed your money well or poorly? How does having a terminal illness affect your attitude toward money? How is the way you manage your money similar to that of your parents? How does it differ? How do you feel about the money you earned, the money you saved, now that you have a terminal illness? What will you do with your money before you die—and after you are gone?

With regard to money, Florence said,

You don't put away money when you're paying a mortgage and raising four children. Sure, salaries are bigger now, but so are your expenses. We had lower salaries, but we had $1.49 day at the local department store, where we bought running shoes for our children. We didn't pay a hundred dollars for running shoes for a little child in those days.

When you have children, you give yourself over to them. At times it feels as though you're held hostage to their needs and demands. You do the best you can with what you've got, but you have no guarantees. This is what I learned in my life: no guarantees. So what is it—luck? If there are no real guarantees, how do people go on having children? It's a big question. It's just as profound as, "How do you feel about having cancer?" The answer is faith, you have faith. I guess I had faith when I had four children. How many young people stop to think about it? If they did, there'd be fewer people in the world, wouldn't there?

After my husband died, there was nothing in the bank, no savings, because we had been paying a mortgage on the house and bringing up four children. You don't expect to die when you're fifty-six. I had to think about my future. I had ten more years in my job and was able to secure my future. I wasn't very smart, it just worked out. So at this time in my life, I'm not looking to get something that I haven't already found. I'm not looking for something new. I make the best of what I've got.

I'm retired, I'm comfortable. I can do anything I want to do. If I drop dead tomorrow, you couldn't say, "Poor woman, she never had a life."

Health and Body Image

Your overall health and body image are a complex part of who your are. There are objective features that make up who you are physically, and there are subjective features that contribute to how you feel about yourself—your self-image. This often involves comparing oneself to others as to appearance, strength, frequency of illness, physical ability, and attractiveness. Consider those features through your lifetime, beginning in infancy and moving through childhood, adolescence, and early, middle, and late adulthood. What part of your body do you like most? What part do you like least? If you could change one feature, what would it be? Does all or part of your body embarrass you? How has your body changed through the course of your present illness? How do you feel about your body since you learned about having a terminal illness?

Florence also spoke about having cancer, which had been diagnosed five years before I met her.

When I heard that I had cancer, I sat up in bed and thought to myself, *I want everything!* Then I thought, *Well, what have you not got?* I've got everything. Whenever I went to Whistler to visit my daughter, I looked at those houses out on Bowen Island and said to myself, "I'll never have one of those." But then I phoned my daughter that very day and said, "I want a house on Bowen Island and I don't want to wait. I want it right away." And so I went and bought it. It was heaven on earth, just heaven. I was at the top of a slope, with a gorgeous view, a mile to one beach and the other beach right there. I walked miles and miles while I could: took part in the community there, joined the little cancer group, went to the fall fair. I had no time to be sick. I really think it was like those people who go home to die and start to write a book. They don't die—too busy writing a book!

Experiences of Death and Ideas about Dying

Death affects people in many ways. Some people might consider any major loss as a death. Others regard death only as the death of another person. You may have experienced the death of a pet in your childhood. You may also have experienced the death of a family member (grandparent, parent, spouse, sibling, child), a friend, a hero. How have your experiences and thoughts about death affected who you are? Have you ever felt abandoned by someone who died? How was death talked about or experienced in your family? How have you grieved with regard to death or loss? What role, if any, has war played in your life? Have you ever killed someone? How did you feel about it at the time? How does that compare to your current feelings about the event? Try to recall the first funeral you ever attended. How did it affect you? How has your previous experience regarding death and dying affected your current experience of knowing that you have a terminal illness? Is it changing and, if so, how? How would you like to die? Do you have fears about dying? Do you have fears about being dead? If you could ask a dead person one question about the dying process, what would it be?

Florence spoke about death: "I had no experience with death. Doris was the first death in our family. I didn't have a chance to do anything, because by the time I saw her she was already brain dead. She was alive one day and dead the next. It was all very fast. I'm still angry, as you can tell. It doesn't matter how long your life goes on after that, it's never the same. This is why you have couples separating after the death of a child—life is completely different. Some people are drawn together, and some people are separated. But I think more people are separated by the death of a child." The grief of those who survive the death of a child, whether it is a death due to illness or an accident, or a violent death or a suicide, will have its own features and complexities.

Of her own response to Doris's death, Florence said, "You know, I was back in the classroom ten days later. I never dealt with it. As you can see even now I can't think about it, and it's been over thirty years." She spoke repeatedly about guilt. "There's a lot of guilt around the death of a child. I think I mentioned that I believe that's what sometimes ends up driving a man and a wife apart when a child dies. A lot of guilt. It's not the kind of guilt that you feel for neglecting to give her something that she wanted. I think to be absolutely honest, it's the guilt for every time I was less than perfect as a mother. I don't think I've ever forgiven myself. You know, it may be one of the reasons why I'm not afraid of dying. That thought just came to me, never thought of it before. It would finally be the end of that guilt."

Hearing Florence speak of her experience was like a lightning bolt to my heart. At the time that she spoke of her experience, I was one of several physicians working at a hospice for children. Some of us were palliative care physicians, others pediatricians. I was confident that we, along with the other team members, were providing care and comfort to the children and families who came to the hospice. Until Florence told me about the death of her daughter, I had not realized how the death of a child and the suffering resulting from that death could threaten the "intactness" of a family. According to her experience, "The death of a child means the death of a family." Her statement exposed the limitations of medicine; too often, its focus is the physical pain and suffering of the dying child, not the effect of that experience on the family. Florence described her own grief in being robbed of her role as a mother to Doris. In the death of her child, she seemed to realize that she could not protect her child from all harm, that the natural order of parents dying before children is not absolute, that life is not predictable, and neither is it fair or just:

My husband sat. He didn't mourn the way I did at all, but he mourned in his own way. He sat all night, in the armchair in our living room with his face covered with his handkerchief. He just sat there the whole night like that and then when he got up, he seemed to have dealt with it. We both had a great sense of guilt.

It was very obvious that we were dealing with something that was not only foreign to us but we had no idea how to deal with it. We were dealing with it differently. He was ready to get on with things and I wasn't. This makes for a very difficult relationship. And a lot of anger.

Aspirations, Life Goals, and the Meaning of Life

Meaning, values, and purpose in life are often difficult to describe or speak about. The simplicity of childhood—right and wrong, black and white, true and false—changes to shades of gray and uncertainty in adulthood. Some people find comfort in religion or other spiritual practices. What was the religious tradition in your childhood, in your home, in your community? Have you ever had a religious experience? How did it come about? What were the immediate and long-term effects? Are there symbols in your life that are important to you? What principles guide your life? How does nature fit into your understanding of meaning or spirituality? What has given your life meaning in the past? Have there ever been times when your life felt meaningless? How has your sense of spirituality changed since you learned about having a terminal illness?

Florence reflected on features that brought meaning to her life:

I was where I wanted to be. I was in the forest, surrounded by nature. When I woke in the morning, I looked out my window at a tree and in it was a little nest of birds. I think it helped me to live.

The home on Bowen Island was great for my children and grandchildren, my nieces and nephews, too. They would come out to visit. I let my friends use it when I wasn't there; they could bring their families and spend a week or ten days. It was a source of joy and healing for everyone.

I'm here on earth for something. It's a feeling—a feeling of worthiness, a feeling of mystery. I don't want anybody to define it for me, but I sense that it's not for nothing that I got cancer.

I feel that it would be horrible to live without having some sort of meaning in your life. No matter how long you live, there should be some meaning to it. Had I not had cancer, I wouldn't have met most of the people for whom I now seem to have some meaning, people who certainly have a lot of meaning in my life. These are the people I support and who support me in return. If I didn't have that meaning in my life, I wonder what meaning there would be now.

Florence was deeply involved in a cancer support group.

My life is tied in now with the young people who are going through this. I hope to be a symbol of the possible. Many of them come in newly diagnosed and really depressed. There's a difference between hearing that your life is threatened when you're in your twenties and thirties and hearing the same thing when you're seventy-eight. You don't want to die, but you probably have children, grandchildren, you've traveled, you've seen things, you've done most of what there is to do. At forty, you haven't accomplished your goals, you have a young family, you're only halfway up the ladder—you know, there are things to do.

When there are new people in the group, I say to them, "Five years and look at me! I don't look sick. I fought, I fought all the way and you can do it, too." I hope to be a symbol of what's possible.

A very mysterious thing goes on when we sit together and talk. It's not all talk about cancer, you know; a lot of it is talk about life and nature—and beauty. I'm convinced that some sort of healing process occurs, a very mysterious thing that goes on when people get together and talk. I don't mean just one on one—I'm talking about a group of people who are there for the same purpose. We're certainly different, A to Z, and some are complainers and some are so courageous, it just tears your heart out. But there is something mysterious that happens in the group. My own theory is that your body chemistry changes when you feel this kind of loving surrounding you. It's an empathy, it's an understanding of what this other person is saying. I've seen people in the depths of despair, unable to speak without crying—maybe they've just had a terrible diagnosis, and an hour and a half later they walk out with a smile, saying, "I'm going to take hold of this myself." It may not last, but they come back the following week and get a little more of that strength. Where does that come from? You have to be there to see it.

Florence found meaning in giving of herself. "I've knit over six hundred pairs of slippers for cancer patients. They've been sent all over the country. I'm still knitting, as long as my eyes hold out. I have all sorts of little projects, and it keeps me going."

Florence also spoke of the value of music in her life:

My mother was an opera singer and our family was all very musical. We all studied some musical instrument. I played the violin, and my three brothers played the piano. One brother sang beautifully, he had a lovely voice. Throughout our childhood we made music. There was no TV, radio. We made all our own entertainment. It was a rich, rich life. Instead of watching other people do things, we did them. We entertained ourselves and we entertained other people. I can remember when we were little children taking part in concerts. You know, that gave us self-confidence. We'd get up there and people would clap no matter how awful it was. It gave us a sense of who we were in the community.

A Lifetime of Loves and Hates

Love and hate are powerful emotions. Love is a strong emotional attachment to a person, place, or thing, and hate is a strong feeling of dislike or animosity toward a person, place, or thing. What have been the major loves and hates in your life (persons, places, ideas, behaviors, things)? What were your loves and hates during your childhood, adolescence, and adulthood? Were you allowed to express both of these feelings throughout your lifetime? Have you lost a love or learned to appreciate something or someone you once hated? Have you ever been consumed by love or by hate? Have you ever disliked someone so much you wished they would die? Knowing you have a terminal illness, do you think there is something left to do with regard to the loves and hates in your life?

Sexual Identity, Sex Roles, and Sexual Experiences

Sexuality includes our sense of sexual identity, that is, of being male or female; our thoughts, ideas, and practices regarding sex role behavior; and our sexual experiences. Do you remember when you first learned about being a boy or a girl? What toys, games, and activities made up your play as a child? Was anything forbidden? How did you parents view your sexuality? Where and from whom did you get your sex education? What were your sexual experiences like, beginning in childhood and moving into adolescence and adulthood? Have you ever had a traumatic sexual experience? If so, how did it happen and who was involved? How would you define the "ideal" relationship? In terms of being masculine or feminine, how do you define yourself? Has that been affected by your illness and, if so, how? How do you relate to members of the same sex and those of the opposite sex?

Grief

Life review begins with remembering and reflecting on the past—the choices you've made, your sense of self, your relationships with others, and your connection to a higher power such as God. This type of reflection leads to a range of insights and emotions. The probity—that is, the goodness—in your life can result in a sense of affirmation, accomplishment, and contentment. If you remember features of your life as tragic, negative, or evil, you can experience feelings of guilt, anxiety, and depression. You may be left struggling to make sense of the life you have lived, to find meaning and purpose in your own history. You might recognize the need to resolve issues within yourself or with another person. You may come to a new or deeper understanding of events and relationships that were part of your life.

If we do not examine the past, its burdens will weigh us down. It will impede our ability to make choices for the future. In fact, as philosopher George Santayana said, "Those who cannot remember the past are condemned to repeat it." Conducting a life review and speaking about it to another person can begin the process of understanding and finding meaning in your own life. It may also serve to reduce the pain and grief associated with some life experiences.

For Florence, her life review resulted in the acknowledgment of her deep-seated grief over the death of her daughter, her husband, and the loss of relationships with her surviving children. At the same time, she recognized how she had reconnected with her mother before her mother died and that within that reconnection she had experienced some kind of higher power. In contrast to the pain and grief associated with her familial relationships, she enjoyed a sense of status and recognition in her career.

Grief is often part of the process of looking back over one's life story. For example, Florence could not speak of her children without sadness. Her sadness contained both anger and remorse. In fact, it was more than sadness; it was grief, deep grief, which had been part of her life for over thirty years.

Grief is born out of wanting what you will never have again. For some people it stems from realizing that they will never get what they truly deserved—unconditional love, being taken seriously, or being seen for who they truly are. For others it results from no longer having what they would like—the company of someone who has died, a job they lost or didn't get, failing a significant exam. Florence's grief did not melt away. It needed to be expressed in order to rid her of its often numbing and paralyzing effects. Florence's grief belonged not only to the death of her daughter, Doris, at age eighteen, but also to the loss of intimacy with her husband at the time of Doris's death, as well as the loss she felt in not being a supportive and nurturing mother to her three surviving children: Robert, who was in his early twenties at the time of Doris's death; Willie, who was in his midteens; and Melody, who had just turned twelve.

People grieve differently, and it can be said that to some degree men and women grieve differently. Grief is not rational; it is a pain, a great pain—not in one's mind, but in the heart, the soul, at the core of one's being. It numbs the emotions, diminishes spontaneity, isolates. Grief signals loss—of what we do and who we are, of self, of a relationship. Grief resides in the conscious and the unconscious, in dreams, thoughts, and feelings—that which is within can be brought to the outside. Grief does not melt away. It must be felt, experienced, and expressed in order to be resolved. Often people who are filled with grief expend a great deal of energy suppressing it, as expressing grief causes pain and generally is not welcomed by others. As much as grief is suppressed, so are the other emotions we might experience. Only people who feel and express their grief recover from it.

About grief, Florence said, "Grief fires grief, fed by the wood of guilt, and vice versa—guilt brings grief. I think one feeds the other." Grief in the present often links to unresolved grief from the past.

Unless grief is resolved through expressing it, we remain emotionally attached to the object, person, or relationship that is lost, that we long to be with. In this case, a mother who has been unable to fully express her grief over the death of her teenage daughter is emotionally paralyzed by her grief attachment to her. This became an impediment to her ability to focus affection on her surviving children. Grief isolates. In Florence's case of unrelieved isolation, estrangement set in:

> I was angry. If you want to know, I'm still angry. People would say to me, "God has a purpose, you know." This to me was such a horrifying thought. I have studied religion. I went to a university that trained Anglican clergy, and I was in the second group of women allowed into the university. You had to take comparative religion. I've always enjoyed reading about religions, but I'm nonreligious— especially after Doris died, that was the end of that. That's when I became angry. My mind was filled with that son-of-a-bitch sitting up there watching the damn sparrows. . . . Why wasn't he watching my daughter? I was very bitter, very bitter.
>
> The loss of a child and the loss of a dearly beloved husband—it's apples and oranges. There is no emotion equal to the loss of a child. It's a different kind of pain because it's flesh of your flesh; some women who have a miscarriage feel the same type of pain. It doesn't matter whether it's a newborn infant or an eighteen-year-old girl.

With the death of her daughter and husband, a part of Florence died as well. Emily Brontë's poem "Remembrance," which she wrote many years after the death in her family that inspired the poem, expresses this well.

> *No later light has lightened up my heaven,*
> *No second morn has ever shone for me;*

All my life's bliss from thy dear life was given,
All my life's bliss is in the grave with thee.

Florence continued: "I used to drive my car out into the country somewhere and roll up the windows and scream and yell and bellow for awhile and then drive back and prepare supper. Willie did tell me about climbing a mountain on his own, some place very private where he just screamed and yelled. I don't know what Robert did. I think he probably chopped wood, or went kayaking, something physical. And as far as Melody is concerned, I think that she cried a lot."

When the death of a close family member has occurred, it must be talked about—again and again and again. Until that happens, meaningful topics will not be engaged, potentially intimate conversations won't get started—nothing will change until someone has the courage to speak what seems to be unspeakable. Florence's family skirted the issue that was isolating them from one another; thus, intimacy was sacrificed for silence and for "being in control." Their relationships with one another, like their voices, were silent. And silence, like death, brings relationships to an end.

Once silence is broken, reconciliation can be considered. Only then can it become a reality. Florence spoke about her hopes for reconciliation with her children:

I plan to take the bull by the horns one of these days and really try to get my three children to talk to me about it, but they are as emotionally constipated as I used to be. I just want to ask how they felt, and whether they could talk about it now—that it was important for me. It might relieve me of some guilt if we could just sit and talk about Doris. I still bring her up. I'll say, Remember when Doris did this or that? That seems to be okay with them. They know that on the anniversary of her death, I always light a candle—it's a Jewish tradition—and they phone and say, I remember what day it is, Mom.

They ask, Did you light the candle? I'd like to hear about their personal pain.

Florence had a very different experience with her mother. One day, Florence received a call from her mother. They had not spent a great deal of time together for more than forty years, ever since Florence and her husband had moved to the West Coast. Her mother told her that she had to move into a retirement home, and she wanted to live close to Florence. "My mother was ninety-four when that phone call came. She lived another seven years, and I was in my seventies. It's like having a baby at that age, you know."

It was the first opportunity I had to spend any quality time with her. It was very difficult because I had to take over everything and watch her lose her independence. She had stayed in her own home in Ottawa, and at ninety-four she was getting on the bus and going downtown, conducting her own business. It wasn't until I brought her out here that she became helpless. I used to go over [to the care facility where her mother lived] and bathe her, and wash her hair. I had to be responsible for the insurance, for her clothes, for her medication, and for her all visits to the various doctors. I was diagnosed with cancer two years after she arrived here. So I had to deal with chemotherapy and radiation *and* my mother. I visited her there nearly every day.

For the first time, we became loving. She and I would hug, and she'd roll her eyes up in her little old skeleton and say, "Oh Florie, only He knows!" I understood that she meant, only He knows what you do for me, and that was compensation. And she was not a believer, but we all say "God" in times of need. Isn't it funny?

Florence wanted to arrange a meeting with her three grown children, and she asked me to participate. She wanted very badly to have them know who she was and for her to know them. She asked whether I might facilitate such a meeting. In making the request, she started by saying, "You know, David, I have given you a lot over the past months, and now I ask for something in return." She was absolutely right. She had given me a great deal. In the process, I had grown very fond of her and was pleased to agree to work with her on the meeting she described. But it never happened, for she was soon admitted to the hospital for the last time. When I visited her there, I offered to hold the meeting in her room. She said it was too late, and the next day she lost consciousness. Through her final days I wondered—but would never know—whether her episodes of agitation and peaceful-ness, even though she was unconscious, mirrored the conscious emo-tions she had experienced—the peaceful resolve about her career, her commitment to friends and to others who had cancer, the agitation and grief of her family relationships. She had hoped to reconnect with her children but did not have the time to complete that part of her journey. Apart from speaking about her family, her friends, her work, and her experience of illness, Florence also spoke of her experi-ence of spirituality (see chapter 9).

Some people will find that it is painful to complete a life review, especially as they experience grief that has been unresolved or unex-pressed through the course of their lifetime. It is valuable to do this work in a group, as described above, or to get the help of another individual who is willing to support you through the process. At a time in my life when I was filled with grief, I was given a valuable piece of advice: Express your sorrow with another person, a trusted friend. Repeat your story with all the emotion it involves until your friend fully understands you.

As one goes through the process of a life review, unexpected emo-tions will likely be aroused—despair, hopelessness, anger, rage, sad-ness. For some these emotions can be overwhelming. If that is the case, contact a friend or family member who will respect emotion without judgment. Ask the person to respond only with questions for clarification. It is important to state that you remember a tragedy, and in remembering you are experiencing a very powerful emotion. Invite the person to be with you. Then, in great detail, remember the event, the person, the loss. Include the features and characteristics that you value. Stay in the emotion until it comes to resolution. At that point, grief becomes mourning, an emotion that is likely to recur throughout one's lifetime. Some people might have to contact a professional counselor if this emotion is severe and does not subside.

Some will remember the wisdom and compassion that emerged in their lives through the expression of grief. We grieve someone or something only if it has value to us. Through our grief, we come to see that that which is lost may still be within us. Of the process of life review, Birren states: "Reviewing their past helps individuals feel that their lives have had meaning and purpose. Furthermore, it helps them resolve continuing or resurgent conflicts, reconcile internal contradictions, overcome problems, and master complicated feelings or relationships with loved ones. Last, but not least, autobiography becomes a cherished legacy to younger generations."

Although the research project I conducted did not follow the life-review process that Birren and Deutchman developed, it provided people the opportunity to review their lives. For many, this was a positive experience. They frequently said two things: that they had never spoken to anyone like this before; and that they felt better after telling their stories, after reviewing their lives. For Florence, the opportunity to speak of her losses, her grief, her achievements, and her relationships resulted in a desire to invite her children to hear her story and for her to hear their stories. Although she died before she was able to do that, I can say with confidence that she had reached a point in her process of life review that would have allowed her to achieve a renewed sense of intimacy with her children.

I will remember Florence for many reasons. One of my fondest memories is one of our first visits. I was preparing to leave her apartment—briefcase, video camera, and tripod in hand. She gave me a warm embrace, saying, "I know you can't do this [referring to the hug], but I can. I'm grateful for the time we spend together. I don't care about rules and protocols, I care about relationships, about caring for people and about letting them know I care."

CHAPTER SIX

Speaking the Truth

Truth spoken by those we love may be painful to hear and provide insight necessary to change one's life.

Isabel

If you bring forth what is within you, what you bring forth will save you. If you do not bring forth what is within you, what you do not bring forth will destroy you.

The Gospel According to Thomas, 70:1,2

Healing occurs to the degree I welcome all my feelings and let myself be loved in them.

Matthew Linn

The Prisoner in the Dark Cave

There once was a man who was sentenced to die. He was blindfolded and put in a pitch-dark cave. The cave was 100 yards by 100 yards. He was told that there was a way out of the cave, and if he could find it, he was a free man.

After a rock was secured at the entrance to the cave, the prisoner was allowed to take his blindfold off and roam freely in the darkness. He was to be fed only bread and water for the first thirty days and nothing thereafter. The bread and water were lowered from a small hole in the roof at the south end of the cave. The ceiling was about eighteen feet high. The opening was about one foot in diameter. The prisoner could see a faint light up above, but no light came into the cave.

As the prisoner roamed and crawled around the cave, he bumped into rocks. Some were rather large. He thought that if he could build a mound of rocks and dirt that was high enough, he could reach the opening and enlarge it enough to crawl through and escape. Since he was five feet, nine inches tall and his reach was another two feet, the mound had to be at least ten feet high.

So the prisoner spent his waking hours picking up rocks and digging up dirt. At the end of two weeks, he had built a mound of about six feet. He thought that if he could duplicate that in the next two weeks, he could make it before his food ran out. But as he had already used most of the rocks in the cave, he had to dig harder and harder. He had to do the digging with his bare hands. After a month had passed, the mound was nine and a half feet high and he could almost reach the opening if he jumped. He was exhausted and extremely weak.

One day just as he thought he could touch the opening, he fell. He was simply too weak to get up, and two days later he died. His captors came to get his body. They rolled away the huge rock that covered the entrance. As the light flooded into the cave, it illuminated an opening in the wall of the cave about three feet in circumference.

The opening was the opening to a tunnel which led to the other side of the mountain. This was the passage to freedom the prisoner had been told about. It was in the south wall directly under the opening in the ceiling. All the prisoner would have had to do was crawl about two hundred feet and he would have found freedom. He had so completely focused on the opening of light that it never occurred to him to look for freedom in the darkness. Liberation was there all the time right next to the mound he was building, but it was in the darkness and he could not see it.

❋

As much as there is light in our stories, so there is darkness and shadow. But like the prisoner in the cave, we avoid the dark shadows and move only toward the light. The prisoner could have found freedom by finding his way in the darkness. In fact, it was the only way out, the only way he could have survived. Like the prisoner, only by embracing the darkness are we able to "step into a new light."

Jill and Doug had been married for four years when Ron, their first child, was born. He was a wanted and much-loved child. As is the case with many first-born children, he was exceptionally cute, exceptionally bright, walked at an early age, spoke before most other kids, and was the pride and joy of his parents.

Ron's mother worked in the home like most mothers during the postwar era in North America. Doug enjoyed his job as the principal of one of the high schools in a city of 60,000 people in Illinois. He always looked forward to the summers when he would be able to spend more time with Ron and, eventually, the other three children born into the family. The actual time he spent with the children was limited by his projects around the house—painting and other renovations—and, during some summers, the university courses he took to continue his education. He hoped someday to become a school superintendent.

Ron did well at school in the early years. Doug's pride in Ron grew with each report card. As Ron reached early adolescence, he made less of an effort to do well in school. His interests shifted to spending time with his friends and finding a job so he could buy a set of wheels.

Gradually, the relationship between Ron and Doug changed. The two of them had fewer common interests. Ron no longer wanted to take the courses that Doug suggested, the jobs Doug lined up for him, or the extracurricular activities that Doug thought he should take part in. Doug felt the strain and dismissed it as typical of the teenage years.

Ron realized that his father had little if any interest in allowing him to pursue his own goals and desires. Ron did not want to go to university. He did not want to be a teacher, a doctor, or a lawyer. He wanted to build things, to repair cars. Doug would not hear of it. Ron was dismissed whenever he attempted to speak to his father about switching to the industrial-arts courses at school, getting a part-time job at the local gas station, or the racing he would like to do with the motorcycle for which he was saving.

Ron dreamed of living the life he chose to live rather than living the life his father wanted him to live. As Ron tired of the confrontations at home, he began to dream of escape, of being with friends who would accept who he was and not try to change him. One day that dream became a reality. At age fifteen, Ron walked out of the house, moved to the city, and joined a street gang. Later he joined a gang of bikers.

The day he left home was the day he chose to walk away from the burden of living the life his father had been choosing for him. From that moment forward, his life changed. As much as he may have believed that he was leaving his father, he remained connected to him. He didn't realize it at the time, but there were "rules of the road" that were as powerful as the "rules of the house" had been. As much as Ron felt the pressure to live up to the expectations of his father, he subsequently felt the pressure of living up to the expectations of the gang.

I met Ron thirty-five years later—an articulate, dark-haired, brown-eyed man with a tentative smile. We met because Ron had agreed to participate in the study. On several occasions he was unable to follow through with the interviews we had arranged because of pain or nausea. I learned from him that in the midst of physical discomfort it is practically impossible to entertain the thought of intimate conversations. His physical discomfort meant that he didn't want to converse about anything. In fact, it seemed that he didn't want anyone else around.

Ron chuckled a lot as he spoke. At times it seemed that the chuckles masked his pain. I listened to him month after month as he responded to the question "What is it like to live with the knowledge that you have a terminal illness?"

Ron spoke of his childhood home as being typical middle-class: Mom stayed at home; Dad was a high school principal; Ron fought with his siblings. He spoke of his marriage, which had ended in separation, his two children, and of the woman who had recently left him. He told me of his frustration at being so physically weak that he could not work as a mechanic any longer, despite the fact that he still enjoyed cars and took pride in knowing how to keep them tuned to top performance.

Ron also told me of his experience as a patient in hospitals, intensive care units, and palliative care units. He reviewed conversations with health care providers and some remarks he had overheard. He felt that some health care providers were prejudiced toward him because of his illness.

On the day the study was to end, I went to visit Ron for the last time. Through the course of the previous months, the smell of freshly baked bread had greeted me at the entrance to his apartment, as did the sounds of a TV talk show host or Ron's flute playing. The microphone I taped to the collar of Ron's shirt picked up the hum of the bread machine, and when I replayed the conversation, I could hear that sound and recall the smell of home-baked bread.

On that day, I arrived at Ron's apartment building with the recording paraphernalia in hand and identified myself through the intercom system. He buzzed me in. Once at the door to his apartment, something felt different. No smell of fresh bread. No TV voice, no flute—just a stale silence. I knocked. Almost before the door was open, he announced, "You're going to be angry with me today."

"How's that?" I asked.

"Because of what I have to say."

"Is this on the record or off the record?"

"It doesn't matter to me." Ron continued to speak in his usually rapid manner. I scrambled to set up the audio- and videotapes and to clip the small microphone to the collar of his shirt. He never stopped talking:

A lot of my guilt, shame, and defenses came out of just simply being human, just simply being human in certain situations. I took a few wrong turns when I was in my teens, but there was a reason for that. That was my way of lashing out. There is pain there. My dad and I fought like cats and dogs. I had low self-esteem. My whole life was mapped out for me, even the sports. My first job had to be at the Dairy Queen. I wanted to work at the gas station as a mechanic. "No, no, we're gonna have you work at the Dairy Queen, a little swing-shift so you can be in all these other little goofy things." Like I say, my whole life was dictated as a teenager.

I eventually stewed to the point where I said to hell with it. I left home and went on a wrong course, definitely a wrong course. I kinda got sucked in deeper and deeper and deeper. You know, it's very easy with peer pressure to just keep going. It doesn't matter who your peers are, even if it's only four or five peers, it doesn't matter—you're a unit, you're a group. It's pretty hard to say no. In my case, it would have been suicidal. I tell you, I could've taken a bullet if I'd tried to stop a rape. You have specific tasks to do if you're a nonparticipant in a gang, and one job is watching your buddies while they're off looting and raping. There, I said it.

Oh my God, it's painful, but I kept silent for so many years. I knew a couple of weeks ago that it was time to actually sit down and work out the chronology of those years—the events, the emotions, the breakdown that happened afterward. It hurt, let me tell you it did hurt. I haven't talked about this to anyone. Confession is supposed to be good for the soul. It came out because I didn't want to sit here and talk any more about my sanitized life. That would've been duplicity. Now I'm facing it all and telling people the truth. I hated the duplicity. Except for that damn fiasco, I'm fanatical about the truth, being honest with people, and I want them to be honest with me.

Ron finished by saying, "I'm glad I talked with you today." Other people in the study said the same thing. Some stated how they had never had the opportunity to speak their truth to someone before participating in this study. For Ron, decades of guilt, shame, silence, and duplicity were followed by a strong desire to review the events of his life, to have the courage to tell his story, to speak his truth aloud.

Truth. What is it? Truth has to do with telling your personal story—"showing life as it really is," according to one dictionary. In this case, Ron's story was about ordering the events of his life to see who he was and who he had become. Ron's story combined *chronus* and *kairos*—chronological and psychological time. It included the delight he felt about his career, the pride in his children, the regrets in his marriage, his political perspectives, and his sense of adventure in traveling.

However, the dominant feature of Ron's story was an overwhelming sense of having lived a duplicitous life. He had come to a juncture where the duplicity was no longer tolerable. For three decades, Ron's secrets held him hostage, isolating him from others. Now he wanted to speak to what really happened, to be free of the secrets, lies, despair, and memories. By telling his story, Ron's past was brought into the present. His emotions could be expressed, his guilt relieved, his spirit rejuvenated. In order to speak *his* truth, Ron first had to be honest with himself. This was followed by courage in telling someone else about these events. Ron's secrets were no longer secrets; his story had been told.

Individuals, families, groups, and organizations keep secrets. In turn, secrets keep individuals, secrets keep families, secrets isolate and hold their keepers hostage. Essentially, people keep secrets and secrets keep people. If those secrets are linked to guilt and shame, they are all the more powerful in their ability to isolate and silence the secret-keeper, to prevent him from speaking the truth. As long as Ron lived in the duplicity of his secrets, intimacy evaded him.

Intimacy is based on clear and honest communication (by word, behavior, and touch) as well as attentive listening. In this way, safety, trust, and inclusion are established, and it becomes possible for an I-Thou relationship to be created. The other person is wholly appreciated for who that person is.

I made another visit that day, this to Frieda's home. She lived alone in a small two-bedroom home. There were books everywhere, for she was a reader. She spoke easily of her three adult children and was especially proud of who they had become professionally: a lawyer, a hospital administrator, and a teacher. She enjoyed their company and wished they could spend more time with her, but she was hesitant to express that wish to her children.

Frieda retired early. In her retirement, she spent time with friends, reading novels, doing crafts, going to movies, and occasionally caring for two of her grandchildren. Frieda spoke of reviewing her life. She described it as an involuntary process—memories surfaced, feelings emerged. She felt that in the process of reviewing her life, it was difficult to ignore or suppress the negative. For her, the bad was more prominent than the good. Things she had tried to forget about or that she believed were forgotten came to the fore in reviewing her life. "I do a lot more thinking now, about how my life was or is, what I've done and things like that. Trouble is, you reflect mostly on the bad. And it's as much over the good that I might have done. Most of the stuff I wish I could forget about, it's all coming up, which is very strange. I'm not proud of myself, in no way, shape or form."

Frieda felt she would experience a sense of peace if she could be relieved of her feelings of guilt. "I've done too many things that I feel guilty for, that I wish I didn't have to think about. All of a sudden you think, *Oh God, I did that or I didn't do that and I should have*—and you're not free of it. I don't think I'll be free of it until I die, and then maybe not. Who knows?"

Unlike Ron, Frieda chose not to divulge the past details that caused her such anguish. She stated that she had no one with whom she could speak about such issues; she felt that her family and friends were not open to hearing *her* truth. She did not want to burden her children with past events that were resurfacing and causing her guilt. And friends seemed not to want to hear what she really had to say. This guilt had a caustic effect on her ability to experience joy in the present. She longed for freedom from the ties to the past so she could experience pleasure in the here-and-now—and hope in the future.

If I were to speak to Frieda outside the context of the research project, I would encourage her to speak to someone about her past. Frieda would come to understand that she was neither as guilty nor as innocent as she believed. As Alice Miller says in *The Drama of the Gifted Child*,

> The confrontation with our own reality will help us give up the illusions that disguise our past, and if we then discover that we have hurt or damaged another person, we must apologize. This will make us free to resolve the old, unconscious, and unjustified feelings of

guilt stemming from our childhood. ... If we don't allow ourselves to recognize our wrongdoings in the present and take steps to correct them, we will not be able to resolve our unreal guilt feelings from the past.

Guilt. What is it? Guilt is the fact of having committed an offense against civil or religious law or the unwritten rules of human relationships. Guilt triggers the conscience. It is a healthy mechanism, a signal to pay attention to an action that may have hurt another person, a reminder to act responsibly and with integrity. Guilt can also be described as the *feeling* of having committed an offense. It is a response, the belief that we should not have done something, or the belief that we *should* have done something when we did not. Guilt arises from what we do and what we do not do.

Ron felt he should have spoken up when he witnessed the rape. Because of his silence, he lived in isolation, alienated from the person he really was or wanted to be and from the people who cared for him—family and friends. That changed the day he chose to tell me his secrets, to stop hiding from himself, to speak his truth, to admit to living a life of duplicity. The secrets no longer held him hostage or maintained power over him. Unlike the "prisoner in the dark," who did not know that escape into the light could only follow a walk through the dark, Ron stepped into his darkness, thereby finding a new light. This is a universal theme of transformation: going through the dark night of the soul to find the light.

Feeling guilty is an emotional response to a choice or an action that has violated a relationship or resulted in suffering. Resolution of guilt begins when a person recognizes his error and assumes responsibility for that action and the hurtful consequences that have resulted. Such recognition can occur only after we stop blaming others. Over the course of our lives, we avoid taking full responsibility for our actions for a variety of reasons—fear, the desire to avoid discomfort (emotional pain), indifference. As a result, we live with guilt until something moves us to an awareness of that emotion and a desire to repair the relationship.

The diagnosis of a terminal illness can usher in an overwhelming flood of memories and heightened self-awareness. For some people, that includes memories that trigger feelings of guilt, as they did for Ron and Frieda. Many people who become conscious of their guilt work toward resolution. In some instances, they seek forgiveness. Until that happens, they may be preoccupied with thoughts and feelings related to guilt.

James Hollis speaks of "recognition, recompense, and release." To those three R's I add remorse, for it often follows recognition. As people remember their past, they recognize the harm to themselves or others because of something they did or did not do. At that point they can acknowledge the part they played—or they may yet blame others. But to blame another is to continue living in the cloud of denial; to assume responsibility for the action is to move toward resolution and release, from despair toward integrity. In assuming responsibility for one's actions, there can be a sense of remorse, true regret for that which one has taken, for the suffering that resulted from words or actions. Frieda was filled with remorse. At times she seemed to be paralyzed in that experience; she was unable to forget the past and equally unable to move toward recompense or reconciliation. "Recompense" means one returns that which has been taken. Because much of what has been done cannot be undone, it is usually a symbolic return, a gesture of giving back. It is only effective if done with sincerity and "only makes sense in the context of genuine contrition." In the context of a religious perspective, one might seek forgiveness or reconciliation.

What was Ron's guilt? Was it his presence while a woman was being raped, his fear of screaming to stop what he witnessed that night, or the silence that enveloped him for several decades thereafter? Ron acknowledged the choice he made to leave home and join a gang. Many years later, he no longer blamed his father for that choice; neither did he blame the gang for his participation in the looting and raping, even if only as a silent witness.

Frieda spoke of guilt as well as shame, but she was unable to move from the general experience of those emotions to the specific actions and events that contributed to how she felt. She did say that the process seemed to be unavoidable and that it was increasing as time passed. I wonder whether she might have been more forthcoming if the study had continued, if I had been able to listen to her story for a few more visits.

It took many months for Ron to feel safe enough to trust that I would respect his story. Only then could he speak about the guilt and shame he had experienced for years. The truth-teller must be able to trust that the listener will not judge but will simply seek to understand. By suspending my judgment, I was able to offer Ron a sense of safety within which he could speak his truth. Ron needed to be understood by another person in order to understand and accept himself. That is true for each of us. That is why it is important to develop a relationship with one or two people with whom you can share the details of your life. At the end of this chapter I offer some suggestions for conducting a meaningful conversation with another person. Perhaps you already can do this. If not, you might want to consider who among your friends you feel most comfortable with. Before telling *your* truth, tell this person that everything you say is to held in confidence—that your truth is not to be disclosed to anyone else.

Barbara Derrickson stated: "Through life review we hopefully tally a ledger that allows us to affirm an essential goodness in life and to bless our participation in that goodness. To the extent that our lives have been tragic or that we have participated in life in an evil or negative way, and these issues remain unresolved, we will struggle."

I could sense the struggle Frieda was having: "If we live decently, we're gonna have a decent life. If we don't, we're gonna face problems." It reminded me of the times when, as a physician, I needed to lance a boil to drain it so it might heal from the inside out. In essence, it is necessary that we open the wound so that it can begin to heal from within. It was not my role as a researcher to open the psychological wounds that troubled Frieda. No, I was there to listen, to understand the experience without judgment. I could feel her anguish, her despair, her longing for resolution.

My hope for Frieda is that she had the opportunity to speak to someone about her feelings of guilt and shame before she died and that the disease had not progressed so rapidly that she was unable to find the time and courage to speak to another person about her emotional distress. It is best to have these difficult conversations as soon as one becomes aware of the need to do so.

The definition of "difficult conversation" varies. For some, it can mean expressing positive feelings toward another; for others it can include expressions of anger, sadness, or grief. It may be telling someone why they are important to you, what they mean to you, and how your life was positively affected by knowing them. You might ask for forgiveness of another. When I'm asked as a physician when it is most appropriate to visit a dying relative, I always advise "sooner rather than later." It is difficult to predict when the illness will hamper meaningful interaction. I usually add that if there is only enough money to make one trip to visit the dying person, go while the person is still alive (i.e., as opposed to attending the funeral after the fact). And if you are someone who has a terminal illness and has something to say to another person, I recommend that you arrange a visit as soon as possible. If you are too sick to travel, invite them over for a visit. If you have the resources, offer to help with travel expenses.

Although the dying process is experienced by the individual, it affects many people. What does or does not happen during the process will affect the grief and mourning of family members and friends. So don't wait! Sometimes there is an urgency to speak the truth to one another, to understand a past or current relationship, to express the meaning of one's life to another person.

Had any of us grown up in the same circumstances, in the same homes, in the same relationships as Ron or Frieda, we might have responded in exactly the same way. We don't know Frieda's past, and we know only some of Ron's. Each of us has our own story, and we can learn from Ron that truth begins with being honest to oneself. Only after that can it be shared with others. For some relationships, that means taking risks, especially if a wrong needs to be corrected.

Ron spoke of two significant relationships during our last visit: his relationship with his father, and his silent witnessing of the woman's rape by his fellow gang members. In a sense, both relationships were marked by the need for forgiveness. In the first, Ron would be free if he could forgive his father; in the second, he would be free if he could forgive himself and be forgiven by another. Perhaps this recognition—that one needs to be forgiven and to forgive—is the opposite side of the same coin. Only in forgiveness can one be freed of the guilt associated with an action.

Knowledge of having a terminal illness seemed to move Ron to accept the consequences of the actions he had taken many years earlier, to acknowledge his sense of guilt that had resulted in a duplicitous life, a life of double standards and lies. You might be tempted to disregard Ron because his life story is more troubled than your own. If so, consider less obvious types of exploitation: the spouse who held the family together emotionally for years without protest or bitterness; the child who carried her parents through alcoholism, mental or physical illness, or financial distress; the sibling who without question or complaint cared for the younger children when the parents were unable to do so. There are many reasons why it is painful to remember and recognize those acts and omissions in our relationships that caused another person to suffer.

I called Ron a week after his truth-telling. I told him I was calling not as a researcher but as someone who wanted to acknowledge the significance of the truth he had spoken. At that time he said, "I'm a free man now. The duplicity has ended. I can speak my truth."

How does all this become relevant? It has to do with being whole. The life you have lived is part of who you are, your entire life—whether you're proud or ashamed of it or feel guilty about things you've done and you wish you'd done. Only by integrating all of this into who you are can you become whole. The word "whole" comes from the German word *heil*. As an adjective it means "all of, entire, in an unbroken or undamaged state; in one piece"; as a noun it means "a thing that is complete in itself." Significantly, the word "heal" has the same origin and means "to cause to become sound or healthy again."

As you review the events and relationships of your life, what happens when you realize there are things you would like to say, a truth you would like to speak? What if you know someone who is dying and would like to say something, or perhaps you would like to hear what that person has to say? This may or may not have to do with forgiving and being forgiven.

Appreciate the courage it takes to face the truth of who you are. Recognize your desire for resolution and inner peace. And know that your basic goal is this: to speak the truth as you describe key events and relationships in your life. Be careful to identify any sense of guilt and note what that guilt relates to in your life. In other words, recognize the harm you did to yourself and/or to another person—and assume responsibility for that harm.

It is not easy to get started, but once you are under way it can be a deeply rewarding experience. Some people find that a simple formula makes it easier to speak what's on their mind: "I feel [*name the emotion*] because [*state what happened*]." Here's an example: "I feel *great regret* because *I missed your retirement party*." You might want to add some additional comments such as "We had worked together for twenty-seven years."

You might speak the truth to another person or write down a description of the event. Follow the facts of the event with a description of the emotions you experienced at the time of the event as well as the emotions you experience as you are remembering the events. Consider what it might mean to forgive someone, to be free of anger and resentment toward that person or to ask for forgiveness, and to be free of guilt.

Forgiveness

Forgiveness is not only a word, it is a process. According to Robin Casarjian, the founder and director of the Lionheart Foundation, which is dedicated to teaching self-development and forgiveness in prisons and public schools, "Forgiveness is the means for taking what is broken and making it whole.... Forgiveness is *not* condoning negative, inappropriate behavior—your own or someone else's. Abuse, violence, aggression, betrayal, and dishonesty are just some of the behaviors that may be completely unacceptable." For people who have been victim to those behaviors, forgiveness is the process and attitude that brings freedom and relief. In response to apartheid in South Africa and all its atrocities, Archbishop Desmond Tutu said, "To pursue the path of healing we need to remember what we have endured. Restoring one's sense of self means restoring memory, recognizing what happened.... [W]ithout memory there is no healing, without forgiveness there is no future."

Forgiving Others

Forgiveness begins by stepping into our emotional pain, by acknowledging what the real issues are and how we feel about them. It means we can no longer deny what happened. We no longer attempt to explain it away or try to understand the other person and why the "hurt" might have occurred. We no longer pretend it didn't happen, trivialize its effect on us, or try to forget it. It means we look at the hurt and its effect on us; we look at what our lives would have been like without the hurt. To acknowledge and experience the hurt and the pain is the beginning of forgiveness.

As William Meninger states in *The Process of Forgiveness*:

It is necessary to know, not only whom to forgive, but what it is we forgive. We have to recognize the extent of our injuries. We have to see what they have done to our trust, our sense of justice, our self-esteem, and our ability to relate freely to our world. It is not just the act of wounding itself that the perpetrator is responsible for (and must be forgiven for) but all of its repercussions.

For Ron, this would mean remembering how wounded he was because his father seemed unable to accept him as he really was. Ron had to acknowledge what his life had been like, growing up with his dad. "I had low self-esteem. My whole life was mapped out for me from day to day." Finally, he had to acknowledge the price he paid for the choices that were made for him, that is, being rejected by his father for who he was.

It was in Ron's best interest to look directly at his relationship with his parents, particularly his father. As much as the physical umbilical cord is cut at birth, so the emotional umbilical cord needs to be cut. In Ron's case, this didn't happen when he left home. Casarjian writes that the emotional umbilical cord "has grown out of a past of unmet needs and unfulfilled expectations. Often this cord is composed of anger, judgments, blame, shame, and guilt. If it remains connected, it will keep a part of us small, close our heart, and, like all resentment, hold us an emotional hostage to the past.... Forgiveness serves as the merciful scalpel with which the umbilical cord is cut and we are all set free."

To enter into the process of forgiveness, Ron would first identify what it was he would like his father to give him: respect, freedom to develop his own interests, time, love. Casarjian identifies the type of questions he might use at this stage.

- What would your life [have been like and] be like if you were not struggling with your father?
- What would your relationship be like?
- What characteristics of your relationship would still be present? Would they be different? How?
- What feelings would you have about yourself? Toward your father?
- Would there be any interaction with your father after the struggle? What would it be like?
- How would you feel?
- How would your life be different?

The next step would be for Ron to express the emotions he felt about being shortchanged: anger, resentment, guilt, shame. These emotions must find a place for safe expression. Otherwise, they remain denied, suppressed, repressed, seeping "out at the edges of the personality as fear, sarcasm, withdrawal, hostility, self-deprecation; or [as] anger, rage, depression, passive-aggressive behaviors, self-abuse, abuse toward others, an inability to be effective in the world, and the inability to have emotionally intimate relationships." Throughout his childhood, Ron's feelings were not respected by his father. If he does not treat his feelings with respect now, he perpetuates the negative pattern.

How might Ron release his feelings? It is important to be aware that the emotions have been stored in Ron since he was a child. That means he must express the anger of the child even though he is an adult. He must be allowed to express the true emotion just as he is encouraged to provide a true description of the events of his life. Some methods of emotional expression benefit from the presence of another person serving as a guide, but others do not. Those that you can do alone include writing a letter; punching a pillow, mattress, or punching bag; screaming in a place where you don't feel inhibited; and physical workouts (running, chopping wood, lifting weights, rowing, etc.).

There are many other approaches that facilitate emotional expression: meditation, visualization, journal writing, dream work, dance, singing, painting, crafts such as pottery and weaving, and playing a musical instrument. Casarjian includes "techniques that trigger awareness and physical and emotional release and integration through working directly with the body. Some of these techniques include Rolfing, massage, bioenergetics, Feldenkrais, the Alexander technique, Lomi Body work, and Soma." For some people, working with a counselor or therapist is of great benefit.

Being Forgiven

Ron recognized that his silence during a woman's rape equaled collusion with his fellow gang members. After speaking about this, he added: "There, it's tough, but I said it. Oh my god, it is painful."

For many years, Ron carried his remorse without expressing it. Now, it was important for Ron to forgive himself and then to express his remorse to the woman who was raped as he stood by. In situations like this, where it is not possible to contact the person directly, this could be done in several ways: with a counselor, by writing a letter to her even though he could not send it, or imagining that she was present and he was having a conversation with her. In a letter or imagined conversation, it would be important for Ron to explain to the woman why he kept silent while she was sexually violated. He would then state his regret about the silence and ask her for forgiveness.

Other examples might be less extreme, such as asking for forgiveness because you missed a significant event in the life of a good friend, or you didn't provide support when a friend first learned that he had a terminal illness, or you said something years ago that you wish you'd never said.

Forgiving Ourselves

The process of self-forgiveness is similar to that of forgiving another person. It begins with acknowledging the truth, by being entirely honest with yourself regarding your actions, your attitudes, and your words. Subsequently you take responsibility for what you have done. You don't deny it, trivialize it, ignore it, or exaggerate it. Allow all your feelings to emerge. All feelings are important and legitimate to the person experiencing those feelings. Some will be painful: regret, remorse, sorrow, grief, envy, shame, guilt, betrayal, loss, anger. As the deeper feelings emerge, identify how these and other feelings have motivated your behavior and thoughts in the past, resulting in feelings of guilt, self-loathing, or self-judging in the present.

Have an open heart and accept yourself. Try to acknowledge the dark emotions as well as the pleasant emotions, remembering that all human emotions contribute to a sense of wholeness and integrity. Acknowledge how past actions, attitudes, and words have affected who you are today. What would your life have been like if you had made different choices? How would you feel? How would you be different?

What would Ron's life be like if he could embrace all the emotions of that night? He would need to listen to his fears and his deep desire to be rid of the guilt he carried. At the same time, it is important for him to understand how he came to behave the way he did, how his secret was controlling him as well as limiting the relationships he had with his family and friends. The purpose would be to appreciate the consequences of his actions, and then—through the years and in the present—to forgive himself. It would help if Ron could say to himself: "I forgive you, Ron, for being silent while your fellow gang members were raping. I also forgive you for all the self-loathing that followed that event."

Life events are like the pieces of a patchwork quilt. I remember the quilt my grandmother made as a wedding gift for my wife and I. She had seen the pattern on a calendar I gave her as a Christmas present—multiple triangles of brightly colored material with various textures. On our quilt, I recognized pieces from shirts, dresses, and blouses that had been worn by family members over the years. While the triangle pattern resembled the picture on the calendar, the colors and textures were unique to the quilt my grandmother stitched.

The pieces of material triggered different memories for others who saw the quilt. Such differences are best seen as enhancing the total picture as opposed to contradicting or negating the value of each memory. If the quilt were on display over a long period of time, more and more of its history would come to light. Meaning is altered over time as understanding is enhanced. How you see your life—remembering events, understanding the importance of your relationships, appreciating the sense of meaning you gain in knowing who you are—all this is *your* story, *your* quilt.

Our families are like that quilt. Each of us sees and experiences something unique to who we are. Whenever a child is born, it's a different family. The dynamics change immediately. And each child will have a unique experience with the same parents. In fact, those parents are not quite the same as before the child was born; there is an additional responsibility to which they must now respond. Also, their relationships with each child are different. Whether within the family or outside it, no two relationships are alike.

Your recollection of the events is your truth. Others might

remember events differently, perhaps even exaggerate or trivialize your role. However, your truth, your recollection, is essential to knowing yourself and to assuming responsibility for the action or the event. Some memories can be exhilarating, satisfying, factual; others can be devastating. When you come up against a devastating memory, you might feel like returning to denial, living as though the memory were not part of your reality. But remember, that makes change impossible; it ties you to the past.

To assume responsibility for your actions is the key to compensation for the injury or insult you experienced or caused someone else. This is true for those who know they have a terminal illness, as well as for those who are in good health. If assuming responsibility for your actions includes another person and you are able to contact that person, ask to speak to her. Have the conversation in private, in a place where you will not be interrupted. Ask her to listen to what you have to say. In some instances, it may be important to tell her that you are truly sorry for what happened between you; ask her to forgive you, if that be the case. This could be followed by asking what would be necessary for reconciliation. I recommend that you practice what you want to say beforehand.

In many instances, what we have done cannot be undone. She may no longer be a friend, or perhaps she's moved away or died. In those cases, a symbolic recompense can be offered. Write a sincere letter; have an imaginary conversation. Whatever you choose, be as sincere as possible. Some might chose to provide a service as a gesture of contrition and compensation. Ron might have donated time and/or money to a rape crisis center, for example. A symbolic gesture can be easier for some people who hold to a religious tradition, who pray, or who meditate. In Judaism, this process would be regarded as reconciliation with another human being, atonement with God; in Christianity, resolution of guilt would include asking for forgiveness from the person who has been offended, as well as from God.

When remorse is genuine—whether real or symbolic—you will experience release. In religious tradition, this is often referred to as the "grace of God." It is something that cannot be earned but is gifted to the individual who has a "contrite heart." For those outside religious tradition, the process of remembering, recognition, recompense, remorse, and release can serve the same purpose. I recommend this so that the individual is free to live the rest of her days in a "clear space," not a place of despair.

Despite their desire and need, many people fail to connect with others. This occurs for any number of reasons—fear, discomfort, going out on a limb. This is especially true for people at the end of life. As a result, conversations are often restricted to small talk like the weather, sports, current events, food, money. This was the experience of Ivan Ilych as described by Leo Tolstoy in "The Death of Ivan Ilych."

> What tormented Ivan Ilych most was the deception, the lie, which for some reason they all accepted, that he was not dying but was simply ill, and that he only need keep quiet and undergo a treatment and then something very good would result. He however knew that do what they would nothing would come of it, only still more agonizing suffering and death. This deception tortured him—their not wishing to admit what they all knew and what he knew, but wanting to lie to him concerning his terrible condition, and wishing and forcing him to participate in that lie. Those lies—lies enacted over him on the eve of his death and destined to degrade this awful, solemn act to the level of their visitings, their curtains, their sturgeon for dinner—were a terrible agony for Ivan Ilych. And strangely enough, many times when they were going through their antics over him he had been within a hairbreadth of calling out to them: "Stop lying! You know and I know that I am dying. Then at least stop lying about

it!" But he had never had the spirit to do it. The awful, terrible act of his dying was, he could see, reduced by those about him to the level of a casual, unpleasant, and almost indecorous incident (as if someone entered a drawing-room diffusing an unpleasant odour) and this was done by that very decorum which he had served all his life long. He saw that no one felt for him, because no one even wished to grasp his position."

Mary was confident that her daughters knew her story; Frieda couldn't bring herself to tell her children hers; Florence asked whether I could be present while she told her children; Peter asked that I write a book so that his children could hear his story, hear what he had to say, what he was unable to say in person. All these people wanted their families to hear their stories, to know *their* truth. In all likelihood their families also had something to say to them. If no one begins to speak the truth, families and individuals are essentially estranged from one another, paralyzed in silence. In order to end the conspiracy of silence, someone must speak first, either the person with the terminal illness or the family member. It could have been Ivan Ilych or one of his family members. In his case, no one spoke. Silence prevailed, suffering increased. People who are dying want to speak and want to be spoken to. Who speaks first is not important; the fact that someone speaks is very important.

In some instances, especially if life expectancy is short, family members can have difficulty speaking to a terminally ill relative. How do you break through safe but superficial conversation to a more intimate level? With a little guidance, it can be easier than you think. How might Ivan Ilych have broken the silence? How might you break a silence? Let me outline how that could happen.

1. Create a private space. If you are living at home, invite the person to come to your house. Make arrangements for an

uninterrupted visit. If you are meeting in someone else's home, ask for privacy until the conversation is complete. If you are meeting at the hospital, find a private space if possible. If you are in a private room, invite the person to meet you at the hospital, informing them of your intent to speak about some private matters. Ask the nurse for an hour of privacy with the door closed. Check whether you require any medication or other care during that period. Put the "Please do not disturb" sign on the door with the message that private time is required.

2. This is an important time. Extra noise (radios, CD players, cell phones), pets, other people, can easily distract you from the conversation you want to have.

3. Make certain both of you are physically comfortable; in a position that fosters eye contact and being in touch. Sit near enough to easily touch each other. Ask if it's okay to hold hands, if that's best.

   - I would like to hold your hand/put my hand on your arm or shoulder while we speak. Is that all right with you?

4. Be aware of your emotions as you begin. You might say that this is difficult.

   - I find this difficult ...
   - I feel a little awkward about this ...

5. Explain why it is important to speak to one another.

   - You have always been very important to me ...
   - We have always been honest with each other ...
   - I have a few things I would like to speak to you about ...
   - I want to stop pretending that I might get well again. I know how sick I am. At times that scares me, keeps me

awake, makes me feel very alone ... I would like you to share this journey with me.

6. Assure the person that you will end the conversation whenever they want it to end. Agree that it is not your intent to hurt, but be aware that hurt or pain might occur. If it does occur, agree to work toward resolution:

   - I did not want to hurt you in any way, but I am aware that some of the things I will say to you might cause some discomfort for both of us.
   - I would like to know if what I am saying to you is causing you pain. I would also like you to know that if something you say is painful for me to hear, I will let you know.
   - I don't want you to keep from saying something that you want to say because you think that it might be painful for me to hear. As far as I am concerned, pain is not a reason to keep silent.

7. Begin the conversation. Speak clearly, and slowly. Avoid euphemisms and metaphors. Say exactly what it is you want to say. Because I don't know what it is you want to say to another person, I have included a few examples of how a conversation might begin:

   - Some of what I have to say is very easy to say. Other parts are more difficult. First, I want you to know how you have influenced my life. I want to remind you of some of the events that were particularly important to me.
   - I want you to know why I value you, and our relationship.
   - I want to clear the air between us as we have always worked hard to be honest with one another. Do you remember the time that...? It affected me for a long time and in some way came between us.

- Something that happened some time ago made me very angry. I wish I could have spoken about it earlier, but I was afraid of your reaction. I had two fears, one of being rejected by you for the anger, and another that you might be offended, and I didn't want to hurt your feelings. I see now that it would have been better for me to talk about it earlier. It has created a barrier between us. It has compromised our relationship.
- I feel that I hurt you when ... and I'm very sorry about that. Could you forgive me for...? or I felt hurt by you when ...
- I want you to know that I care very deeply about you. I want you to know that I love you.

8. Provide opportunities for the other person to speak as well. As you listen, suspend all judgment.

- I'm sure there must be some things that you want to talk about.
- I wonder whether you might want to say some things to me as well. How can I make that easier for you?

9. While the other person is speaking, listen with your full attention. When the person is finished, ask questions for clarification.

- If I understand you correctly ...
- Could you tell me more about what you mean, what you feel, or what you think?
- Are you saying that ...
- Avoid asking questions that begin with "why."

10. Let the other person know how you feel about them. Speak honestly. Don't exaggerate. Keep the conversation simple.

- I don't want to say goodbye to you.
- I love you.
- Your friendship has meant a great deal to me.
- As a close family member, you ...

11. If you sense any agitation or restlessness as you speak, stop. Make statements like:

    - I sense that you might be uncomfortable about what I just said.
    - I'm wondering if you have something to say in response to what I just talked about?
    - Would you prefer to continue this conversation at another time?
    - I would be interested to hear about how you feel concerning the things I just talked about.
    - While I sense that you might be a little uncomfortable, I would like to finish this conversation if that's all right with you.

12. Express gratitude for the time you spent together and arrange for another visit if desirable.

    - I appreciate having had a chance to talk to you. I would like to talk with you some more. Could we do this again some time?

13. If it is someone from whom you have been estranged and you feel that you would like to continue spending time together, ask whether the other person feels the same way.

    - I value the time we spent together today.
    - I wonder whether we could meet once a week for the next several weeks. That would be very important to me. Would you be interested in doing that?

Peter knew he had a terminal illness. He was estranged from his family. "I believe in the truth. I believe that truth only hurts once, but a lie lasts forever. Other than my younger brother, everybody seems to be playing games. If everybody was acknowledged and put on the same playing field, we could talk—we could look each other in the eye and speak. You look at my family. What do I have? I've got a son and a daughter who don't speak to me. I have a grandson I'll never hear from, or see. I have a brother I haven't spoken to in twenty years."

A person who is terminally ill does not have unlimited time or energy. In the desire to optimize the meaningful time remaining, they want the truth from doctors, from friends, from family members. As Peter said, "Let's solve the problems before I die. The only way you can do that is by telling the truth. If you don't tell the truth, you play games and you're just wasting everybody's time. And I don't have time to waste. I would like to make peace."

The last time Peter saw him, his son stormed out of the house, yelling back, "Why don't you fuck off and die!" Time had passed, and now Peter longed to speak to his son, to tell him that he loved him and that he forgave him. He did not want to die without speaking *his* truth.

As stated previously, Peter was one of the people who asked me to write this book. It was Peter's hope that his son would read it some day and realize that I was writing about his father—a man who loved his son and forgave him. "I'm at peace because my son will know I forgive him. I've been around other people who have died. I've seen what it's like when they have unfinished business. You can tell when a person is struggling because they don't have that peace. But if your relationships are defined, they either continue or they end. Then you can die with a smile on your face—a whole person. You can sit there and die with a smile on your face."

Consider a situation in which someone would like to speak with a friend who has a terminal illness. Essentially the process is the same as that outlined above. Recently a colleague told me about a close friend of hers named Keith who had been diagnosed a few weeks earlier with pancreatic cancer. Often when such a diagnosis is made, the disease is already advanced. My colleague added that Keith, his family and his friends, would speak only about cures because they felt that speaking about the other possibilities would be to admit defeat. It is in this way that a conspiracy of silence begins, which in turn means the person who is dying is truly alone.

It is my sense that fear keeps people silent—fear that if they speak the truth to one another, then all hope will be lost. But truth and hope are not mutually exclusive. In fact, in speaking the truth new hope might emerge. Life is full of multiple hopes, most of which can coexist.

Imagine how Keith's story might show how it is possible to open up the space for one person to be in contact with another.

Keith is in his mid-forties and runs a computer business. He and Liz lived together for twenty-four years, but they never had a formal marriage ceremony. They have a seventeen-year-old son and twin girls aged fourteen. Keith's father died of lung cancer seven years previously. His mother is alive and lives in the same city. He has two brothers, Glenn, who lives in the same city, and Darryl, a divorced lawyer who lives in the suburbs.

The three brothers get along well. That wasn't always the case, but following the death of their father they decided to work out their differences and try to spend more time together. All three grew up playing hockey; one of them as a teenager had hopes of playing professionally. As adults, they became avid hockey fans. The brothers cheer for different teams and try to get together to watch a game once a week.

Keith was diagnosed just as the Stanley Cup playoffs started. Even though Keith wants to talk with his brothers about it, he doesn't know how to begin the conversation about his terminal illness. His brothers are afraid that speaking about death will make it happen sooner. And for some reason they don't want Keith to know that they think he is dying. So the three men continue to enjoy each other's company and conversations about hockey.

Rich is one of Keith's closest friends. He watches the occasional hockey game with Keith, Glenn, and Darryl. Rich is very aware of the conspiracy of silence. One day, on his way home from work, he called Keith to ask whether he could drop by for a short visit. Keith welcomed the company. Liz was still at work, and the kids were involved in after-school activities.

Arriving at Keith's house, Rich knocks on the door and walks in. He enters the living room, where Keith is lying in a rented hospital bed. Keith is reading. He puts the book down and takes off his glasses. They shake hands. Rich grabs a chair, placing it so he can comfortably speak to Keith.

He begins by saying, "Keith, I have something to say to you, that I've wanted to say ever since you got sick." He continues:

It's my sense that no one here wants to speak about what's happening. I want to respect you, cause I care about you. It's for that reason that I've come to say what I need to say. Is that all right? Do you mind if I continue? We're all pretending that you're going to get better. I want to believe that as much as anyone. And I certainly don't want to take any hope away from you. At the same time I've got to tell you that what I see happening to you and what we're pretending is happening to you are very different. And I don't want you to get any sicker before we have a chance to talk. I need you to hear me out. Are you still all right with this?

You've always been a good friend to me. We've had our arguments and our differences. We even thought we were in love with the same girl in high school. But we have always worked out our differences and agreed to be honest with each other.

What I see, Keith, is that you are getting sicker. You seem to be more tired; you lose your ability to concentrate every now and again; and I see you losing weight. This process isn't just about you. It's about you, Liz, your kids, your family and a few good friends. All of this has happened very fast. And you know, Keith, I have something to say to you. I'm sure everyone else I named also has something to say.

We need to start talking, man, 'cause what happens if you don't get better? What happens if you get so tired you can't talk to us anymore? I'll only say this once: Your kids need to hear from you. The rest of us would like to hear from you. And I put money on everybody having something to say to you as well. It's not going to be easy, but it will only get harder as you wait longer. There's a conspiracy of silence. We're behaving as though you don't have a diagnosis of a terminal illness, but you do. We're acting as though you're the healthy, active jock you always were.

Like you, I hope you get cured. I also hope that you won't have to deal with a lot of pain or any other physical discomfort. I hope that your kids know you love them, that they hear you tell them that, that Liz knows that you love her as well and that you appreciate the last twenty-four years together. I hope she knows how you want to spend your last months, weeks, and days. Don't you think she might have something to say to you as well and likely doesn't find it any easier than you do?

And then there's your mom. After your father's death she probably thought that, in time, she would be next and not you. She's got to have something to say to you. You're her kid. You're not supposed to die before her. To her, you're still her freckle-faced kid who became a very successful businessman overnight. And now that kid is dying. That's just not how it's supposed to happen.

So that's the conversation I came here to start. I hope I didn't offend you and, if I did, I have every confidence that we'll work it out. I just couldn't be silent any more. Sometimes I'm scared to look this in the face, but I'm more concerned that someday I'll look back and wish I had said a bunch of stuff I never said, and that I had heard you say some things as well.

Keith was relieved that the conspiracy of silence had been broken and the two men could finally talk about Keith's death and their friendship. They shared specific memories, times when they appreciated the support of the other and episodes of conflict when trust might have been jeopardized. But because of their commitment to friendship, their relationship weathered the storm, and their trust in one another was actually strengthened.

CHAPTER SEVEN

Longing to Belong

Though I was not loved, I was not as unlovable as I had
often believed myself to be.

Anne

What you do speaks so loud that I cannot hear what you say.

Ralph Waldo Emerson

Love is our true destiny. We do not find the meaning of life
by ourselves alone—we find it with another.

Thomas Merton

Naomi and Ruth

Because of a famine in the land of Judah, Elimelech, his wife, Naomi, and their two sons emigrated to the land of Moab. The two boys married women from Moab, one named Orpah, the other named Ruth. All three of the men died, leaving the women to grieve and to fend for themselves. Naomi suggested that each of the women return to their families of origin, to their mother's house, "Return, my daughters. Why should you go with me? Have I yet sons in my womb, that they may be your husbands? Return, my daughters! Go, for I am too old to have a husband. If I said I have hope, if I should even have a husband tonight and also bear sons, would you therefore wait until they were grown? Would you therefore refrain from marrying? No, my daughters; for it is harder for me than for you, for the hand of the Lord has gone forth against me."

And they lifted up their voices and wept again; and Orpah kissed her mother-in-law, but Ruth clung to her. Then she said, "Behold, your sister-in-law has gone back to her people and her gods; return after your sister-in-law."

But Ruth said, "Do not urge me to leave you or turn back from following you; for where you go, I will go, and where you lodge, I will lodge. Your people shall be my people, and your God, my God. Where you die, I will die, and there I will be buried. Thus may the Lord do to me, and worse, if anything but death parts you and me."

When Naomi saw that Ruth was determined to go with her, she said no more to her.

❀

"Longing to belong" means we want and need to be loved. It is a basic human need. As such, it was true of Ruth and Orpah. They had a longing to belong: Orpah chose to return to her family of origin; Ruth chose to stay with the family of her adult life, the family of her husband who had recently died. This biblical story rings true with what I have observed in caring for people at the end of life. For some, the longing to belong is fulfilled by members of their nuclear family; for others it is fulfilled with members of their nuclear family as well as with other people they chose to be with; and for some it is fulfilled not by blood relatives but those with whom they have chosen to share their lives, their intimacy, their love. Everyone needs to belong. In that context, for some people deep family-of-origin issues surface at the end of life.

In some ways Brent's story is similar to that of many people. He had some things to say about his hospital experience and the way in which health care professionals spoke to him. As he reviewed his life he became very aware of what he never had with either his biological or his adoptive parents. He understood how the relationship with his adoptive parents was fractured and how his longing to belong was met in relationships with close adult friends. Brent was a man in his late thirties who spoke with ease of his relationships: with his partner, his parents, his siblings, his friends, his neighbors, the doctors and nurses who were involved in providing care to him. He grieved over his relationship with his mother and mourned the loss of his relationship with his father, which had never been close. The mourning left him with a deep yearning, a longing to belong.

Sitting in Brent's living room, I became aware of the gift he was giving me by telling the story of his life, his pain, his suffering, the meaning he had found. As I listened, I realized that he had confronted issues I skirted—that he *knew* dying while I only knew *about* dying; and in some way he also knew life and living in a way that was real and true and different from my own understanding. That became more apparent as I listened, as I heard and worked to understand what was really being said.

There was a talk show on the television, which was muted. Looking out the patio doors, I saw a deck covered with plants, a gray skyline from the light drizzle, typical of the Pacific Northwest during that season. A fish tank gurgled in the background. Brent's golden retriever rested on the floor next to his chair. He had an occasional cigarette, although he was working to beat the habit. It was our fifth visit. Brent spoke about his family and his childhood. "It was lonely, it was very lonely. We were reminded constantly that we were adopted and that this was something to be grateful for. We were always made to feel we owed them something."

Memories of his childhood were painful. He realized that his mother had been harsh.

I'll never forget an incident when I was about five years old. I think this has a lot to do with my fear of abandonment. But first I should say that my mother told us that we were adopted when we were very young, far younger than I think a child should be told. It was an adoption arranged through a priest she worked with, in the Children's Aid Society. In those days, that's how it was done. There was no home study.

My mother, my brothers, my sisters, and I were at the breakfast table. My sisters and I were fighting over something and I said, "You're not my sisters anyway!" My mother said, "What did you say?" I said, "They're not my sisters anyway." So she said, "Go to your room and pack up all your stuff." I packed up one of those wicker baskets with handles. I put in all my toys, my teddies, my pillow, and my blanket. She came into my room and dumped the stuff out on the bed, then she took the empty basket and me to St. Claire's Hospital, which I thought was the Children's Aid Society, and left me there all day. She was telling me two things: that they could take me back at any time, and that nothing belonged to me. I remember sitting on the upturned basket on the curb in the parking lot behind this big building. I remember people coming and asking me what I was doing there and answering that I was waiting for my mom to pick me up.

My mother was parked, oh, six blocks away or something; it wasn't far. When she picked me up, she said, "Are you ever going to say that kind of thing again?" and I said, "No." She brought me home. I was so thankful. It was getting dark, and I was hungry and scared. I didn't know what was going to happen, but from that moment on I was aware that nothing in that house belonged to me.

People who know they have a terminal illness speak of a desire to be in a relationship. They refer to their family of origin, sometimes with fondness, warmth, and love, sometimes with indifference, anger, and resentment. They seem to have a desire to understand their relationships with parents, siblings, and other relatives. Those who have close relationships with their children and grandchildren often have a sense of hope in the legacy that they will leave; those with "broken" relationships with parents or children long for resolution before death. "Resolution" can mean restoring communication, reestablishing trust, or understanding and defining the relationship. Sometimes resolution means letting go of one's hope for a relationship you wanted but never had.

Most people have a sense of belonging with someone. Everyone longs to belong. The psychologist Abraham Maslow described the longing to belong as the human need for love, affection, and belonging. He established a hierarchy of need based on his understanding of actual needs based in the body. The individual longs for affectionate relations with people in general, for a place in the group or family, and will work hard to achieve that place. Without it, the individual will experience "the pangs of loneliness, of ostracism, of rejection, of friendlessness, or rootlessness." The longing to belong is a deep desire; it is the yearning of one person to be attached or connected to another.

The human sense of belonging begins at birth. The degree of intimacy between parent and child is experienced through the senses—

how the baby is held and caressed, the tone of voice, eye contact—all of which reflect the physical and emotional availability of the parent. This occurs throughout the routine of the day, whether the infant is being fed, bathed, changed, or simply held. These features communicate messages of unconditional love or, in contrast, resentment that the needs of the infant must take precedence. It is the emotion by which the care is delivered that transmits the true message from parent to child. Even as the child grows up and begins to understand language, the content of the verbal message is not as important as *how* the message is spoken.

"Unconditional love" is love given to another person without expecting anything in return. In the context of the parent-child relationship, the parent can have expectations with regard to the behavior of the child but does not expect the child to meet the needs of the parent. Ideally, unconditional love is given to the child regardless of the situation. The child deserves it simply for being born into the family. In this way, the child develops a strong sense of attachment to the parent.

Everyone has physical, psychological, and spiritual needs. For example, physical needs include food, clothing, and shelter; psychological needs include the sense of self and the relationship to others; spiritual needs include the awareness of and connection to a source of power or strength bigger than oneself. Adults recognize and meet their own needs, the needs of other adults, and the needs of children. Children are not meant to meet the needs of adults. That, however, was not the situation in which Brent grew up.

I had no sense of safety. None. Then the same woman who abandoned me at the hospital for the afternoon died of cancer when I was only twelve. I took care of her, you know. I bathed my mom when I was eleven. An eleven-year-old boy should be out playing games, not bathing his mother. And then when she died, my whole world was confused because I hated this woman and yet she was gone. My mother took me in, raised me and abused me. That's the only way to put it.

In order to know unconditional love and have a strong sense of belonging and attachment to the parent, the child must not be expected to carry the burden of fulfilling the needs of the parent. If a child is made to feel that he owes the parent something, the sense of belonging will be impaired. Brent was right: an eleven-year-old boy should be out playing games.

Brent's desire to play games at age eleven was as legitimate as the anger he felt toward his sisters at age five. But Brent's mother taught him that the expression of anger toward his siblings was unacceptable. Brent internalized that message and came to believe that anger in general was unacceptable to his mother. "Anger seems so real and so much a part of me, but it was unacceptable to my mother," he said. "That made me feel that I was unacceptable to my mother." Subsequently, anger was not expressed, and Brent's sense of self was altered.

As much as he had longed for a relationship with his mother, so he also wanted a close relationship with his father.

After my mother died, my father, who had been an absentee parent, became even more absent. He was concerned with his daughters more so than with his sons, and so my sisters got a lot of his attention. I never seemed to get much of his attention; he says it's because I pushed him away. I've never thrown a baseball with my father, I've never played soccer with my father, I've never gone to a hockey game with my father, a football game, nothing.

I don't want him in my life because he's caused me so much pain. But the pain that he causes me I can let go of, because I know that he will never understand. I wish I could say, "Dad, I want to talk to you about something that's important to me. I want you to understand that if I die before you do, I will have missed out on a whole life.

You've had your life." He doesn't understand, or he can't understand, or he won't understand. I'm just tired of trying to figure out which one of those three options it is. So I make new friends and a new family.

Brent longed to be close to his father—to be held physically, emotionally, and spiritually. Although that did not happen, Brent developed intimate, loving relationships with other people that came to be family. Through them, his longing to belong was fulfilled. When Brent spoke about living with a terminal illness, he spent much time explaining how the fracture happened in his family. He wanted me to understand the complexity of his relationships with his father and mother beginning in his childhood. It was my sense that he wanted others to know that it is important to understand one's family of origin and that meaningful relationships can happen outside that context, such that one's longing to belong can be fulfilled in different ways. It was a message of pain, understanding, and hope.

Brent had worked hard to belong to his family. To realize that he didn't belong in the true sense of the term was very painful for him. "All I can do is continue my journey with or without them. I think they've made the choice that it's going to be without them. I have to accept that and stop trying to make it work, 'cause it isn't going to work." He began to understand that he would never be accepted by his family; he didn't fit the mold they wanted him to fit. He couldn't be the son and brother they wanted him to be, and he knew for the first time that he could belong only if he became the man his father and siblings expected him to be. They expected him to be there for them, to care for them, and to care about them, to meet their needs, regardless of what his needs might be. The real Brent was a stranger in that environment, a stranger who was not welcome.

The complex nature of the parent-child relationship surfaces at the end of life. Some people struggle to understand its significance;

others choose to ignore or dismiss it. Because of the profound struggle that some people experienced with regard to their parent-child relationship, I have included an explanation, which I hope will enhance your understanding of it. You, like many people I spoke to, may have the perspective of both parent and child. One's longing to belong originates in the initial relationship between the infant and the adults who provide care for that infant. Unconditional love is the necessary ingredient for a child to have a secure attachment to his parents. For the child to develop a secure base, the parent must be present and available physically and emotionally. If the parent is too busy, damaged emotionally for some reason, or unaware of the child's situation or emotional experience, secure attachment to that parent will be compromised. This results in a tremendous challenge for the parent, as there are endless demands on time and energy.

How does attachment happen? John Bowlby describes the process as "the provision by both parents of a secure base from which a child or an adolescent can make sorties into the outside world and to which he can return knowing for sure that he will be welcomed when he gets there, nourished physically and emotionally, comforted if distressed, reassured if frightened. In essence, this role is one of being available, ready to respond when called upon to encourage and perhaps assist, but to intervene actively only when clearly necessary." When the child knows that the parent is available, accepting of and responsive to his needs, he will have a strong and consistent feeling of security. This enables the child to explore and discover the self. As a result, he will more likely grow into the adult he really is, as opposed to the adult that the parents want or expect him to be.

Brent did not feel accepted in his family, and he felt that way for much of his life. He struggled with it again once he realized that his illness would likely cause his death. That was when he fully acknowledged the reality he had been living with. "My family has an image of me that they project to you and to other health care providers, which is not the person I am. They don't see me the way I see myself; they don't see me for who I am. Once you get to know me, you'll wonder who they're talking about." For many years Brent was the person his parents wanted him to be. Only when confronted with death did he choose to become who he felt he was and choose to be in relationships with people who liked him as he was. He wanted to be with people who could accept his emotional expression, his anger, his sadness, his loneliness; who could accept his personality, his career choice, his sexuality. He did not want to be expected to be only happy, only agreeing, only taking care of them. His friends were not trying to change him or expecting him to be anything other than himself.

In reading this book you, like Brent, may also wonder about relationships with family members or other people who expect you to be something you feel that is not true to your character, your personality, your sense of self. You may realize for the first time that your relationship with your family of origin is not, or was not, what you wanted it to be. This might result in emotional pain or discomfort.

The parents' relationship with their children has an intergenerational component. Parents generally treat their children as they were treated by their parents. In Brent's case, this means that Brent's mother brought the experience of her childhood and his father brought the experience of his childhood to their new relationship to one another and to their children. The influence that Brent's grandparents had on his parents had a significant impact on him. Psychologist Carl Jung shed some light to this when he states that "children are driven unconsciously in a direction that is intended to compensate for everything that was left unfulfilled in the lives of their parents." James Hollis, a Jungian psychologist, puts it another way. He says that the greatest burden a child must bear is the "unlived life" of the parent. In this situation, the unlived lives of the grandparents are projected onto Brent's parents, whose unlived lives are then projected onto Brent. In that way patterns are passed on from one generation to another. Thus, one of the greatest challenges for the parent is to be aware of his or her sense of self. Otherwise the unlived life of the parent will be projected onto the child.

Whether it's a profession or education left unpursued, a sports team not joined, a value not expressed, a religious faith unfulfilled, a musical instrument that went unplayed, or travel opportunities missed, the conscious and unconscious desires, attitudes, and values of the parent are projected onto the child. Giving the child what the parent never had then becomes the focus of child-rearing. The parent is reacting to his own childhood rather than loving the child with spontaneity and acceptance for who she is and will become. In that way, the desires of the parent impede his ability to provide unconditional love—the condition being that the child must become what the parent was unable to become. This will undermine the ability of the parent to provide a secure base for his child and weaken the attachment between child and parent.

Without attachment, one feels abandoned, like Brent. One longs to belong, to be attached, to be part of a family, group, or community. It is a matter of survival as well as emotional development—and this is true at the end of life as much as at the beginning. In fact, once people learn they have a terminal illness, the process of understanding their childhood can become more powerful than ever. And as much as they review past lives, so, too, they seek to understand their relationship with their parents, and the effect it had. You may find that true yourself.

Two psychologists, Mary Ainsworth and John Bowlby, know about early parent-child relationships. In 1971, Ainsworth published the results of her work with infants in Uganda. Her work sheds light on your longing to belong in this context, regardless of whether you consider your relationship with your parents to be positive or negative. It may also help you understand your relationships with your children. From her work with children less than one year of age, Ainsworth developed the theory of attachment and described her technique as the "Strange Situation." First, researchers observed mothers for seventy-two hours during the first year of a child's life, noting the mother's response to the child while the child was feeding, crying, or being cuddled. The smiles of the mother and the eye contact between the two were also noted. When the infant was twelve months old, infant and mother were brought to an observation laboratory. This time, the infant was observed as he was separated from the mother. During two intervals, there was a stranger in the room; during another interval, the child was alone.

Ainsworth identified three patterns of reactions: infants were either securely attached, ambivalent in their attachment, or avoidant in that attachment. Securely attached infants cried when separated; when mother returned, the infant expressed pleasure, reaching to be picked up and molding to mother's body once in her arms. Bowlby, who commented on the study, states that these young children are confident that their parent will be "available, responsive, and helpful should they encounter adverse or frightening situations." This means the child is able to boldly explore the world. "This pattern is promoted by a parent, in the early years especially by mother, being readily available, sensitive to her child's signals, and lovingly responsive when he seeks protection and/or comfort." The mother's attention, responsiveness, and caring are always and consistently available, that is, the child receives unconditional love. There are no conditions under which love is withheld.

The ambivalent infant is uncertain whether the parent will be available, responsive, or helpful when the child calls. Such infants are clingy when the mother is present and afraid to explore a room on their own. They get anxious and agitated when mother leaves and may cry upon separation. When the mother returns, the infant moves to contact the mother and also expresses anger, with resistance to being comforted. According to Bowlby, this pattern is created by a parent who is available and helpful on some occasions but not others; it is exacerbated by separations and by threats of abandonment used as a means of control.

A common example would be the situation in which a two-year-old boy is slow to respond to his mother's request that he hurry up as they leave a grocery store. Finally, the mother says that she will leave without him—the threat of abandonment used as a means of controlling behavior. The child believes that the parent will leave without him if he doesn't follow. Children thrive on trust in their parents, just as an infant thrives in a trusting relationship with those who provide care—feeding, clothing for warmth, cuddling for nurturing, a diaper change, and a bath to keep clean and comfortable. Breaking that trust, even in seemingly harmless ways, undermines the parent child relationship.

Avoidant infants gave the impression of being independent. They explored their new environment without returning to their mothers for reassurance. They didn't look around to see if their mothers were present; when mother left the room, the infant did not seem to be affected. These children have no confidence that they will receive help and therefore do not seek care. Because the child is attempting to live his life without the love and support of those around him, he becomes emotionally self-sufficient. The child who grows up in an ambivalent or avoidant relationship with parents will experience some anxiety.

Studies that follow children over years show that each pattern of attachment tends to persist as parents respond to their children in unchanged ways. The child's pattern of behavior also persists. As Bowlby describes it, the secure child is "a happier and more rewarding child to care for and also is less demanding than an anxious one. An ambivalent child is apt to be whiny and clinging; while an anxious avoidant child keeps his distance and is prone to bully other children." In the two latter cases, the child's behavior will be met with an unfavorable response from the parent; patterns of behavior become ever more entrenched in the characteristics of the child and in the relationship between child and parent.

If the parent looks at the child with love, the child will internalize the message that he is lovable. This is reinforced by the parent's tone of voice and touch. If, for whatever reason, the parent looks at the child with mixed emotions, indifference or resentment, he will internalize that message. "I don't know if I am lovable. I'm not wanted. I'm not appreciated." In these circumstances, the child feels insecure. As he matures, his perception of self continues to be affected by the parent's responses.

A consistent and secure childhood results in an adolescent and later an adult who has a strong sense of self. By contrast, the insecure child is hampered by an unconscious defensiveness. Information that could potentially change the internal message, which the child needs to strengthen the sense of self, is excluded. In this way the adolescent loses the opportunity to enhance his sense of being secure. That child, as an adult, will imagine that others are relating to him just as his parents had, even if those individuals treat him completely differently. Understanding your early relationship with your parents, whether biological or adoptive, can help you understand your relationship with them throughout your lifetime and especially if you are living with dying. You may have wondered about the power of that relationship, that it has accompanied you for much of your life. The relationship may still result in some anger, resentment, or discomfort.

For Brent, a strong attachment to his parents seemed to be lacking, and he no longer wanted to pretend that there was any intimacy. He was aware of his inner struggle because of what was lacking in the relationship with his father. Brent wanted to let go of that anger and sadness. He appreciated the other close relationships he was able to develop. Those relationships did not substitute what he lacked as a child, but they served as a basis for respect, caring, and intimacy. If you have experienced a secure relationship with your parents, it can be difficult to appreciate the fact that Brent no longer wanted to be in association with his father. However, if you have been rejected by your parents, you may well appreciate a similarity. Through the research, I learned that some people speak fondly of their parents, others recognize strengths and weaknesses, and a few don't want to speak about parents at all.

The theme of longing to belong also emerged in Peggy's story as she reexamined her life. Peggy, in her sixties and suffering from lung cancer, had breast cancer thirty years earlier (see chapter 2). She spoke of her childhood experience: "I think the big thing is that I was an only child. I was a thing owned by my parents. I was dressed up and brought up to say 'good evening' during the cocktail hour. I didn't realize it at the time, but it probably was a very lonely life."

Peggy had a longing to belong. "There was a lack of connection because I was brought up by nannies and governesses. For that reason, I loved boarding school. (As a mother, I went in the other direction: I didn't want a nanny and practically never used a babysitter.) My sense of self was not to be found. I couldn't satisfy my parents. If I got an A, why didn't I get an A-plus? My mother was an alcoholic, and everybody around her was an alcoholic." The pattern of her family of origin was repeated. She married a man who, like her father, disregarded her efforts. Peggy became an alcoholic. "My husband was very, very British. You know what it's like: He walks in the door, the baby's crying. 'Can't you shut it up?' The kids ended having the same upbringing I had. The kids were seen and not heard. My life changed once I started to accept that I was an alcoholic. I looked around and saw hundreds of people around me who enjoyed life." At this point, she had to confront the isolation she felt in her family of origin and recognize that her sense of belonging was met outside her home.

Children develop attachment to their fathers in a similar fashion as to their mothers, but usually with a delay of several months. Again, touch, eye contact, facial expression, and sharing of positive emotions result in strong and intimate attachments between father and child.

Primarily, the longing to belong of the secure child is met within the family of origin. For the insecure child, the longing to belong is not met within the family of origin. That child will usually seek to belong, either by working harder to meet the expectations of the family of origin, or by working to belong in some way to an alternative family. That could be a group of friends, members of a social organization, or colleagues at the workplace. Some people will choose isolation rather than risking another difficult or impossible attachment. For them, the fear of a second rejection limits their relationships with others.

A sense of belonging becomes heightened for many who know they have a terminal illness. People yearn for this sense of belonging to their family of origin as well as their family of choice (spouse, partner, children, close friends). You may have known for some years that this need was not met in your family of origin yet be secure and satisfied in your other relationships. However, if you have recently come to realize that this need has not been met by your family of origin, you will likely experience a sense of betrayal and pain.

For your own well-being, it is helpful to confront or face pain. In fact, the only way to be free of pain is to move through and beyond it. Work to understand your longing to belong. The need for love and acceptance, if not received from a parent, will motivate a child to seek it elsewhere. It is a powerful force. And unless you face your pain, the search can result in relationships that are no more satisfying than was the relationship with your parents. Patterns persist, and patterns repeat. The love and sense of belonging that was lacking in childhood cannot be replaced. That is extremely sad and difficult to accept, intellectually and emotionally. Yet it is important to experience the emotion—whatever it might be—that is associated with recognizing that things did not turn out as you would have wished. In expressing that emotion—whether sadness, anger, rage, or bewilderment—you will move from despair toward integrity. You will gain a greater acceptance of yourself. And, primarily, this journey is about *you*. An unmet longing to belong will likely interfere with your ability to establish trusting, intimate relationships with other adults. It may also have affected your relationship with your own children. However, all is not lost. Although it might not be possible to recapture the unconditional love of a parent, it is possible to love others and to be loved by them, to have very deep and satisfactory relationships. It is still possible, at the end of life, to deepen relationships with people you love and with those who love you. That was experienced and very clearly stated by those who participated in this study.

In reviewing parent-child relationships, many people recognize that their experience lies on a continuum between security and abandonment. The nearer the experience lies to abandonment, the greater the sense that a basic trust has been broken. When trust is broken, people feel betrayed. When a child has been betrayed by abuse or neglect, later relationships in adulthood are usually characterized by the same pattern, that is, they form bonds with adults who are likely to betray them. Eventually, they learn to avoid intimacy for fear of being hurt again.

When a sense of belonging is absent from your family of origin, there is a feeling of being ostracized, of grief. When a sense of belonging is present, there is inner peace and comfort.

Brent felt the shame his family felt toward him. This was most apparent with regard to his homosexuality and his illness.

The whole truth of the matter is that they still think that this is my own fault because I am gay. I think that the typical reaction by a family who is in denial, which is what I believe a lot of families go through, is that it's only at the very end that they realize that you're dying. Deep down inside they think it's for the best, not for you but for them, because this is like a big thing hanging over them, this big black cloud of shame.

My family has a real problem with me being gay; it's something they've never dealt with. They also have a real problem with me having AIDS, which they don't want to deal with either. It's just something that they cannot understand. They've distanced themselves so far now that when the time comes, I probably won't have them around because they don't know me, they don't know who I've become, how different I am than what I was before, and what my needs are.

Betrayal is felt when trust is broken. Brent felt betrayed by both parents as well as by his siblings. He felt a strong sense of loss. His mother abandoned him, not only at the curb outside the hospital when he was five years old but also by dying when he was twelve. As far as he was concerned, she betrayed her role as mother. That was true of his father, too. Brent's father did not provide a secure base; he was not accessible and constant in a world where the only constant is change. Brent did not have a secure attachment to his adoptive parents, and so he was destined to satisfy his longing to belong through other relationships. In order to have intimate relationships with others, he would need to find people who would not take advantage of him, who would not expect him to meet their unmet needs. Brent had to find people he could trust—and he did.

The longing to belong that characterizes all relationships can be met within a family of origin, with a spouse or partner, with children, and with friends. Florence felt estranged from her children. Her sense of isolation left her with a deep longing. "At the top of the list of things that matter in a person's life, I would put family and friends. But I do feel alone where family is concerned. I kept thinking, all through my married life, that I was so glad I'd had children. I thought I had good relationships with my children, but I don't." She continued:

I say I'm glad I got cancer because it has turned my life around. Now I can see what's worthwhile in life and what's not—what's not worth spending any time on, the kind of stuff you used to spend days and months worrying about, or being angry about, or fretting about and only now you look at it and say, What for? The things that really matter are relationships with other people. Love matters. I'm not speaking necessarily about physical love. I'm speaking about a feeling that doesn't even have to be expressed between people. The kind of love we show in our support group. And that kind of love is very, very healing, very important. What I like to call "the theory of relativity" takes hold—you understand what's relative to life and what doesn't matter at all. And at the top of the list I put relationships with family and friends.

What will bring you the most happiness in life will be loving relationships with people because out of that closeness to other people will come everything else. You can have all the material things in the world, but if you do not have loving relationships, I don't know how you can say you're a happy person. I don't think that things bring you happiness. It's nice to have them, of course, and I'm glad I'm able to live in a nice place at this time of my life and that if I want to give gifts I'm able to do that, but what I need more than anything else is loving relationships. I'm taking them where I find them now, you know; I'm not distinguishing between the love of family and the love of friends. They're all loving.

Even if there is no sense of belonging within one's family of origin or adult family, it can be developed through other relationships. Florence found connection with others through her cancer support group. It symbolized hope, life, and healing for her.

Brent found a sense of belonging among friends. "I've developed a new family. When the disease progresses and things change about you physically, you have to learn to adapt and then you have to deal with people differently. You find out who your real friends are." He speaks of the relationships he treasures, those people from whom he receives love and to whom he gives love. "I'd rather spend even a short period of time with my friend Kevin talking about things that are really spiritual. Kevin and I can talk about very deep things. We may only see each other every two weeks or so, but we share more in that two weeks than I've shared with some people in years." And especially of his friend Susan:

> We share our soul stuff. We share stuff that you don't share with just anybody. I remember saying to her that one of the reasons I haven't taken my own life is because I couldn't do that to her. It would cause her too much pain, and I would never be at peace with myself if I hurt her. For me to say that was very difficult but very important, because I let her know how important she was to me. When I'm with her, we have a great time together. We laugh, we smile, we talk about nothing and we talk about serious things. We know each other because we've talked about our pain, about all the real important issues in life.
>
> There are a lot of people in your life, but people you can really trust and count on to be there for you, those are few and far between. So I feel very fortunate that after all I've been through I've met one person I feel is a true friend, someone I can trust implicitly with anything I have to say, anything I need to do. I know she will be there for me. That's a gift, that's a gift to me.

By speaking of relationships with parents, siblings, partners, children, and friends, people express their need for belonging. Some of my coresearchers spoke of the pain they experienced in feeling rejected and ostracized; all valued the need for love, affection, and belongingness, especially at the end of life.

Through the following exercise, I invite you to explore the sense of belonging in your own life. The purpose of the exercise is to review and examine your significant relationships, beginning with your parents, your siblings, and other family members. This may be of value to you in defining and understanding your own sense of belonging.

Starting with your childhood, describe your relationship with your parents. Appreciate who they were and, if they are still alive, who they are to you today. But keep in mind that this exercise is about you, not about them. Do you remember your mother and father being warm, caring, open, and responsible for you? Or do you remember them being unavailable? How did they react when you made mistakes, when you said things they didn't want to hear, when you messed up, when you were rebellious?

If you experience deep pain with regard to these questions, you can choose to speak to someone you trust about your feelings. If, through the course of your conversations, you are unable to finish speaking about your feelings without crying uncontrollably, you may want to seek help from a professional (counselor, psychologist, member of the clergy, etc.). If you have not cried for a long time, you may feel sad without actually crying. Just because you have not expressed an emotion does not mean it does not exist within you.

What emotions do you feel when you remember your childhood? Which memories result in pleasant feelings? Which memories result in unpleasant or painful feelings? Could you approach your parents with questions on any topics, any emotional issues and concerns, all ideas that were important to you? Were there unspeakable topics in your home, unmentionable activities and ideas? Were you loved unconditionally? What about your relationships with your siblings, aunts, uncles, grandparents?

How do you feel about the other relationships in your life (spouse, partner, friends)? Are your relationships to those people based on trust, a sense of safety, a feeling of inclusion, or do you fear closeness, intimacy, and trust even with them? Have you been in long-lasting friendships and relationships, or do you have a hard time building a trusting relationship?

You might consider writing letters to some of these people, again beginning with your parents. The letters are for your benefit, to enhance your understanding. You do not need to send them; you can choose to destroy the letters or file them away as part of the legacy you leave behind. You could begin your letter by expressing gratitude for what the person gave you and then state what you think was missing in the relationship, what you wish you could have received from them. If you have become estranged from the person to whom you are writing, you might want to tell them who you have become, what is important to you, and that you have met people in your adult life who have been there for you, have understood who you are.

When you have completed the letter, you might become aware of things you want to say to someone. Chapter 6 provided some examples of how that might be done, how you might speak your truth.

I witnessed some of the emotion Brent experienced in longing for a connection with his father. He spoke about despair, anger, grief, the pain in his soul as he acknowledged what he never had and knew that he would never get. It would have been easier for me to avoid the topic, not to witness the pain, not to work to understand his experience. It would likely have been more comfortable for him as well. However, in the process of searching for meaning, Brent realized that he had to confront his past and embrace his truth regardless of the degree of pain he might experience. The wound begins to heal once it is cleansed.

As for his father, Brent knew at the core of his being that he would never know unconditional love or acceptance for who he was as a child or as an adult. At the same time, he felt a new sense of freedom as he emerged as his own person, not the man someone else wanted him to be, but the man he knew he was. And so, Brent experienced a great triumph.

You will likely require some courage to complete this exercise. It is the courage I often witnessed in people who knew they had a terminal illness. They looked inward despite the fear, the desire to ignore the past, and the pain. May their courage provide inspiration to you as it has to me.

CHAPTER EIGHT

Self-Realization: Who Am I?

It is only in the face of death that man's self is born.

Saint Augustine

I have faith and belief in myself now that I never had before. I'm not afraid of being who I am.

Peggy

A new consciousness starts when we ask, "Who am I, apart from my history and the roles I have played?"

James Hollis

The Roar of Awakening

A tiger cub was brought up among goats. Its mother had died in giving it birth.
Big with young, she had been prowling for many days without discovering prey,
when she came upon this herd of ranging wild goats. The tigress was ravenous
at the time, and this fact may account for the violence of her spring; but in any
case, the strain of the leap brought on the birth throes, and from sheer exhaustion she expired. Then the goats, who had scattered, returned to the grazing
ground and found the little tiger whimpering at its mother's side. They adopted
the feeble creature out of maternal compassion, suckled it together with their
own offspring, and watched over it fondly. The cub grew, and their care was
rewarded, for the little fellow learned the language of the goats, adapted his
voice to their gentle way of bleating, and displayed as much devotion as any kid
of the flock. At first he experienced some difficulty when he tried to nibble thin
blades of grass with his pointed teeth, but somehow he managed. The vegetar-
ian diet kept him very slim and imparted to his temperament a remarkable
meekness.

One night, when this young tiger among the goats had reached the age of
reason, the herd was attacked again, this time by a fierce old male tiger, and
again they scattered; but the cub remained where he stood, devoid of fear. He
was, of course, surprised. Discovering himself face to face with the terrible jungle being, he gazed at the apparition in amazement. The first moment passed;
then he began to feel self-conscious. Uttering a forlorn bleat, he plucked a thin
leaf of grass and chewed it while the other stared.

Suddenly the mighty intruder demanded: "What are you doing here among
these goats? What are you chewing there?" The funny little creature bleated.
The old one became really terrifying. He roared, "Why do you make this silly
sound?" and, before the other could respond, seized him roughly by the scruff
and shook him, as though to knock him back to his senses. The jungle tiger
then carried the frightened cub to a nearby pond, where he set him down, com-
pelling him to look into the mirror surface, which was illuminated by the moon.
"Now look at those two faces. Are they not alike? You have the pot-face of a

tiger; it is like mine. Why do you fancy yourself to be a goat? Why do you bleat? Why do you nibble grass?"

The little one was unable to reply but continued to stare, comparing the two reflections. Then it became uneasy, shifted its weight from paw to paw, and emitted another troubled, quavering cry. The fierce old beast seized it again and carried it off to his den, where he presented it with a bleeding piece of raw meat remaining from an earlier meal. The cub shuddered with disgust. The jungle tiger, ignoring the weak bleat of protest, gruffly ordered: "Take it! Eat it! Swallow it!" The cub resisted, but the frightening meat was forced between his teeth, and the tiger sternly supervised while he tried to chew and prepared to swallow. The toughness of the morsel was unfamiliar and was causing some difficulty, and he was just about to make his little noise again, when he began to get the taste of the blood. He was amazed; he reached with eagerness for the rest. He began to feel an unfamiliar gratification as the new food went down his gullet and the meaty substance came into his stomach. A strange, glowing strength, starting from there, went out through his whole organism, and he commenced to feel elated, intoxicated. His lips smacked; he licked his jowls. He arose and opened his mouth with a mighty yawn, just as though he were waking from a night of sleep—a night that had held him long under its spell, for years and years. Stretching his form, he arched his back, extending and spreading his paws. The tail lashed the ground, and suddenly from his throat there burst the terrifying, triumphant roar of a tiger.

The grim teacher, meanwhile, had been watching closely and with increasing satisfaction. The transformation had actually taken place. When the roar was finished he demanded gruffly: "Now do you know what you really are?" and to complete the initiation of his young disciple into the secret lore of his own true nature, added: "Come, we shall go now for a hunt together in the jungle."

❋

In the midst of bleating goats, how can you hear the roar of a tiger? How do you know you are a tiger?

Most of us live a life that is routine and familiar, from our work and other activities to our relationships with family and friends. Death is a reality for all of us. And yet for many it is a reality that lies dormant within us. Some of you know that reality because you have been told that you have a terminal illness. Some of you have been told you have a terminal illness yet still do not know that reality. And some of you know that reality for reasons other than having a terminal illness—perhaps because someone in your life has died. Life is full of dying; life is full of death. When the reality of death strikes, it strikes with a "roar of awakening."

When people no longer deny death and know they are dying, the new awareness often inspires a process of life review. As an inherent part of that process, people speak their truth, recognize a longing to belong since birth and throughout their lifetime, realize who they really are, and ultimately achieve or discover a transcendence, a spirituality that extends from the core of their being to a spirit that cannot be contained. For some the process may follow this sequence; for others the process happens all at once or in a different sequence, in part or as a whole. One cannot predict who will be affected by the reality or when it might hit them. Through life review, we recognize patterns, successes, and failures. We understand in a new way that the end of life is affected by a lifetime of relationships, activities, values, and beliefs. The ending is not divorced from the beginning, the beginning is not separate from the end. In time, some of us wonder what happened to the dreams and aspirations we once had, the lives we lived. Ultimately, we may feel estranged from who we really are and yearn for a life that has more meaning.

To connect with the inner self—what many call the "soul"—we must go on an inward journey. Many people say to themselves, "My life is going to end and I have never been me. I don't even know who 'me' is. I feel that something or someone has been lost and that someone is me. Am I living by the norms and expectations of 'the herd' without recognizing my unique roar? Have I realized who I truly am?"

Three people whom you have already met in this book asked themselves the question Who am I? To answer that, they went through a process of self-reflection (life review), acknowledging their longing to belong, were truthful about their past, and had the courage to persevere in seeking an answer. This trio realized that the only way they could be free of emotional pain was to move through and beyond the pain and the suffering. They were able to acknowledge pain's presence without allowing it to impede the process of inner resolution.

For Peggy, the roar of the tiger occurred when she realized that she had been using alcohol to drown her pain and that even though she had stopped drinking she was still an alcoholic. Before that realization, she wanted to avoid pain at all cost, to be distracted from the work of looking in the mirror to see who she really was. For Ron, the breakthrough occurred when he confronted a life of duplicity and saw the price he paid for running away from home, running away from pain and anger. And for Brent, a near-death experience taught him in a dramatic fashion that death was in fact imminent, and it was then that he realized he had lived by the expectations of those around him for most of his life.

Virginia Satir, a pioneer in family therapy, stated, "Many people in the world still feel moving beyond their status quo means risking death. This attitude toward change can be one of the greatest hindrances to personal growth and effective therapy. In this frame of mind, people sometimes prefer a familiar dysfunction to an unknown improvement or comfort." For many, the diagnosis of a terminal illness or the experience of that illness serves as a roar of awakening. It ends the routine and indifference. People are no longer paralyzed by the fear that moving beyond their status quo means risking death. They know that death is inevitable and therefore experience a new freedom to live authentically.

Because they know that they cannot escape death, they embrace life—their own life. The "prescription" of how to live given by family, culture, profession, religion, or friends loses its grasp. Perhaps, in this way, knowing that you have a terminal illness is of value. Knowing that dying is part of living might also be experienced as meaningful by those of us who do not have a diagnosis of a terminal illness? What about those who are living with a chronic illness? Those who are aging? When do I begin asking the same questions that people who know they have a terminal illness are asking? What can each of us learn about living from those who know they are dying?

For Brent, the stimulus to ask the question Who am I? arose from his close encounter with death. His process of awakening began with a near-death experience:

> I'm really taking control of my life and that's because, in coming so close to death, you realize that if you don't take control no one will do it for you. You can't expect the doctor to do everything, the nurse can't do everything—no one can—but you can certainly make an effort yourself . . . to learn to be an individual. You have to separate from your family to become a person. I realized when I was dying that I was going to die alone, that no one was coming with me; I was going alone. Then I realized that each person's journey is truly one of aloneness and that whatever happens in your life it's only you, it's always going to be only you.

Furthermore, for Brent, asking Who am I? was linked to speaking his truth and hearing the truth of others. "If you can't be bothered to tell me the truth, don't tell me anything, because there's nothing else but the truth. This is who I am, take it or leave it. I don't put on airs. I used to think it was really important what clothes you wore. All the things that used to matter so much, they don't matter any more."

By looking inward, he reexperienced the pain of his childhood. "My childhood was painful. You know we were adopted children. We were treated poorly by our parents, two people who were very religious. They must have thought that they were doing their duty, that they were giving some poor children a good home. I do believe that's what they honestly felt. They believed they were doing the right thing, but what they actually did, and I think they forget this, is they took the lives of four children and potentially ruined them."

That was a difficult statement for Brent to make. He could appreciate that his parents had done their best. At the same time, he realized that his life was about *him*, not about his parents doing their best. He had to learn to separate from his family in order to learn to be an individual. That was as true for his parents as it was for him. Everyone needs to separate from their family of origin in order to become their own person. For Brent, that meant going through a process of self-reflection, which helped him to become aware of his own unique psychology.

With regard to family expectations, he said, "I don't want to play that game any more. I want to live in the truth. And whether they want to deal with it or not is irrelevant at this point." Resolution lay in understanding and speaking the truth. Brent believed that without resolution within himself, he would exist in a state of turmoil right up to the moment of his death. "Dying bottled up would be horrible. I can only imagine it's like going to hell. I think that would be awful because you'd carry that around with you for all eternity. And if there is such a thing as reincarnation, you would come back with that turmoil within you. It has to be resolved in this lifetime, I believe."

Brent spoke about his wishes for his last days. "If the family or friends can't or don't want to deal with these issues, then at least you face up to that. Everybody can pretend they're getting along, but I don't want to pretend. That doesn't get you anywhere." For Brent, that meant stating that his father could not bear to be at his bedside as he died. His father could not say that he loved his son. Brent could no longer pretend that there was a loving relationship between them. He wanted to move beyond the shame he felt. For him, "Resolution is simply the truth—good, bad, or indifferent. It's the truth, and that's all that seems to matter when you're at that point. You know where you're going, and you feel good about where you're going. You just don't want to bring this negative stuff along with you." He realized he would never have his father's love. To come to that understanding and to say it aloud was, for Brent, a painful process. In experiencing such pain, Brent integrated the truth into his reality. He not only spoke the truth; he accepted it into his sense of himself. He moved through the despair experienced in that truth, toward integrity.

In being confronted by death, Brent realized who he was. He also realized that to be truly alive it was important to be real—to be himself—regardless of his remaining time on earth. "When you're dying, you're stripped of everything that's important to society—money, image—so all you have left is that honesty. It takes so much energy to pretend when you can use that energy for other things. Part of me died in that hospital, a part of me died, the part that was bitter, angry, resentful, hateful and spiteful, died. Now there's a new person."

After suffering through the anger he'd lived with all his life, Brent began to experience a new compassion and ability to listen to others. When a nurse helped him after a bout of incontinence, he said, "If I was still worried about what people thought about me, I think I wouldn't have noticed her care or listened to what she was saying because I would've been so concerned about being dirty and the humiliation of needing her to clean me. But she did it with such dignity and made me feel like there was nothing wrong. And it wasn't just small talk, I wasn't just pretending to listen, I was listening."

In dying, many people find their true self. Brent experienced a new level of perception. "You do wake up. It's like a revelation of some sort. All of a sudden, all these things that were hidden are now front and center. There's no hiding from them any more. I belong to me now, and that's how I think I've survived."

When you confront your own mortality, the person other people expect you to be falls away, and a new self is born—or rather, your original self surfaces. "And that's what I think makes us lucky. When you come close to death, all that crap just flies off of you; it just sort of comes off you like layers of skin. All of a sudden, you're starting from scratch, like when you were born. And all of those messages that you were taught, all of the negative stuff is replaced with positive things, loving things, caring things, things that make you a better, happier person. I believe in myself now. I never had that before. And I am not afraid of being who I am."

In becoming true to yourself, a new person emerges, one who may not be recognized by others. "Well, you are a different person—and they don't know this new person."

Wearing a mask is how we present ourselves to others (the perfect mother/father, the wise teacher, the compassionate doctor, the successful business person, etc.). The clothes we wear, the words we speak, how we say them, and our actions tell others about who we are. Carl Jung spoke of this mask as being the "persona," the Greek word for mask. We can choose to hide features of who we are our weaknesses, for example—if we do not want others to see them. Hiding weaknesses reduces our vulnerability. In that way, the mask provides a protective covering. It also means that some features of who we are do not come to light. In essence, they are what Jung described as our "shadow." Often, these are qualities of which we are ashamed. The shadow also includes "aspects of ourselves that might yet be lived out, our unlived life—talents and abilities that have long been buried or never been conscious." Perhaps another term we could use to define or describe our shadow is our "wild side"—the part of us that is unknown, untamed, unrecognized.

Wearing a mask is our attempt to compromise between our real identity and the expectations of others; it is a compromise between who we are and what we are willing to reveal. It helps us interact with other people. Sometimes people take their mask so seriously that they believe it truly reflects who they are. They forget about or ignore their shadow, their wild side. It is only when people distinguish between their mask—that is, the person they appear to be—and their real identity that the process of answering the question Who am I? really begins. This results in a decreased identification with the mask and an increased assimilation of the shadow. You can stop playing games and be honest and truthful with yourself and others.

To die outside the truth is to die wounded, whereas to understand one's truth and accept it is to die healed—not cured, but healed. To heal is always possible, even when cure is impossible. As Brent says, "Don't lie to yourself, because that only makes it more difficult to fight the physical disease. By telling yourself the truth, you allow yourself to heal. You're not so busy trying to play games, and so your mind has more time to work on your body. The mind and body really do work together. If your mind is so busy trying to keep you from thinking about the truth, your body is going to be neglected; it's not going to get that chance it needs to heal. It's funny how people will just deny it 'til they die."

Consider the tiger cub who, upon looking outward, assumed himself to be a goat with all that being a goat entailed—his diet, his stance, his expression. He was wearing the mask of a goat, taking himself seriously as a goat, never doubting that he was a goat. Then something happened that forced him to stop acting: He began to look inward. He could no longer see himself as a goat, no longer felt like a goat, no longer sounded like a goat, for his true self awoke to who he really was. Part of that process included being taken away from the herd, looking in the mirror to see who he really was, and responding to some very pointed questions. Did the roar of awakening occur when he heard the roar of the other tiger—or when he himself produced the roar?

Like the tiger cub we, too, adopt the stance, the culture, the habits, the bleating of the world around us—the world of our families, communities, institutions, workplaces, and professions. What is it in us that results in an awakening to our true self?

Frederick Buechner, a theologian, describes the situation:

[T]he world sets in to making us into what the world would like us to be, and because we have to survive after all, we try to make ourselves into something that we hope the world will like better than it apparently did the selves we originally were. That is the story of all our lives, needless to say, and in the process of living out that story, the original, shimmering self gets buried so deep that most of us end up hardly living out of it at all. Instead we live out all the other selves which we are constantly putting on and taking off like coats and hats against the world's weather.

James Hollis, a Jungian psychologist, also describes this process:

[W]hatever reality may be, it will to some extent be shaped by the lens through which we see it. When we are born we are handed multiple lenses: genetic inheritance, gender, a specific culture and the variables of our family environment, all of which constitute our sense of reality. Looking back later we have to admit that we have perhaps lived less from our true nature than from the vision of reality ordained by the lenses we used.

And though each person is born with multiple lenses, she also makes choices to become the person she is.

The process of "waking up to oneself"—that is, the process of individuation—beckons everyone at some point in life. As a process, it is never complete and becomes more of a quest than a goal. For some it may begin in adolescence, for others it is manifest through the emotional despair of a midlife crisis, some catastrophic event, or difficult circumstances (divorce or threat of separation, financial difficulties, problems at work, illness, or the death of a family member or friend). And if it has not occurred before learning that one has a terminal illness, the longing to know and understand one's self—to answer the question Who am I?—often emerges in the experience of living with a terminal illness.

Consider again Ron's story, which appeared in chapter 6. In asking the question Who am I? he saw a new person, one who chose to step from a life of duplicity into a life of truth.

There's a new Ron. I want to live in the now, I don't want to live in the "what if"—what if before or what if future. I don't want to dwell on things, but I do feel like I've learned from my experience. I've been down there, I've seen myself, and I've seen what led to what—all the combinations of events and emotions that led to what happened.

I'm not a horrible character, you know. I took a few wrong turns when I was in my teens, but there were reasons for that. Other than a lot of fighting with my father, I don't have too many clear memories of those years. I didn't want to go to university. I couldn't get into the army. So I went with a bunch of bikers. That wasn't power and glory; that was nothing but shame and dishonor. So that's why the double life.

I'm tired of duplicity. I've made my confession to myself. I've confronted my demons. You know, I'd blocked out the looting and the rape to some extent. I think it took about a year after, before I thought about it. I was actually back in this country, and I was just drifting aimlessly. I was pretty screwed up, and I was shut out by my family. I needed escape and of course it was women first because I needed that close human contact. Then drugs, and a drug addiction came along with it.

I'm glad I talked to you today. I've been giving out quite a few of my secrets. I'm feeling much better, you know, getting back on the straight, so to speak. That's probably one of the reasons I just had to tell you the whole truth—because I'm feeling a lot better.

To know who we are as adults we must understand who we were as children in the context of our family of origin. This is strengthened by knowing the context of our family history through past generations. For in understanding the context of our family of origin, we begin to understand and appreciate "who the world wanted us to be." A feature of knowing one has a terminal illness is visiting or revisiting one's place in, one's relationship to, the family of origin. Even for someone who has already done this, the need recurs at the end of life. It can happen in the context of an adult relationship with one's family, whether that's the family of origin or of choice. It pertains to one's understanding of self. With the understanding comes a sense of peace and, for some, a sense of meaning. This process seems to mark the experience of living with a terminal illness. One's experience of childhood is a reality throughout life, whether that person remains in the family community or moves far away. Understanding that context is part of answering the Who am I? question.

Here are two important things to remember with regard to your childhood and your family of origin. First, each pregnancy changes the family in that it will either result in a miscarriage, which is a death, or a birth, which marks the addition of a new family member. Your parents and, to some extent, your siblings would be affected by your birth. That is also true for you as to subsequent births and deaths in the family. Second, your memory is your story and your truth. Your family members will have experienced the same events differently and will likely have different memories. Your experience and understanding of events is legitimate; the same holds true for other family members.

Peggy (see chapter 2) was the sixty-eight-year-old dying of lung cancer. She spoke of being what the world of her childhood wanted her to be. She described her ancestors. "They're old families. On my French-Canadian side we're sort of settlers in Canada, way back. On the other side, my father was a lord, and there's a lot of history there too. My girls are very proud of it. They don't capitalize on it or anything, but family history has been very much a part of their upbringing and who I am. I was an only child. Although I didn't realize it at the time, it probably was a very lonely life."

Peggy was right about the significance of being an only child. The author of *Family Constellation*, Dr. Walter Toman, studied 3,000 people and concluded that personality and relationship profiles are related to birth order—that of the child as well as each parent. "[M]uch of personality development has to do with parents' sibling positions. The parents' personality characteristics, in large part derived from their own sibling positions, become important determining factors in personality development. The way parents relate to their children has a great deal to do with the relationships they formed with their siblings. For example, a youngest brother of brothers, as a father, may tend to relate more easily to his older son who is an older brother of brothers, just as he had at an earlier time of his life related to his own older brother." According to Toman, as a female only child, there might be a tendency for Peggy to "structure her life around older people, people in authority and superiors; to obtain their approval and hopefully their preferential treatment."

Peggy recognized that pattern in her own relationship with her father: "My sense of self was not to be found. I just couldn't please him." She had a sense of not being good enough. On one level, she was determined to do better next time in the hope of pleasing her father. On another level, she came to believe that there was something wrong with her unless she was perfect (in most cases like this, the child strives for perfection). Peggy believed that she was valued for her performance rather than for who she was as a person. She learned to live according to expectations, ignoring her own sense of self, ignoring her own limitations. She would continue to strive for perfection and parental approval, always falling short, always reminded that she was failing. At times she might have believed that she was a failure as a person. She discounted her own feelings, gradually losing her identity; like her mother, she would come to numb her pain with alcohol.

The pattern recurred in Peggy's relationship with her husband, for she recognized in it the same demand for perfection. A child in a situation like this would internalize the message that there was something wrong with her. This usually results in a sense of shame, described by John Bradshaw, a well-known family therapist, as "toxic shame."

Shame. What is it? According to the dictionary, it is a painful feeling of humiliation or distress caused by the consciousness of wrong or foolish behavior. As such, shame serves a purpose in our relationships with one another and in society as a whole. Who I am and what I do are separate entities. If I feel shame for what I do, I can correct the behavior; if I feel shame for who I am because I have been lead to believe that I am flawed, that there is something inherently wrong with me, my sense of self suffers. That means I and perhaps my family would be better off if that part of me did not exist, if that part of me died. This is toxic shame, or "the shame that binds you, [which] is experienced as the all pervasive sense that I am flawed and defective as a human being. Toxic shame is no longer an emotion that signals our limits, it is a state of being, a core identity. Toxic shame gives you a sense of worthlessness, a sense of failing and falling short as a human being. Toxic shame is a rupture of the self with the self." In the context of that definition, Bradshaw speaks of developing a false self from the pain of being unacceptable as one's true self. The false self is as commonly found in the superachieving perfectionist as in the addict in the alley. "[T]he most paradoxical aspect of neurotic [i.e., toxic] shame is that it is the core motivator of the superachieved and the underachieved, the Star and the Scapegoat, the 'Righteous' and the wretched, the powerful and the pathetic." Think of "toxic" as synonymous with "poison." Poison damages, injures, and/or destroys. Shame that damages, injures, or destroys who we are could certainly be regarded as poisonous or toxic.

Peggy spoke about her mother: "My mother had some very good qualities; she was a very clever lady. But she had an unhappy upbringing. She was an alcoholic and everybody around her was an alcoholic." By seeking counseling and by acknowledging that Alcoholics Anonymous had become her lifeline, Peggy began to change the course of her family history. She *stepped into and through* her pain. She understood the source of her toxic shame. She became more aware of her shadow and so became more wholly who she was.

Peggy wanted to look at the whole picture of who she was, for only then could she truly begin to like herself. She also realized that she mattered to some people. "So that sense of no self-worth is leaving. I am very grateful I can see it that way, and I'm hoping it comes through with those close to me. I think it will." Peggy spoke of her sense of self: "You know, I guess it has changed. I think that I can face death liking myself now. I think that's the big difference. Facing death has shown me that I've got the inner strength. I'd say that's the essence of it." A hope-filled essence indeed!

In speaking of her family of origin as well as her adult family, Peggy was addressing who she was. Knowing and understanding the relationships in her family of origin enabled her to understand herself more fully and clearly. Although this process had started several years prior to her diagnosis, the issues surfaced again as she reviewed her life. Peggy seemed to appreciate that her real self grew out of a complex interaction of her genetic composition (nature), the experience of being a product of her family of origin (nurture), and her own choices.

The wounds of the first generation hurt the second, the wounds of the second hurt the third, and so on, until someone like Peggy suffers enough to break the chain. Peggy's father expected her to be perfect, most likely because that was expected of him as a child. Peggy's mother was an alcoholic. Peggy followed the script of her childhood—being a perfectionist, trying to meet all the expectations of her parents, failing to acknowledge, feel, or express her pain—into adulthood, where she continued to live by the same script. But she suffered enough psychologically that she was prepared to break the chain by changing her behavior and pattern of relationships. This is summarized by James Hollis: "Fate provides the initial wounding and the flawed parenting of each subsequent generation, and yet all are responsible for the lives they have chosen—as we too are responsible for our choices and their consequences. That one has made choices from a wounded vision, a flawed perspective, is usually clear only in retrospect, with the consciousness our suffering has brought."

This was apparent in Peggy's life: For a time she followed a course similar to her mother's. However, the difference between the two women was Peggy's choice to live a different life, to alter the course of her family history such that her children would benefit from living with a mother who was not an alcoholic.

Brent, Ron, and Peggy all looked inward. They had been living under the guise of the world around them. Each experienced toxic shame because their parents were unable to accept them as they were. In stepping into their true selves, each of them had to leave home. They worked to understand who they had been during their childhood years, how they had lived up to the expectations of their families, and how they had thereby denied the expression and development of who they were as individuals. Brent was able to articulate that his father and sisters could not accept who he was as a gay male. Ron acknowledged that his father's agenda for him was so powerful that he had run away in order to keep some sense of himself alive; in his adolescent confusion, he had substituted one powerful agenda for another. Peggy suffered through an addiction to alcohol before she realized that she did not need to measure up to the expectations of anyone else, that she had her own worth—her self-worth.

In chapter 7, I refer to the concept of attachment. When a child is not accepted by parents for who she is, she begins to perform for acceptance. That means she is unable to grow into her uniqueness but instead becomes the product of the expectations of the home and community. Dr. Murray Bowen, a psychiatrist who produced a new theory of human behavior—the family systems theory—describes the need to differentiate. He uses the formation of the embryo in his explanation:

> In the developing fetus groups of cells that are identical in the beginning become different from each other. They "differentiate" in order to form the different organs of the body [heart, liver, lungs, etc.]. The concept as applied to the self describes the variation that exists among people in their abilities to adapt—that is, to deal with the exigencies [difficulties, needs, requirements, or demands] of life and to reach their goals. People fall along a theoretical spectrum of differentiation, depending on their unresolved emotional attachment to the family of origin.

The more children are accepted for who they are, the greater their ability to differentiate, to cope with the demands of life and reach their goals. All children learn who they are through the people around them. For most children, that begins with their parents, who mirror and echo the child. That message is transmitted primarily by action and attitude; even the infant receives the message in the preverbal years. Children who are loved unconditionally learn that they are inherently lovable and acceptable. Parents who have misgivings about themselves or poor self-esteem will project that message onto the child. The child will see and experience that attitude, interpreting it to mean that it arises from how the parent feels about her. For the child, looking into the parent's face is like looking in a mirror, hearing the parent's voice is like hearing an echo. The child has no reason to doubt the message the parent is giving. That is why it is particularly important that in the first years of a child's life she be taken seriously, that she be accepted for who she is. What does that mean specifically?

Alice Miller, the author of *The Drama of the Gifted Child*, describes the dynamics of effective mirroring, an essential feature of parenting. To begin with, the parent knows that the child is a separate being and loves him as a separate being. When the child is aggressive or expresses anger, the parent is not threatened but is able to respond to the child's behavior. As an example, consider the young child who has a temper tantrum in a grocery store. A parent who is self confident, not threatened, would remove the child from the public space in a gentle yet firm manner. Once the two are outside the store, the parent might hold the child very securely, speaking calmly to the child. This would eventually eliminate the child's own fear about the emotion. He would learn that anger is an acceptable emotion, that it can be expressed, and that the parent will not withhold love from him during the temper tantrum.

Similarly, a child may be allowed to express ordinary impulses— jealousy, rage, sexuality, defiance—because the parents have not disowned these feelings in themselves. The child can leave or approach the parents as necessary, confident that the parents will be available when the child needs them. His natural striving for autonomy is not seen as a threat by the parents. Such children are able to develop their own needs at their own developmental pace. Parents live their lives and allow children to live theirs. Until we understand how the influence of childhood affected who we are as adults, our understanding of who we are as adults will be limited. We may be children who grow old, or grow older without growing up, rather than children who become adults and take their place in the world.

The experience of learning about a terminal illness can propel someone into a search for the true self, a search for healing, for the courage to care for psychological wounds. It is the only way to live life to the fullest until one dies. One discards what's imitation and embraces what's real. This is a continuous process, which seems to move people from depression toward hope, through anxiety toward peace, and from despair toward integrity.

Erik Erikson developed a theory of the life cycle that divided life into eight stages. He presented the cycle such that each stage could be understood in the context of the laws of individual development and social organization. An understanding of the eighth stage—integrity versus despair—enhances one's understanding when learning about a terminal illness.

Erikson defines despair as a "feeling that the time is short, too short for the attempt to start another life and to try out alternate roads to integrity." Following the work of Erikson, Judith Herman, a psychiatrist at Harvard Medical School and director of training for the Victims of Violence Program at Cambridge Hospital, defines integrity as "the capacity to affirm the value of life in the face of death, to be reconciled with the finite limits of one's own life and the tragic limitations of the human condition, and to accept these realities without despair."

Brent, Ron, and Peggy lived with integrity. They were willing to look at themselves, warts and all. They were prepared to acknowledge what it meant to live in dishonesty and pain from wounds generations deep. In so doing, they experienced despair. Despair might include anxiety and depression, experiences that are generally seen as threats to one's sense of well-being, particularly at the end of life. But they knew that what leads to despair, no matter how painful, can also lead to enhanced self-awareness and meaning.

It is *meaning* that delivers people from despair to integrity. To find meaning, we must be willing to embark on a journey—an encounter with the past, with the core of one's being. As Hollis states,

[It involves a] more honest encounter with the shadow, some deepening of the journey into places we'd rather not go. . . . To experience some healing within ourselves, and to contribute healing to the world, we are summoned to wade through the muck from time to time. Where we do not go willingly, sooner or later we will be dragged.... Soul work is the prerequisite not only of healing but also of maturation.

This is no different for those with a terminal illness or those who are not ready to confront mortality. For many people who know they have a terminal illness, that in itself provides the impetus and the courage to go places to which they would rather not go. Therein lies the irony. For one person, knowing you have a terminal illness can result in the belief that the real opportunities of life have passed; for another it is an indication that life has just begun.

I have been telling you about others, how they made and found meaning in their lives. But perhaps this is an opportunity for *you* to begin thinking about your life and who you are. The following is a self-reflective exercise that you can do right now to begin the process. It might lead to a fuller understanding of who you are. In doing this exercise, you might discover that there is more to be explored, that is, beyond the questions I pose. If that's the case, I recommend you contact a professional counselor or therapist. By working with one, you can more fully complete the work you have yet to do.

Find a space where you will not be interrupted. Make yourself comfortable. Sit quietly for a period of time, thinking about who you were as a child. Imagine that you are seven years old. Draw or imagine a triangle (adapted from Birren and Deutchman, "Metaphors and Triangulation of the Self"). Each point on the triangle has a label: your *ideal self* (how you would like to be), your *social image self* (how others see you), and your *real self* (how you see yourself). For each of these selves choose something that most accurately describes you at that age. If you like, choose an animal, a character from literature, or a piece of music. Remembering your favorite activities, friends, stories, music, and games might help you. How did you relate to your parents and your siblings at that time?

Describe in thought or in writing how you understand yourself to be each of those labels, each of those points on the triangle. Repeat the exercise, remembering yourself at seven-year intervals until you get to your present age (i.e., as a fourteen-year-old adolescent, a twenty-one-year-old young adult, and so on). Make certain to do the exercise at your present age. As you look at the collage of who you were and who you have become, in which picture is the ideal self, the social image self, and the real self most similar?

In *Creating a Life: Finding Your Individual Path*, James Hollis suggests some important questions to ask yourself, questions that can be used in the recovery of personal integrity. Work through the answers with a close friend and/or with your journal.

- How am I carrying the unlived life of my parent?
- Where might I be stuck, or blocked, as my parent was blocked?
- Where am I compensating for others, even though it may not be productive for me? How does that shackle me to the consequences of someone else's life?
- How am I passing on to my children that which was passed on to me by my parents? This includes attitudes, strategies, behaviors, and worldviews and can differ from mother to father. How is my relationship with my children similar to the relationship I had with my mother and/or father? What about my other intimate relationships? Are they also bound and defined by familiar patterns?
- What are the memories of playfulness and spontaneity in my childhood? How are those features expressed in my life today?

- Where is the life I would truly want to live, that is, the unlived life that haunts, or summons, or intimidates me?
- Am I asking others to take responsibility for my life? How? Is it subtle or blatant?
- Do I have a sense that I am on the right journey regardless of the approval of others?
- What part of myself do I need to get to know better in order to feel more complete, to feel less like a visitor here? What agenda is now demanding attention? What growing up do I have to achieve? What security, old identity, relationship, or pathology do I need to leave behind?

There is benefit in telling your story to at least one other person, especially if you have experienced toxic shame in your life. Chose the listener carefully. You must feel completely safe; whatever you say must be accepted without judgment. It would be wise to select somebody who has already proven to be able to listen to you—not just hear you—but to *listen* to you. The person you choose must realize that this is about you, not about them. This is *your* story. It is not the time for them to begin to tell you about their childhood, their story, their toxic shame, their psychological wounds.

Speak to that person about toxic shame, looking into the listener's eyes. This will be difficult, for we avoid eye contact when we feel ashamed of what we have done or if we feel shame in who we are. The listener might ask questions for clarification. After you finish your story, ask them what they understand about your experience and what they were feeling as you spoke.

Many readers will be familiar with the story of Moses. He was born a Hebrew in Egypt, at a time when the king of Egypt had commanded midwives to kill all Hebrew male babies. But Moses survived and was raised as an Egyptian by the daughter of the ruler of the land.

After Moses had grown, he saw an Egyptian man beating up a Hebrew man. Moses killed the Egyptian and fled the country. He became a shepherd for his father-in-law in his new homeland. One day he came upon a burning bush, which was not consumed by the fire. In his curiosity, Moses approached the bush. From within the fire, he heard a voice that confronted him and challenged him to stop being a shepherd and become the leader of the Hebrew people, to free them from captivity. In order to take his unique place in history, Moses had to ask the question, Who am I? Am I Hebrew or am I Egyptian? And in order to answer the question, he had to connect to the spiritual level.

That was true for Moses. It was also true for Dietrich Bonhoeffer. He was imprisoned in the infamous Buchenwald camp for two years for working in political opposition to Hitler. Preceding his execution, he wrote this poem while in prison.

"Who Am I?"

Who am I? They often tell me
I would step from my cell's confinement
calmly, cheerfully, firmly,
like a squire from his country-house.

Who am I? They often tell me
I would talk to my warders
freely and friendly and clearly,
as though it were mine to command

Who am I? They also tell me
I would bear the days of misfortune

equably, smilingly, proudly,
like one accustomed to win.

Am I then really all that which other men tell of?
Or am I only what I know of myself,
restless and longing and sick, like a bird in a cage,
struggling for breath, as though hands were compressing my throat,
yearning for colours, for flowers, for the voices of birds,
thirsting for words of kindness, for neighbourliness,
trembling with anger at despotisms and petty humiliation,
tossing in expectation of great events,
powerlessly trembling for friends at an infinite distance,
weary and empty at praying, at thinking, at making,
faint, and ready to say farewell to it all?

Who am I? This or the other?
Am I one person today and tomorrow another?
Am I both at once? A hypocrite before others,
and before myself a contemptibly woebegone weakling?
Or is something within me still like a beaten army,
fleeing in disorder from victory already achieved?

Who am I? They mock me, these lonely questions of mine.
Whoever I am, thou knowest, O God, I am thine.

CHAPTER NINE

Transcendence

The beyond is not what is infinitely remote, but what is nearest at hand.

Dietrich Bonhoeffer

It is only with spiritual knowledge that we can truly face, and understand, death.

Sogyal Rinpoche

Man lives in three dimensions: the somatic, the mental, and the spiritual. The spiritual dimension cannot be ignored, for it is what makes us human.

Victor Frankl

The Buddha's Enlightenment

After Prince Siddhartha left his family to seek understanding of the mystery of human suffering, he sought wisdom through various doctrines and under the guidance of various teachers. But these did not teach him what he was seeking. He continued to wander and then remained for six years on the bank of a river where he practised terrible austerities which reduced his body almost to nothing. (He did not bathe, and he ate sparingly, reducing his body to skin and bones.) For he believed, as many religious people do, that if he denied every desire of the body, he would eventually invigorate the life of the spirit.

But in time he realized that such excessive self-punishment only destroys a person's strength and, instead of freeing the mind, makes it impotent. Siddhartha knew that he must go beyond asceticism, just as he had gone beyond worldly life. Exhausted and thin as a skeleton, he accepted a bowl of rice offered to him by a village girl who was moved to compassion by his weakness. Then he bathed in the river. Five disciples who had shared his austerities abandoned him, feeling betrayed by what they deemed to be his self-indulgence. Perhaps, they said to each other, he was not so enlightened after all.

Siddhartha then started for a place called Bodhi-Gaya, in search of the Tree of Wisdom. As he passed through the forest, such light emanated from his body that the birds were attracted and flew in circles around him, and the animals escorted him. Then he reached the sacred tree. He set a bundle of new-mown hay down and sat on it, uttering this vow: "Here, on this seat, may my body dry up, may my skin and flesh waste away, if I raise my body from this seat before I have attained the knowledge I seek!" The earth quaked six times as he uttered this pronouncement.

A demon called Mara, knowing that Siddhartha's enlightenment would mean his own destruction, decided to interfere. He sent his three beautiful daughters to tempt Siddhartha. The girls sang and danced before him, but Siddhartha remained unmoved in heart and countenance, calm as a lotus on the smooth waters of a lake. The demon's daughters left in defeat. Then the demon sent an army of horrible devils who surrounded the sacred tree and threatened Siddhartha. But so profound was Siddhartha's serenity that they found themselves paralyzed, their arms bound to their sides. Finally, the demon Mara himself rode down from the clouds and hurled his terrible weapon—a huge disk that could cut a mountain in two. But this weapon was worthless against Siddhartha. It was transformed into a garland of flowers and hung suspended above Siddhartha's head.

The demon was finally vanquished. Siddhartha remained in meditation under the sacred tree. Night came and, with it, the enlightenment that he sought. He understood the conditions of all living beings, and then the causes of their rebirth into the world of form. Throughout the world and in all ages, he beheld the birth, life, death, and reincarnation of sentient beings. He remembered his own previous existences and grasped the inevitable links of cause and effect. Finally, he understood the roots of human suffering.

When dawn came, Siddhartha had achieved perfect enlightenment and had become the Buddha. For seven days he remained in meditation, then stayed near the sacred tree for another four weeks. He knew that two paths were open to him. He could at once enter nirvana, the state of ultimate bliss; or he could renounce his own deliverance for a time and remain on earth to teach others what he had learned. The demon Mara urged him to leave the world, but the gods united to implore him, and the Buddha at last yielded to his ultimate destiny as a teacher.

For the rest of his life he labored to teach men and women the mystery of suffering and rebirth. Finally, at the age of eighty, he felt he had grown old and prepared for his end. He lay down beside a river, and the trees about him were immediately flowered. He entered into meditation, then into ecstasy, and finally passed into nirvana. His body was burned on a funeral pyre, which lighted itself and was extinguished at the right moment by a miraculous rain. Thus one human being trod the thorny path to achieve enlightenment and then turned back, sacrificing for a time his own reward, in order to bring light to the darkness in which other human beings lived.

✳

Our lives are a process of enlightenment, of learning, of understanding who we are within ourselves and then in the context of the world in which we exist. This chapter continues with the words and the stories of the people who were living with dying. Among them were those who believed in a particular faith tradition, those who would consider themselves to be agnostics, and others who were atheists. Yet all were spiritual in some sense. This chapter is not a definitive work on transcendence or spirituality. It is a presentation of the experience of the people you have already met, people who knew they were dying.

My study was entitled *Exploring Spiritual and Psychological Issues at the End of Life*. It was exactly that—an exploration of the day-to-day experience of the end of life. I listened and observed as the people told me their stories. The participants didn't tell me when they were speaking about spiritual issues and when they were speaking about psychological issues. They simply spoke about their lives. My division of their words into nine chapters is my effort to understand what they were saying and then to serve as a conduit of information and understanding. They seemed to speak most about who they were. They also spoke about their relationships to others and about the spiritual or transcendent dimensions of their lives. For them, there seemed to be no division of the physical, psychological, and spiritual. They spoke from a place of being. Perhaps they were speaking of all that is psychological and all that is spiritual at the same time. In the words of T. S. Eliot,

> We die with the dying:
> See, they depart, and we go with them.
> We are born with the dead:
> See, they return, and bring us with them.
> The moment of the rose and the moment of the yew-tree
> Are of equal duration . . .
>
> With the drawing of this Love and the voice of this Calling
> We shall not cease from exploration

And the end of all our exploring
Will be to arrive where we started
And know the place for the first time.

Josh, a man in his early thirties, was a patient in the palliative care unit for several weeks. His pain and other symptoms were well controlled; he was comfortable for the most part. His family and friends visited him regularly. One morning when I entered his room I noticed that he was wearing a pair of white silk pajamas rather than the usual hospital attire. When I commented on this, his response was: "I'm going to die today. I wanted to dress for the occasion." I could tell he was serious. Symptomatically, there was no reason for me to believe he would die that day. But at the same time, I trusted he might know something I did not. There was no reason to doubt him. I had seen people predict their deaths before, but rarely in the case of someone who appeared so well. As he spoke, his sister, standing at his side, was weeping softly. She believed him. She knew she would have to say a final goodbye.

I asked him whether he was afraid of dying or death. "No," he said. "It's different from anything I have ever experienced before. I have a calmness within me, and a quiet confidence that my life on earth is complete." We spoke for a time, after which I said, "In one sense, I envy you, in that the mystery of living and dying will be over for you. You will know what that mystery is all about." He chuckled, "I will, and not to worry, I'll send you a letter—that way you'll know too." Josh died forty-eight hours later.

According to the dictionary, "transcendence" is that which is "beyond or above the range of normal or merely physical human experience, surpassing the ordinary." The word derives from the Latin *transcendere* (*trans*, meaning "over," and *scendere*, meaning "climb" or "surmount"). Dying is a time of transition, of moving from one place to another, for people are no longer fixed to the material physical world.

They journey into the spiritual world. For many it seems to "just happen," and yet in some way it requires effort and focus.

People speak of a spiritual component to their experience of living with the knowledge of having a terminal illness. They may call it Nature, the Creator, Allah, God, Jesus, Buddha, or some "higher power"; for others, it is couched in terms of meaning, purpose, and value. Hindus might refer to Shiva, Brahma, or Vishnu, and Sufis call it the "Hidden Essence." Howard Thurman, author of *Creative Encounter*, writes, "It is my belief that in the Presence of God there is neither male nor female, white nor black, Gentile nor Jew, Protestant nor Catholic, Hindu, Buddhist, nor Moslem, but a human spirit stripped to the literal substance of itself before God."

How does one begin to write and speak about transcendence? Transcendence has to do with mystery, which inherently contains some element that cannot be defined. Furthermore, to define mystery is to defy its essence. Yet people who know they have a terminal illness, who know they are dying, speak about the spiritual, the transcendent, as though it were real. Their conversations range beyond the boundaries of religion as they explore their connection to something greater than themselves. This spiritual experience is described variously as love, forgiveness, resolution, self-acceptance, gratitude, and inner strength—all based upon a deep-felt connection to a higher power.

From meeting, in a sense, the people in this book who know they are dying, you know that they speak about a new sense of self and relationships with others. Their sense of who they were and who they had become evolved along with their spiritual nature. Knowing they were living with a terminal illness, they began to pay attention to their inner voice, a voice that guided them to acknowledge the unfamiliar within, the person they had ignored. For some it seemed as though there had been a stranger within them waiting to be introduced, recognized, and acknowledged as essential to their well-being and wholeness. This brought about changes in their psychological and, for some, spiritual consciousness. In becoming acquainted with that inner voice, people felt united with a higher power. And even though each person walked a different path, the common feature was this connection of the inner voice and the higher power.

It seems that knowing you have a terminal illness affects your awareness of yourself, of your relationship with others, and your understanding of your spiritual self; it seems to include a process of transition from an outward journey to an inward journey, from a strength within to a connection to a source of strength outside yourself. Knowing you have a terminal illness pushes you to move from the unconscious and the familiar to a new consciousness and the unfamiliar, from the superficiality of routine to a deeper attention to the soul. Consider the following poem about the need for consciousness that will enable you to move from old patterns to a new understanding of who you are. The poem, written by Portia Nelson, is entitled "Autobiography in Five Short Chapters."

I

I walk down the street.
  There is a deep hole in the sidewalk.
  I fall in.
  I am lost ... I am helpless
    It isn't my fault.
  It takes forever to find a way out.

II

I walk down the same street.
There is a deep hole in the sidewalk.
  I pretend I don't see it.
  I fall in again.

I can't believe I am in this same place.
    But it isn't my fault.
It still takes a long time to get out.

III

I walk down the same street.
There is a deep hole in the sidewalk.
    I see it is there.
    I still fall in . . . it's a habit . . . but,
        my eyes are open.
    I know where I am.
It is my fault.
I get out immediately.

IV

I walk down the same street.
    There is a deep hole in the sidewalk.
    I walk around it.

V

I walk down another street.

As promised, let's revisit some familiar stories—as told by Peggy, Brent, Florence, and Ron. I will begin with Peggy. I learned a great deal about spirituality from her, simply by being with her. I interviewed her only twice, but during the interim I facilitated a family meeting for Peggy, using the process I outlined in chapter 4. Because of the cancer, Peggy had fluid around her heart, which resulted in some pain and discomfort. She also experienced some shortness of breath as the fluid constrained the functioning of her heart. She had several treatment options and wanted to be involved in all decisions regarding her care for as long as possible, which is how the family meeting came about. She was alert and oriented until the last day of her life. She was able to communicate clearly about her physical, psychological, and spiritual experience through the course of her illness.

Our two interviews were only thirteen days apart. She was transferred to the palliative care unit a few days after the first interview. For the last week of her life, I was the physician at the unit. Because there was potential conflict of interest as physician and researcher, I made certain that one of the other physicians was directly involved in her care as well. I saw how her physical energy and strength were waning over the course of that week. At the same time, there was a tremendous sense of spiritual strength emanating from her.

My responsibilities as unit physician for any particular week ended on Friday afternoon. That day Peggy asked to see me as a researcher, not as her physician. She informed me that my study results would be stronger if she were able to confirm, refute, and/or correct the themes I had identified from the first interview. She was right. However, I had witnessed her loss of energy, her increasing weakness, the abbreviated opportunities to have meaningful conversations with family and friends. I suggested that it was unethical for me to proceed with the second interview; I felt that it would be more appropriate for her to spend time and energy with her daughters, not with a researcher. She didn't have the strength to speak aloud and so responded in a emphatic whisper: "It would be unethical for you not to review the themes with me as it is one of my last wishes." She knew how sick she was. For that reason, we decided that her daughters would witness the interview.

The dominant theme was that Peggy's sense of the spiritual was a tremendous source of personal strength and comfort. She perceived this spiritual power as a "force" greater than herself, in the context of which she was able to accept herself, to laugh, to love, and to enjoy life: "I was from a structured religious home, I was brought up a

Roman Catholic and sent to church, then I converted to become an Anglican. The children were baptized Anglican. It was the thing to do. I have no deep beliefs. I knew there was something, but I didn't stop to take time to think of it. So it really wasn't until I got into AA [Alcoholics Anonymous] and started to accept that I was an alcoholic . . . I think that was where I really learned spirituality."

Peggy, in her own voice, makes clear to us what spirituality is in her experience:

> Spirituality to me is a belief in a higher power, a power greater than myself. I happen to be fond of nature; I can take pleasure just looking outside. Spirituality isn't any one thing. It comes from inside for me, and when I find I'm in a very bad space and discontent and everything, I know I have to go back to basics and think of spirituality. Then I can ground myself again.
>
> I'm having to adjust to knowing that I'm not going to get better. I'm not used to a defeatist mind-set, and the spirituality is what's pulling me through. As I mentioned to you, I'm in Alcoholics Anonymous and involved quite deeply and it's done a lot for me. One of our things is to "Let go and let God." I've relied on that. I have to use the word trust in turning myself over and praying for help for my children. I'm acknowledging my spirituality more then I ever have.

"Let go and let God" is a slogan used by Alcoholics Anonymous; the phrase may seem simplistic, but for many it represents the core concept of spirituality. It has been described as easy to say and difficult to follow. Peggy didn't explain the meaning of the term, and in order to more deeply understand it I turned to Frederick Buechner's *Telling Secrets*, which explores the concept.

When Buechner was a young boy, his father committed suicide. After the memorial service, his father was not spoken of again. Then, when Buechner himself was a father, one of his daughters had an eating disorder. In his despair and pain, he decided to seek help by attending an Alanon meeting, despite the fact that neither he nor his family were alcoholics. It was through that group that he became familiar with the slogan "Let go and let God." He explains that it means to

[l]et go of the dark, which you wrap yourself in like a straitjacket, and let in the light. Stop trying to protect, to rescue, to judge, to manage the lives around you—your children's lives, the lives of your husband, your wife, your friends—because that is just what you are powerless to do. Remember that the lives of other people are not your business. They are their business. They are God's business because they all have God whether they use the word God or not. Even your own life is not your business. It also is God's business. Leave it to God. . . .

Go where your best prayers take you. Unclench the fists of your spirit and take it easy. Breathe deep of the glad air and live one day at a time. Know that you are precious. . . . Know that you can trust God.

For Peggy, this simple phrase contributed to her coming to know herself and ultimately to trust in a higher power for her own sense of fulfillment and for the well-being of her daughters. In attending AA meetings, Peggy began to speak her truth, to tell her secrets, to come to a point of accepting who she was, including the pain of her childhood, the anguish of being an alcoholic, and the freedom in knowing who she was. Peggy had to let go—to let go of her painful past, her clinging to the present in recognizing the disease was incurable, her fears of the future—for herself as well as her children and grandchildren.

Jack Kornfield and Christina Feldman tell an interesting Hindu story: In India, hunters had a proven way of catching monkeys. A half-coconut would be hollowed out, and a hole made that was only large enough to let a monkey's open hand pass through. The coconut was then pinned to the ground and tempting food placed beneath. A monkey would approach, intent on getting hold of the food beneath the coconut, but as soon as it grasped the food in its fist, it found itself unable to pull its hand and the food free of the coconut. Imprisoned, it would stay, caught by its own unwillingness to open its fist. They summarize the moral of the story: "Letting go is the essence of the spiritual life, the heart of spiritual practice."

Peggy expressed her awareness that as her physical self was drained of its strength her spiritual strength increased. During the family meeting near the end of her life, she said, "My cup of joy is filled to overflowing and that which overflows is also full, as that which is physical in me gets ever weaker, that which is spiritual gets ever stronger." When asked about the role of health care providers with regard to spirituality, she said,

> It's a very difficult one to answer because if somebody starts spouting on about spirituality, I back off. It's such a private concept, so my answer would almost be that the patient has to call the shots in terms of bringing it up. You asked me about my definition of spirituality. Other people have different definitions and that's fine. It works for them. There's no right or wrong way of looking at it. It's not something I would like to have forced on me.

In her second interview Peggy was very weak and able to speak only in a very soft voice. Two of her three daughters were present. When asked about the spiritual dimension, she said, "My experience of the spiritual changes every day. My sense of the spiritual increases from day to day—it's dynamic, it's changing. I think it's stronger today than it was when we spoke two weeks ago. That's because I'm needing Him more."

At that point, Peggy had transcended her physical limitations. She was not confined by her physical body; she enjoyed a freedom in her spiritual reality. Although she was pain-free, she was unable to care for her own physical needs, for she was too weak. She was entirely content in the presence of her family, acknowledging that her sense of well-being resulted not from looking forward in sadness at what would be missed but by looking back and celebrating what she had been given. Her boundaries of existence had changed from the defined world of the physical domain to the undefined world of the spiritual domain.

Through the course of her lifetime, Peggy came to accept who she was. She also grew to appreciate that she was accepted unconditionally by what she called the "higher power." This provided great solace for her.

Perhaps you have your own concept of spirituality—a connection or relationship to God or some other power, to a neighbor, a close friend, a partner or spouse, perhaps your inner self or the world and environment around you. How is spirituality related to our acceptance of ourselves? Is it only in accepting ourselves fully that we are able to give the attribute of being accepted to the higher power as well? Is this what Saint Paul meant when he said, "When I was a child, I used to speak as a child, think as a child, reason as a child; when I became a man, I did away with childish things. For now we see in a mirror dimly, but then face to face; now I know in part, but then I shall know fully just as I also have been fully known." Is Paul speaking of knowing ourselves fully "in the presence of God," or is he speaking of knowing God fully?

The traditional interpretation of this passage is that our perception of ourselves and of God is limited, as we are confined to a physical body. When we meet our Creator, this will change to a full knowledge. Of this passage, Dr. Deepak Chopra states:

> But that isn't the only way to interpret the passage. St. Paul could be making the point that the observer who is attempting to see who God

is winds up seeing his own reflection. Since there is no way around this limitation [of seeing only oneself], we have to make the best use of it that we can. Like a child growing up, we have to evolve toward a more complete vision, until the day arrives when we can see the whole as God does. Our self-reflections tell our own story along the way, usually in symbolic form as dreams do—hence the clouded mirror.

For Brent, a near-death experience while on the palliative care unit had a profound effect. His experience of spiritual awakening "just happened"—Brent could neither initiate it nor avoid it. Until that occurred, he was living with a stranger. That stranger was himself. The near-death experience altered his sense of the spiritual and ultimately altered his sense of himself. "I'm much more spiritual now than I ever was before, because I do believe that I saw and did things that only someone who comes within a fraction of a second of remaining on the other side could do. I remember being very content there and very happy, even though I was very, very sick." In that context Brent began to hear his inner voice, a voice that seemed to have been mute for decades. His work was to listen, to focus, and to respect whatever surfaced for him. By paying attention to the voice, he became a stranger to those around him but was no longer a stranger to himself.

For Brent, forgiving himself and others was a key element of spirituality, as was addressing the issue of God. "Forgiving those you think have done something to you and forgiving yourself for things you think you've done; dealing with spirituality, dealing with God for the first time in my life, I decided that I had to either believe in God or not. I prayed."

In *The Tibetan Book of Living and Dying*, Sogyal Rinpoche says,

Not everyone believes in a formal religion, but nearly everyone believes in forgiveness. Forgiveness exists in the nature of God; it is already there. God has already forgiven you, for God is forgiveness itself. But can you forgive yourself? That's the real question.... All religions stress the power of forgiveness, and this power is never more necessary, nor more deeply felt, than when someone is dying. Through forgiving and being forgiven, we purify ourselves of the darkness of what we have done, and prepare ourselves most completely for the journey through death.

"I believe in God now." Brent continued.

Not that I didn't believe in Him before, but now I know that there's so much more out there than I'd ever imagined. By praying and asking for forgiveness and giving forgiveness, I think I made a deal. I would never take my own life now. I know it's a gift. I'll never be the same. I mean, no matter how bad my life may seem, I can always find something that makes me feel fortunate. I don't know if that's spirituality. I just have this belief that things are meant to be. Everything will work out. When you pray and your prayer is answered, you've got to believe that something, somehow happened here.

Brent confirmed that for him spirituality meant a belief in God, in prayer, and in the crucial role of forgiveness—both the requesting and granting of forgiveness. He did not associate this experience with a particular religion, but he believed that it provided a connection to those who had died before him. He had a sense of God being with him at all times, which meant that he was never alone. "I felt that somehow I'd been given a gift. Maybe I was just learning that life was worth living. Even on oxygen and unable to walk, life was better than death, but death was not a bad thing either. My Maker is powerful, strong and full of love. In spite of being a homosexual and having HIV and not having fulfilled a 'life of Christian duty,' I know now that God loves me unconditionally."

In spirituality, Brent found a source of strength and freedom from the fear of death. "Where do I get the strength to go on? I believe that comes from within, from knowing now that I'm not alone, that there is Someone there. Whether we call Him Allah, Buddha, Jesus—whatever you want to call Him—there is Someone there. I'm no longer afraid of dying."

Acknowledging a spiritual presence or reality in his life required courage on Brent's part. Many of his friends did not accept his new spirituality. "I tell you, admitting to someone that you believe in God in a gay community is not easy, 'cause right away they think you're strange. They don't want to have anything to do with you."

Through his experience of unconditional love from God, Brent was able to learn to love himself unconditionally. For him, the healing of the soul included healing wounds of childhood and adulthood, and ridding himself of self-hate.

> You can give up, or you can put your faith in someone or something to help you along. That's what I did, I let God take control. You have to love yourself unconditionally, meaning warts and all. No one's perfect. We're all deserving of love and we're all deserving to heal, but healing is something that has to happen in the soul first, I think, and then the body heals. It's funny how you have to heal all those old wounds from childhood. Having been a gay man and a gay young man and a gay prepubescent boy, I grew up with all this self-hate. Once you accept that all of that is just bull, you learn to love yourself as an individual. Then you can start to heal.

For Brent, psychological and spiritual aspects were closely related. In recognizing spirituality in his near-death experience, he broached the psychological by reviewing his personal history and facing his fears and self-loathing. He said,

End-of-life issues, especially for gay men, have to do with God. They're afraid of hell, they're afraid of all of the punishment for being bad, so their fear of death is terrifying. They believe they'll pay for their sins, pay for what they've been. But through God you realize that we're all equal, we're all loved, we're all okay. I like the idea of saying we're created in His image. If we're in His image, we're okay. If we weren't, we wouldn't be here, pure and simple. If He didn't want us, we wouldn't be here. Mistakes of nature don't occur. It's the way we were meant to be, and we should be accepted and loved for what we are.

In confronting death, Brent experienced the fullness of life. "I'm aware of the simplest things in life now: a plant growing, a bird flying. You know you've seen them before but they meant nothing; you see them afterward and they mean everything. I'm taking care of my next-door neighbor now. I took on the role of caregiver because she needed someone, and I could do that for her." And through spirituality, Brent experienced love without fear, forgiveness without guilt. "God loves everybody, and no matter what you've done, he still loves you, you know. You don't have to fear him and you don't have to ask for forgiveness—he's already forgiven you. All of the guilt just flies away, it just goes away." Brent's near-death experience was the ultimate wake-up call, spiritually and psychologically. "It was like being reborn. It was truly being given an opportunity to understand that we all control our destiny to some extent by the way we behave in our present life. A lot of people go through life pretending they're something they're not."

And in truly knowing oneself and believing in a higher power, one finds resolution, wholeness, and integrity. "All of a sudden all the pieces fit. People go around searching for what'll make them happy—drugs, cars, sex, whatever it is that their addictions are and they usually are addictions. But once you find and put the pieces of this puzzle together, you no longer need these outside things to make you feel complete. You understand the wholeness a person achieves when he or she starts to believe in a higher power."

Brent spoke of wholeness; Peggy spoke of accepting herself. Peggy grew to accept herself over a seven-year period, coming to appreciate that the spiritual dimension within her was increasing over time. Brent realized his sense of wholeness through his near-death experience, then underwent a psychological process of accepting who he was. He moved from a place of self-loathing to feeling healed and whole. He believed that in his near-death experience he had been in the presence of a higher power that loved him unconditionally, and therefore he was able to begin to love himself unconditionally as well.

Like Brent, Florence also experienced spirituality as having a component of self-acceptance. "Spirituality, for me, has something to do with self-acceptance. I don't think I knew I was spiritual until I reached a stage in my life very recently where I accepted who I was. I was reading Ecclesiastes yesterday, and the idea of a punishing, judging God seemed so foreign." However, for Florence, the stronger spiritual reality was experienced as inner peace, which she found primarily in nature. "My spirituality is tied to nature, so when I look for help, instead of looking up, I look around. That's where my peace lies." In fact, Florence saw nature as the most powerful component of spirituality:

> For me, spirituality is walking along the path in the park and seeing a fir tree, bigger round than my arms can stretch and reaching up into the sky. I go over to the tree (I wouldn't care who was looking) and, putting my arms around that tree, I take a deep breath and say, "Give me some of your strength!"

One time I was down on the path by the water, and I heard this blowing and puffing, and all of a sudden it came to me—the killer whales were coming! I ran and looked, and suddenly there they were. It was like a religious ecstasy. Now I know what an ecstasy feels like. I'm happy that I have grown from thinking that I was a failed religious person to knowing that I have this spirituality. Maybe that is the reason that I can be as courageous as I have been with what I've been through for the last ten years.

At the same time, she had a longing for faith, for a belief in God. "I would love to believe, I would love to have faith. I'm an agnostic, not an atheist. I know that it's not that I'm not willing, it's just that I don't understand it."

Following the death of her daughter, Florence took solace in nature.

One day I visited a Buddhist temple. It just seemed so right—lighting the incense, which I did in my daughter's name. When I sat down, the priest was talking about the meaning of death. Beautiful. He talked about the tree and the leaf that falls in its given time and nourishes the earth from which the new leaves come. Nobody is at fault for the leaf falling. I liked that. Nobody was guilty of anything. Sometimes a leaf will fall in May or June or July. I went out of there partially healed. This was when I began to see that I could find a religion, a spirituality in the things that I loved.

My mother could hold a leaf in her hand and be as adoring and wondering as a person holding a crucifix or reading a verse in the Bible. In her old age, I used to drive her down to the park, stop the car, go out and take a leaf off a tree, pick a berry, a flower, or a blade of grass and bring it to her. Nature is so beautiful. She would say, "Only man is not so good." I think I'm like her. I see no deliberate cruelty in nature. I see the laws of nature taking place and sure, bad things do happen. But it's not as though you're guilty of anything. It doesn't happen to you 'cause you were bad. It gives me such a sense of rightness, of power, of control, that I'm now trusting my instincts.

Florence also found healing in nature:

I'm not religious, but I'm spiritual. I believe that there is a guiding force in life and in my life especially, which is related to the world of nature. I needed to have some form of higher power in my life because I wanted to put my daughter in the hands of a higher power. I became desperate to find something, without defining it or giving it a name or color or anything. After my daughter died, we took a trip across the country, and my eyes were drawn to the mountaintops, imagining I would see her there. I was drawn to the vision of the Big Bang, which was not Creation as described in the Bible. I knew from science that nothing ever gets destroyed. It's there in some other form, so that the strength and the power is still with us. I saw this as a wind high in the mountains, and I was able then to visualize the path that I needed to take to lay my children at the foot of this mountain and go away feeling peaceful, just as other people go into church and put their cares in the hands of God.

Based on her earlier studies, which included world religions, and in keeping with her religious tradition, Florence's experience reminded her of Psalm 121: "I will lift up my eyes to the mountains; From whence shall my help come?" And as her illness progressed, Florence turned increasingly to a higher power for relief from her suffering. "So this is where I'm at now, looking for spiritual help. I even use the word 'Lord' and I use the word 'God.'"

Ron described himself as an atheist, saying it was difficult for an atheist to embrace spirituality. Ron did not see terminal illness as a reason to change himself or alter his previous beliefs. He respected science but could acknowledge a place for religion in the lives of others, at times longing for components of religion to make his life easier, especially the belief in life after death. He stated clearly that he was not able to talk himself into believing in an afterlife. "I tried to believe when I was dying in the hospital. What a hypocrite! If Jesus wants me, he'll accept me for what I am. I'm not going to change all my beliefs and values just because I'm in a dire situation. I am what I am, and I'm either accepted for what I am or I'll go my own way. I believe in science. I just can't see somebody overseeing this whole big picture. I can see how religion does bring relief, comfort, and a sense of purpose to a lot of people."

Even though Ron denied being a spiritual person, he recognized in himself a component of spirituality when it was defined as having purpose, meaning, value, and integrity. He summarized it by saying that for him spirituality was equal to doing good and what was right. For him, the moral code was based on the Ten Commandments. It was easier for him to consider inner strength from a sense of morality, for with a moral purpose one has guidelines for living and a sense of integrity.

The spiritual experience is one of profound love and acceptance—seeking to live in truth and forgiveness, with a deep understanding of healing and wholeness. For some people, learning that they have a terminal illness is a gift, a gift of time to pay close attention to who they really are, discover the sense of a higher power, and grow in self-acceptance and love. As this spiritual discovery unfolds, the fear of death is diminished or even eliminated.

Based on the interviews and conversations with my coresearchers in this study, spirituality was for them a sense of connection to a higher power. This higher power provides unconditional love, and the individual thus learns to love unconditionally as well. In the context of that love, the individual accepts herself with an awareness of the wounds of lifetime, beginning in childhood. One is then able to extend that acceptance to others. Because the higher power offers forgiveness and love without judgment, the individual is also able to forgive herself and others for all transgressions. In the strength of this higher power, one experiences healing and a deep connection with self and others.

The experience of the higher power is personal, private. One no longer feels the boundaries and limits of self, for strength, love, and integrity result in a wholeness not previously experienced. This is strongly felt in nature, from watching the smallest bird to embracing a tree to looking up at the mountaintops. There is a wholeness, a oneness with nature, which includes an extension of the self—beyond the self—to the higher power. In this context, one is filled with joy, a sense of purpose, and all fear of death vanishes. Being witness to the journeys of these people taught me that in embracing who we are physically, psychologically, and spiritually, dying is not so much about living in fear; paradoxically, it's about finding a way to integrate all of who I am—past and present—into a new wholeness of who I am as a person. Therein I find peace, compassion, and hope.

How do I change my consciousness, my awareness of life? Whether you choose to do so is entirely up to you. And how you do that is entirely up to you as well. This part of your journey, of my journey, can begin at any time. People seem to wrestle with questions such as:

- Who am I?
- Why are we here?
- Is there life after death? If so, what is it like?
- What does reincarnation mean to me?
- What is my purpose in life? What is the meaning of life?

- What makes my heart sing?
- Where is my sorrow, my grief, my pain?
- Is the religious tradition I grew up in the same as what I practice today? If so, why is it important to me? If not, why is it not important to me?
- What does death mean to me? What has been the experience of dying and death in my life?
- If I didn't have to live up to the expectations of anyone else, who would I be?
- Is God, Buddha, Allah, Shiva, Brahman, Vishnu, or any higher power important to me?
- If I knew I had hours, days, weeks, months, or years of life remaining, how would I spend my time? Who would I spend my time with?

The inward journey seems not to be a linear process. This may be a process you have already started, and you may already know your way. If not, and you're interested in exploring your spiritual self, know that your spiritual reality is unique. Ways of exploring this important part of who you are can happen in discussions over meaningful topics, in self-reflection through journal writing, in therapy, in understanding yourself by reading about myths, wisdom literature, and world religions, in religious traditions and in contemplative practices. If you prefer to walk while you contemplate, you might find that walking a labyrinth is effective. To do so is to purposefully walk a metaphor of your life's journey. It symbolizes a walk to your inner being—and back again. It is not intended to confuse you; neither is it a puzzle to be solved. The purpose of a labyrinth is to demonstrate that the way into its center is actually also the way out from its center. It will broaden your sense of who you are.

In *From Age-ing to Sage-ing*, Zalman Schachter-Shalomi and Ronald Miller speak of various contemplative practices:

To a Hindu, for example, meditation might refer to mantra chanting. To a Christian of the contemplative tradition, it might involve concentrating on the sacred heart of Jesus. To a Jew, it might mean chanting the prayer "Shema Yisrael" ("Hear, O Israel") and entering into the stillness pointed to [created by] these sacred words. To a Buddhist, meditation might refer to breath control [controlled breathing] and the impartial observation of thoughts. To others, it might mean quieting the mind and receiving guidance from the Higher Self.

A spiritual journey brings our whole being into question. As we become quiet in order to listen to the voice in our heart, we begin to hear and to see who we really are. Jack Kornfield, a Ph.D. in clinical psychology trained as a Buddhist monk, tells the following story of a spiritual journey:

Aris, a young princess, was betrothed to a fearful dragon in payment for her parents' misdeeds. Upon learning her fate, she feared for her life. In the midst of her fears, she recovered her wits and sought the council of a wise woman who had raised twelve children and twenty-nine grandchildren, and knew the ways of dragons and men. The wise woman told Aris that she must marry the dragon. She also informed her of proper ways to approach him. She gave instruction to Aris about the wedding night, telling her to wear ten beautiful wedding gowns, one on top of the other.

The wedding party took place in the palace, after which the dragon carried the princess to his bedchamber. As the dragon approached his bride, she stopped him, telling him she had to remove her wedding attire before she would be able to offer herself to him. She added, as instructed by the wise woman, that he too must properly remove his attire. He willingly agreed to do that.

"As I take off each layer of my gown, you must also remove a layer." The princess removed the first wedding gown and watched as the dragon shed his outer layer of scaly armor. It was painful for the dragon. It was a pain he knew as he had periodically removed that layer before. The princess proceeded to remove the second gown, the third and the fourth. Each time the dragon did the same, removing a deeper layer of scales. By the fifth gown and the fifth layer, the dragon was weeping copious tears of pain. Yet the princess continued.

As each layer was removed, the dragon's skin became more tender. His form softened. He became lighter and lighter. Upon removing the tenth gown, the dragon removed the tenth layer and the last vestige of dragon form. From the form emerged a man, a fine prince whose eyes sparkled like those of a child, finally released from the ancient spell of his dragon form. Princess Aris and her new husband were left to the pleasures of their bridal chamber.

Of this story, Kornfield says,

As in a dream, all the figures in such a story can be found within us. We find the scaly dragon and the attending princess, the wise grandmother, the irresponsible king and queen, the hidden prince, and the unknown one who cast his enchantment long ago. What this story reveals from the start is that the journey is not about going into the light. The forces of our human history and entanglement are tenacious and powerful. The path to inner freedom requires passing through them. Receiving grace, opening to illumination, becoming wise has not been easy even for the masters. It is described as a difficult purification: cleansing, letting go, and stripping away.... It is painful to cast off our own scales, and the dragons guarding the way are fierce. It requires the inspiration of angels; it requires diving into the ocean of tears.... [W]e cannot just go to the last page of the story and live happily ever after. We have to go through the great fear of marrying the dragon, the seeking of wise counsel, and the long process of releasing the painful habits we have clung to. It is the difficult, slow letting go that allows us to awaken from our enchantment.

Conclusion

Embracing Life

But, Oh for the touch of a vanished hand, and the sound of a voice that is still.

Alfred, Lord Tennyson

And soonest our best men with thee do go.

John Donne

In a dark time, the eye begins to see.

Theodore Roethke

It's 2001, spring, a Monday morning. Every morning begins the same way: the 5:30 alarm wakes me, I let the cat out, then pick up the morning paper from the front porch. I make coffee and check e-mail. Breakfast and the paper. Then a second cup of coffee as I settle in to work on this book. I'm writing the chapter on truth: how to speak your truth, how to hear the truth of another.

A few hours later, my wife calls me. Jean rarely interrupts me when I'm writing. I finish the sentence, then scribble a few words on a piece of paper so I won't lose the thought I'm working on.

My parents are spending part of their vacation with us. As I enter the living room, I sense a tension that didn't exist the night before. My mother tells me that she has just spoken to my brother, by phone. He's worried about Nancy, my oldest sister.

Nancy was diagnosed with breast cancer nine years ago. Five years after the diagnosis, following surgery, chemotherapy, and radiation, she was given the "All-Clear Five-Year Survival Award." That's how it had been interpreted. We assumed she had been granted a long-term reprieve, cancer in remission for decades. She could look forward to celebrating the marriages of her two sons, she would hold her grand-children in her arms, she would travel with her husband, Ray, after his early retirement—something both of them were looking forward to.

Doubt crept into their lives when the cancer spread to her spine six years after the initial diagnosis. For the next three years she rode the roller coaster of hope and despair. She had to travel eight hours by car to Winnipeg for her checkups, for assessment whenever a new symptom emerged, and to get radiation treatments for the lesion on her spine.

On Monday, May 14, when my brother called Nancy, he realized that something wasn't right. Something had changed since he'd last spoken to her. She seemed discouraged and tired, and her speech was different than it had been on previous calls.

I decided to call Nancy. Her "Hello" said a lot. There was no spark, no energy in her voice. She sounded tired—more so than she had in a long while. Actually, she sounded frightened. I asked her how she was. Her voice quavered as she told me about her nausea, the weakness in her right arm, and the fatigue. She denied having pain.

Nancy told me that she had been living with constant nausea for some time. She added that this wasn't living, especially with the increasing weakness she was experiencing at the same time. The gradual deterioration, the roller-coaster ride, had gone on too long. Spring had arrived in her northern Manitoba community. She wanted to be outside in the sunshine, to be going for walks, to be planting flowers in her garden, to be spending time with family and friends.

Something was happening in her body. She couldn't concentrate as well anymore, her right hand seemed not to cooperate at times, occasionally her speech sounded slurred, and she had difficulty walking. She didn't have pain, but she was never free of the nausea. She stopped going out with her friends. Much of the time she worked hard to stay in one position. She didn't want anyone to drop by for a cup of tea anymore. What did this really mean? What were these new symptoms all about?

In the first years after her diagnosis, Nancy had wondered how God could let this happen to her. She had even questioned whether she still believed in God at all. Not now. Now her faith was a tremendous source of strength. At the same time, she wanted either to be free of the nausea or to die. She was getting very tired of living with cancer.

Nancy had never said this to anyone in our family before. She wasn't one to complain or to ask for help. In fact, she was the one who usually took care of others. So I asked her, "Do you want someone to come be with you?" She skirted the issue. It was hard work to get her to answer that question. (She didn't want to impose on anyone. In fact, she had always prided herself on her independence.) By the end of the phone call, she tearfully said that she would really like someone to come to be with her.

My parents' holiday ended with that phone call. The journey they had dreaded for years, ever since Nancy learned that the cancer had spread, had begun. Women with breast cancer that has spread to the bone and the brain do not survive. Any treatment at this point was palliative—for comfort only. They knew they were going home to do one of the most difficult and heartbreaking things they would ever have to do.

After our call ended, Nancy and Ray waited for a phone call from her doctor, who in turn was waiting to hear from the oncologist in Winnipeg. People frequently have to wait for health care, even in major cities. When they live in isolated communities, they may have to wait longer. Waiting for an hour or two, or even a day or two, might not seem like a hardship when you are healthy and busy. When you are in pain, experiencing nausea or fear that you might be in a life-threatening situation, five seconds seems like forever. Waiting added to Nancy's suffering. It also added to Ray's suffering.

The call didn't come that afternoon. It came a day later. Arrangements were made for Nancy and Ray to be flown to Winnipeg for assessment. The cost of the airfare was high, which made the flight prohibitive. But the eight-hour drive was unthinkable given the pain and constant nausea Nancy was experiencing. Because of Nancy's difficulty in walking, the Manitoba health-care system would pay for her to fly with an assistant—in this case, Ray. I don't know whether that would have been true for her in other parts of the country or in the United States.

Nancy was the oldest of four children in our family. We grew up on a farm in rural Manitoba. She knew when she was five years old that she wanted to be a nurse. In fact, her favorite book was entitled *Nurse Nancy*, and in time she lived out her dream. After nurse's training she moved to northern Manitoba. She loved the community, the winter sports, the fishing in the summer, singing in the community choir, meeting with other women to work on crafts, playing the piano for the church choir. It was a great place to raise her sons.

She loved being a nurse. She worked on the surgical ward for many years. The night shifts allowed her to be at home when her family was at home, to sleep during the day. When her sons were older she got a clinical-administrative position, which gave her regular daytime hours. Over the years, she came to realize that there was a need in the hospital and in the community for a program to care for the dying. With her colleagues and volunteers, she developed a palliative care program that continues to grow. Through the program people with a terminal illness, both in the community and in the hospital, receive care and support.

On Wednesday, May 16, Nancy and Ray were flown to Winnipeg, where they learned that the cancer had spread to her brain. It was a five-minute presentation of information. She had at least three tumors. Where were they located? How do they account for the symptoms? What might be expected with treatment, without treatment?

The doctor seemed inclined to give the minimal amount of information. With the number of people he had to see in the course of a day, he couldn't afford to stay for more than five minutes with each one if he wanted to get home at a reasonable hour. And somebody would need more of his time, somebody in crisis, somebody who just couldn't bear what he had to tell them and would need him to go over the information again and again.

I've been there. In fact, Nancy herself was familiar with this situation, with the constant tension between the patient's needs and the doctor's time. She used to talk to me about it. The doctor doing rounds in the hospital has time for only five, at most ten, minutes per patient. You can't expect him to stay longer, given the number of patients he has to see in one day. The health-care system simply can't afford a larger investment of time.

On hearing the results of the CAT scan, Nancy was overwhelmed with both relief and fear. At least now she knew what to expect: radiation, once a day for the next five days—with the hope of decreasing the size of the tumors and eliminating the symptoms. The treatment would be done in Winnipeg. She was told she had three to twelve months to live. "Ray and I will have to make the most of the time we have remaining." She now had an explanation for her symptoms, and she had nursed others who had brain tumors. She knew what would follow.

She hadn't known how to speak of her fears earlier. Perhaps she just didn't want to speak about them. (Only after she died were large quantities of literature on Alzheimer's disease found among her belongings.) Now, she didn't know how to tell her sons that the brain tumors would be the cause of her death. Her oldest son and his wife were expecting their first child. She preferred to say that they were expecting her first grandchild. How could she ever let them know that she might not hold that child, even though to do so was her dearest hope? Her youngest son was thinking about changing jobs, about moving to another city, about getting married. He had his own stresses, his own life to live. How could she burden him with her fear?

Eventually, she told them nothing because she couldn't. She was too sick to speak. The nausea was too great. Her symptoms silenced her. Because of the nausea and exhaustion, she couldn't concentrate. All she wanted was to lie quietly, with minimal movement.

In Winnipeg, Nancy and Ray were staying with their youngest son and his girlfriend in their condominium. There was a steep flight of stairs to get up to the first floor. It was nothing for them, but it was like climbing Mount Everest for Ray because he had to support Nancy, who was weak, unable to rely on her right hand, and feeling as though she might collapse at any moment.

Ray felt that he was forced to be both husband and doctor. He drove her to the hospital for radiation treatment every day. They didn't ask about additional services or equipment that might have been available to them. They managed on their own.

I've seen a lot of people in similar situations. And I've heard similar stories from many of my patients over the years: the determination to function independently, the will to do it on their own, the resistance to being a burden to someone else, to messing up the smooth flow of the system. Then, once the patient has been hospitalized for a few days, the caregiver realizes how tiring it was to provide full-time care for someone they love. The desire for independence can result in two patients instead of one, because the caregiver will suffer fatigue— both physical and emotional—perhaps even injury.

Over the phone, I suggested they call an ambulance for transportation to and from the hospital every day. If Nancy arrived by ambulance, she would get better attention. "They'll see how sick you really are," I told her. "Don't put on your best front anymore. Let them know how tough this is for both of you. My god, Nancy, you of all people deserve to be taken care of through all of this. Ask someone for assistance. Don't do this alone. If you fall down those stairs, both of you could be badly injured."

I was torn between being a brother and flying there to be a doctor as well. Nancy seemed to be suffering more than was necessary. Any doubt about whether I should go vanished when my mother called from Winnipeg to say, "We need you here." I phoned my brother. We decided it was time for both of us to get to Winnipeg as soon as possible. Twenty-four hours later, we were on our way.

I wanted to be there immediately, and yet I didn't want to ever get there. I didn't want what was happening to be happening. I didn't want to see my sister suffer; I didn't want her to die. I didn't want to see my mother's heart breaking. I didn't want to have to hear the truth; I didn't want to speak the truth.

My feet were like lead weights as I climbed the stairs to the condo. When I entered the living room, Nancy was lying in a fetal position on the couch. She was holding her head, the nausea overwhelming. Her doctor had prescribed a new medication that morning, but at that time she felt no relief. Her husband sat next to her, holding her hand, raising a glass of water to her lips every few minutes in the hope that she would take a sip.

This wasn't just another patient—this was my sister. I'd done this for hundreds, possibly thousands, of other people. I'd done this for colleagues, for friends, and for friends of friends. I didn't want to have to do this for my sister. I didn't want it to be her, lying on that couch. I didn't want to see the look in her eyes that told me she knew why I was there.

And I didn't want to know what I knew. I didn't want to feel what I felt—the sadness, the grief, the panic. It's not three to twelve months; it's not even three to twelve weeks. Who told them it would be months? Who planted a seed of hope that won't even have time to germinate?

Ray was providing the most amazing care. His heart must have been breaking; he must have been screaming on the inside *Where the hell is everybody? When is somebody going to give her something that will take the nausea away?*

Another nurse, Pat, who had known Nancy for nine years, saw her name on the local hospital's radiation slate. Pat tracked down Nancy's phone number at the condominium and called her. She called and spoke with Ray at some length, asking questions. What's happening? Who is providing nursing care? Who helps with bathing, assessment of pain or nausea, medications? What additional equipment has been brought into the home to make care easier? When will Nancy be reassessed by the oncologist?

She discovered that Nancy and Ray were on their own. It seemed that Nancy had slipped through the cracks in the system. Her oncologist had retired. Nancy didn't know who was responsible for her care. Who was to guide them through the next part of the journey? Who could let them know what was available to make a difficult time less so? Who would order services? Who would order or recommend equipment, wheelchairs, commodes, or other pieces of equipment that might mean less risk of injury, fewer stairs to climb, more privacy, less awkwardness, less discomfort?

An hour later, Pat called back to say that Nancy would be seen by an oncologist the next day. The family breathed a sigh of relief. We had hoped that Nancy's suffering would be reduced. Ray hoped that someone would recognize just how sick his wife really was, how much she was suffering. Nancy always put on such a good front when she arrived at the hospital for the radiation. And she was only there for a few minutes, so people didn't really get a chance to see how sick she was, how the nausea was overwhelming.

This had been a very lonely experience for Ray. He wanted to believe that Nancy would have twelve months to live, not three; that the radiation would work; that she would improve and then get chemotherapy, as the doctor had suggested; that Nancy would be strong enough to go home.

Ray wanted to trust the health care professionals, but in the city the system is so big and indifferent at times. In his home community, people know each other, word gets out, and eventually you get help. In the city, it's hard to know who to ask for help. He wondered whether there wasn't more that could be done for Nancy. He thought they had an oncologist, but now they find out he's retired. What's happening?

It's the individuals—the Pats in the system—who make all the difference. Twenty-four hours later Nancy was admitted to a palliative care unit. That included an IV for the dehydration, a change in medication for the nausea. She had a beautiful view. She overlooked the forks of the Red and Assiniboine Rivers, a famous Canadian landmark. Her immediate family was with her. One sister-in-law sent a quilt that added a personal touch to the room; nieces sent pictures and cards.

The facility to which Nancy had been admitted was amazing—one of the finest palliative care units in the country. Members of the staff take over the care in a nonobtrusive way. The family is freed to be the family, to simply be present, to provide the care they choose to provide—love, foot rubs, back rubs, hand-holding, stories, music (recorded and live), occasional laughter, prayers, the arranging and rearranging of the many floral arrangements that are sent by family and friends from near and far.

Our family knows what a palliative care unit is. Initially, nobody speaks about it. Hope for a reversal of symptoms, for a tumor that will decrease in size and perhaps disappear, prevails. That hope overshadows the reality. Nobody dares to speak the truth out loud.

The change in medication was beneficial. The nausea diminished and eventually cleared. And although the improvement was minimal, it triggered a great hope in those Nancy loves: *This must mean that she has twelve months, not three.* At the same time, we knew at some level that the signs and symptoms of the severity of the disease process were no longer masked. The hope that the radiation could eliminate all the symptoms was waning. I struggled with what to do, what to say.

The voices of the people who have spoken in this book are with me. I hear their words. I remember writing that when someone has a terminal illness, that person will have something to say to those who are close, and in turn they will have something to say to the person who is dying. I am no longer researching it; I'm no longer writing about it. I'm living it. We're living it. This is very different. This is very sad and very painful. It is too hard.

We all knew how sick Nancy was. Nancy was dying. But nobody was saying a great deal. My brother sensed the urgency. He spoke about it. So did my other sister, Bev. It confirmed my feeling that I must apply my professional knowledge to my personal experience. I suggested a family meeting. That is what the people I interviewed for this book would recommend at this point. They said: "Truth is showing life as it really is" and "Truth is paramount at the end of life."

We had convened a family meeting about a year and a half earlier. At that time, we hoped to connect and reconnect as adult family members who had been geographically and in some ways psychologically separated for much of our adult lives. We had left home, married, had children (some of whom were married or getting married, others in elementary school, one traveling in Europe), moved to different parts of the country, and planted roots in new communities. We knew each other as children and as siblings; we didn't know each other as adults.

During that first meeting, we told Nancy what we would want her to know if the cancer she was living with would result in her death. We were very honest with her as to what she meant to us, how our lives had been affected by her, and what our lives would be like without her.

It was time to reconvene. This time, the meeting would be held in a hospital. We chose a time convenient for everyone: Saturday at 5:00 P.M. A room was reserved, and the nurses made certain that Nancy would be prepared.

Riding to the meeting with Bev, I said, "Wouldn't it be miraculous if Nancy cleared up enough to participate in this meeting, to speak her truth, to say what she needs to say, to hear what each of us would like her to hear from us, to know that she is loved, that she will be held in the hearts of her family forever, and that she is regarded as being very courageous."

I got my wish. When we arrived at the hospital, Nancy was sitting up in bed. Although she wasn't her usual talkative self, she was more alert than she had been in many days. And she was talking. We all gathered in the room that had been set aside for the meeting. We rolled her bed into the room and arranged our chairs around her. It was a "family circle." Then we went through the decisionmaking process as outlined in chapter 4 of this book. We spoke about the medical reasons for her being in a palliative care unit, what her wishes were (personally, physically, with regard to her family, and spiritually), where she wanted to be, and how we, her family, might work to give her what she was asking for.

We learned what Nancy wanted and what she didn't want in terms of the time and energy she had remaining in her life. And just when I thought we were done, each family member said to Nancy what they wanted Nancy to hear and to know. This was different from any other family meeting I had attended. I stopped facilitating—what was happening could not be facilitated. It was a true expression of the heart and soul of each person present. I had never experienced or witnessed that level of intimacy in the context of a meeting like this. Everyone was saying what only they could say only to Nancy. Nancy spoke as well. Our hearts were open. Our tears were shed. Truth was spoken. Love was present, love was expressed, love was holding each of us.

Through the course of Nancy's illness I applied the ideas in this book to our family experience of sharing Nancy's journey. In the end, I realized that the people I have known in my work over the past fifteen years and those who participated in the latest study gave me an incredible gift when they offered me their stories. The gift made a huge difference to Nancy's journey, as well as to the journey of my whole family. We were able to do and say what needed to be done and to be said. For that, I will be forever grateful.

Nancy died sixteen days later. Thanks to the care providers on the palliative care unit, she died free of nausea and free of pain. Thanks to the family members who were present, she was held and surrounded by their love as she died.

What was it like to sit with my sister as she was dying? As a health care provider, I learned that I have a great deal more to learn from the people who speak to me about living with a terminal illness. I need to work to understand the psychological and spiritual as much as I work to understand the physical—the pain, the disease process, the symptoms. Dying is as much a matter of the psychological and spiritual as it is of the physical. It involves the whole person—body, mind, and spirit. Being with Nancy during her final days was one of the most difficult experiences I have ever known. It was also one of the greatest honors. I wanted time to stop; I wanted to do what was right for Nancy; I wanted to do what was right for her family.

I was angry and frustrated with a system that seemed to allow her to slip through the cracks. In fact, at one point I was filled with rage. I understand the system, and I understand that things happen unintentionally. These same things have happened to people under my care over the years. But I understand it differently now. The system will never be perfect, but because it was my sister, I wanted perfection for her.

I still don't know what it means to have a terminal illness. Only those with a terminal illness really know. But I do know what it means to be the brother of someone who is dying, and now I know grief in a way that I have not known it before. I also understand a lot of other things differently than I did before Nancy's death. In the past, I have not always spoken clearly with patients and their family members. I assumed that family members understood what I understood as a health care provider. Now I realize how personal wishes affect one's understanding of what is being said. And while I am very aware that it is not possible to predict how much time remains in the life of another person, I now know how hope can spring eternal. I also know how difficult it is to address the issues pertaining to death and dying for a fifty-three-year-old woman who wants nothing more than to become a grandmother.

I am even more aware now of the value of the family meeting. I also learned that the exercise as I have facilitated it to date is incomplete. My family showed me a new way to bring love, integrity, and honor to the process. Although I facilitated most of the meeting, my family showed me how it could be done differently. They added the intimate conversation, the part that did not require any facilitation.

If I had it to do again, would I do anything differently? Absolutely. In one sense, the course of Nancy's illness was like a chronic illness. It went on for nine years, and I believed it would continue for considerably longer than it did. I waited too long to deepen my relationship with her.

Nancy and I shared similar interests professionally. I always believed that this book would be complete well before she died and that it would provide many opportunities for us to have discussions, professional and personal, about its content, about ourselves, about each other. We had some discussions, but from my point of view we weren't finished.

I wish I had said more along the lines of what I prescribe in this book when I learned about the change in Nancy's disease process three years prior to her death. I wish I had told her then what people were telling me about living with a terminal illness—that a process of life review emerged, that they had a longing to belong, that they wanted to speak their truth, to know who they were, and to experience the transcendent. I wish I had said that if she ever wanted to explore or talk about any of that, I would be honored to listen and work hard to understand who she was as an adult who happened to be my sister.

I knew that Nancy had to say goodbye to a lot of people and I only had to say goodbye to her. I am very thankful for the opportunity I had to do so, in that I was able to say to her "I want you to know how my life is better because you were in it. I want you to know what I learned from you that has made me who I am today. I want you to be aware of what I will take with me, that you have given to me." After that I said, "I love you" and I held her. Our tears ran down each other's cheeks onto her pillow. If I could do it again I would then sit by her side and hold her hand, until she fell asleep. After that, I would walk away and keep her in my heart forever.

I'm angry at myself for waiting too long. One would think that fifteen years of being with people who are dying, listening to the stories of their lives through a research project, and writing a book about it would be enough to teach me that waiting is a risky business. And I'm angry at her for her being so private, so independent, so alone in her suffering that she didn't invite me to stop waiting and come to be with her. But I know that I need to respect her for being the private person she was. I know that anger is part of grief, but it feels that we ought not to be angry at those who have died. I'm angry because I love her and I miss her. I am working to forgive myself for waiting too long. I know she knew I loved her and I know that she loved me— that's the beginning of forgiveness.

I write about this because I believe it is a common experience. Perhaps it is especially common among those who live with a chronic illness or a terminal illness of a lengthy duration. And what about people simply growing older? When do those who care about them begin to address issues that might concern either party?

The only answer I can come up with is that it is never too early to connect with the people we care about. Both people in a relationship are responsible for exchanging information, feelings, and concerns. If you've got something you would like to say to someone, it's important enough to say right now. What are the fears you have about living or dying as you are at the moment?

Many people don't want to discuss these issues. All I can do is encourage you to have discussions about your lives, about who you are, about what you want at the end of life. Begin these discussions sooner rather than later, for you may run out of time. And if your children or siblings approach you about issues pertaining to dying, work to be open to them. Your death will affect them as well. The more they know about you, the less awkwardness, discomfort, and tension there will be for you and for them. Procrastination in talking about the end of life is not in anyone's best interest. Through such discussions you might also benefit from a new intimacy. It is fear that keeps us silent about difficult topics; it is courage and compassion that allow us to begin to speak. You may have to make several attempts before you are able to have those conversations.

Just as people live unique lives, so they die unique deaths. The ideas in this book can be used to guide, direct, and facilitate the process of dying. They can also be used to facilitate the process of living. For the truth is that we are all dying all the time. Some of us get advance warning, and some of us don't. All of us at any moment have to answer the question: Do I embrace life, or do I prepare to die? And for all of us, the answers are ultimately similar. Living fully and dying well involve enhancing one's sense of self, one's relationships with others, and one's understanding of the transcendent, the spiritual, the supernatural. And only in confronting the inevitability of death does one truly embrace life.

Eros

The sense of the world is short,
Long and various the report,—
To love and be beloved;
Men and gods have not outlearned it,
And how oft soe'er they've turned it,
'Tis not to be improved.

Ralph Waldo Emerson

Appendix

Talking to Terminally Ill Patients:
Guidelines for Physicians

Communicating a diagnosis of terminal illness is a challenge to even the most experienced and highly trained physician. It is best if this message is given in the context of a close relationship between physician and patient, one characterized by mutual respect, trust, and honesty. Needless to say, such a relationship is not created overnight but is built up gradually over time.

In *How We Die*, Sherwin Nuland states that there is need "for the resurrection of the family doctor. Each one of us needs a guide who knows *us* as well as he knows the pathways by which we can approach death.... The clinical objectivity that should enter into our decisions must come from a doctor familiar with our values and the lives we have led, and not just from the virtual stranger whose superspecialized biomedical skills we have called upon."

Unfortunately, we sometimes don't have the luxury of having such a relationship with a terminally ill patient when we are called on to give them difficult information. In that case it is vitally important that we be as sensitive as possible to the whole human being to whom we are delivering our message.

Before you, the physician, enter the room to give someone bad news, to discuss code status, or to inform a patient that they have a terminal illness, stop and think about your own feelings about the message, the person, and the process that is about to happen. To know and understand your own emotions at this point is significant to reducing the iatrogenic suffering that can occur when a doctor speaks with a patient. How you speak is usually based on how you feel, and how you speak is louder than what you say. Be honest with yourself about your own sadness, frustration, discomfort about confrontation, dread, feelings of ineptitude, and desires to run away and have some-one else do this very hard job. These are normal feelings, and you wouldn't be human if you didn't have them. Simply, be aware of what-ever emotions you feel.

Let your patient know that she is about to hear some bad news. You could begin with any of the following: "I have some information to give you which may be difficult to hear" or "The results of the test are not what I had hoped for. We need to talk about it as soon as possible."

It is important to give your patient the option of having someone else present, perhaps a family member or friend. In fact, for some it is the cultural norm to have someone other than the patient receive the news and discuss the options. If one senses that this might be the case, it is appropriate to ask: "If I needed to make some decisions with regard to your physical health, who might I speak with?" Give the option to meet at another time, when other family members or friends can attend as well.

Once the meeting takes place, make certain there will be no inter-ruptions—turn off your pager and portable phone—and let the patient know that the meeting will last twenty to thirty minutes. Assure your patient that you will meet with her again if necessary. If you don't have the time, consider the elements of this process. Be aware, first, of your own feelings about informing someone that she is going to die. Then remember to speak with respect, clarity, and sim-plicity without using medical jargon or metaphor.

At the start of the meeting, remember to introduce yourself to any people in the room who you have not met before. If you have met them but don't remember their names, ask them their names. Wearing a readable name tag is also helpful, as some people are more comfortable if they can see how your name is spelled. Make certain the people present are sitting comfortably and will be able to hear what is said. (Turn off radios, CD players, etc.)

Sit down, on the same level, so as to allow direct eye contact with the patient. Touch her in a reassuring manner—hands, arms, and shoulders are generally safe. It might be wise to say, "Do you mind if I touch you like this?" There are some people who experience physical or psychological discomfort by being touched; it might also be culturally inappropriate.

Speak clearly and simply, using nonmedical terms as much as possible. If medical terms are necessary, explain their meaning in a straightforward manner. Simplify the content of the message so that all of the people in the room are able to understand. Begin by asking the patient what she understands about her illness—symptoms, tests, results, diagnosis, and prognosis. Ask how the disease has progressed and how it has affected her lifestyle. Listen carefully to what is said and to what is not said. Even though you may have explained some of this before, your patient may not have heard the information or may not remember it. Explain it in a different way from the previous time.

Once you have a sense that everyone in the room has a common understanding, move to the next piece of information. For example, "As you know, all the test results are in, and unfortunately I have to let you know that the results are not what I hoped they would be. I have reviewed them with a colleague of mine to be certain that I'm not missing something. We have tried a few treatments. Unfortunately, they have not stopped the disease from progressing. That means this disease will likely be the cause of your death."

Never say, "There is nothing more that can be done for you."

Throughout the course of the conversation, ask your patient whether she understands the message she's being told: "Do you understand what this means?" Invite anyone present to ask questions, especially for clarification. It is unlikely that anyone will remember everything that has been said. Each person will remember some component of the information you have given them. Everyone may need to meet again for further discussion.

Invite someone to take notes if the group wishes to have a written record of the meeting. It might also help if you highlight in writing two or three points important to the patient's understanding of the diagnosis and treatment. Offer to have subsequent meetings to review the content or to repeat the information for others who might be significant to the care of the patient.

Be aware that bad news is always bad news, even if it is given in a respectful, compassionate manner. No one wants to hear that they themselves or a loved one is dying. "Shooting the messenger" is a typical response, and because you are the messenger in this case, is important that you reassure your patient she will not be abandoned, that there will be as much attention paid to pain and symptom management as is necessary to achieve an optimal degree of comfort. Reassure your patient that you will be there for her regardless of her experience from that point until the time of her death.

Notes

Introduction: Facing Death

xxiv   "A story is not just a story . . ." Clarissa Pinkola Estés. *Women Who Run with the Wolves: Myths and Stories of the Wild Woman Archetype* (New York: Ballantine Books/Random House, 1992, 1997), pp. 508 and 519.

xxviii   "One Stick, Two Stick" story adapted from Estés, p. 120.

Chapter 1: Time and Anxiety

1   "As time is the most valuable thing . . ." Dietrich Bonhoeffer. *Letters and Papers from Prison: The Enlarged Edition* (London: SCM Press Ltd., 1953, 1967, 1971), p. 134.

2–3   Gilgamesh story adapted from Liz Greene and Juliet Sharman-Burke, "Gilgamesh and the Tree of Life." In *The Mythic Journey: The Meaning of Myth as Guide for Life* (New York: Fireside, 2000), pp. 102–105.

4   "What is the most wondrous thing in the world?" From the *Mahabharata*, quoted in Joseph Goldstein and Jack Kornfeld. *Seeking the Heart of Wisdom: The Path of Insight Meditation* (Boston: Shambala Publications, 1987), p. 142.

4   "If no one asks me, I know . . ." St. Augustine's *Confessions*, Book XI, Chapter XIV, 17, quoted in K. R. Eissler. *The Psychiatrist and the Dying Patient* (New York: International Universities Press, Inc. 1955), p. 265.

11   Anxiety is "a free-floating dis-ease . . ." James Hollis. *Swamplands of the Soul: New Life in Dismal Places* (Toronto: Inner City Books, 1996), pp. 92–93.

17   "Narrative time" is defined in Ken Wilber. *Eye to Eye: The Quest for the New Paradigm* (New York: Anchor Press/Doubleday, 1983), pp. 77–78.

18　"When you have a ... terminal disease..." from "Tutu Says Life with Cancer Has Added 'New Intensity,'" *The Globe and Mail* (Toronto), April 16, 2001, p. A2.

19　"According to Diggory..." Irvin D. Yalom. *The Yalom Reader: Selections from the Work of a Master Therapist and Storyteller* (New York: Basic Books, 1998), pp. 192–193, referring to J. Diggory and D. Rothman, "Values Destroyed by Death," *Journal of Abnormal and Social Psychology* 63 (1961): 205–210.

19　"One dreads ... losing oneself..." Yalom, p. 193.

20　"If we can transform fear..." Yalom, p. 194.

26–27　"And now here it is! ..." Leo Tolstoy, "The Death of Ivan Ilych." In *The Death of Ivan Ilych and Other Stories* (New York: Penguin Books, 1960), pp. 132–133.

27　"Five domains for quality end-of-life care..." Peter A. Singer, Douglas K. Martin, and Merrijoy Kelner, "Quality End-of-Life Care: Patients' Perspectives," *Journal of American Medical Association* 291, no. 2 (January 13, 1999): 163.

29　Life time line adapted from B. de Vries, J. A. Blando, P. Southard, and C. Bubeck, "The times of our lives." In Gary M. Kenyon, P. Clark, and B. de Vries, eds. *Narrative Gerontology: Theory, Research, and Practice* (New York: Springer, 2001), p. 142.

Chapter 2: Bad News

34　Achilles story adapted from Liz Greene and Juliet Sharman-Burke, "Great Expectations." In *The Mythic Journey: The Meaning of Myth as a Guide for Life* (New York: Fireside/Simon & Schuster, 2000), pp. 12–13.

54　"One must realize that in any relationship..." Aldo Carotenuto. *Eros and Pathos: Shades of Love and Suffering.* Translated by Charles Nopar (Toronto: Inner City Books, 1989), p. 65.

56–57　Danae story adapted from Bernard Evslin, Dorothy Evslin, and Ned Hoopes, "Perseus." In *Heroes and Monsters of Greek Myth* (New York: Scholastic, 1967), pp. 7–32.

Chapter 3: Physical Pain

72–73　Chiron story adapted from Melanie Reinhart. *Chiron and the Healing Journey: An Astrological and Psychological Perspective* (Arkana Penguin Books, 1998), pp. 24 and 26. The story is also told in Michael

Kearney, M.D. *Mortally Wounded: Stories of Soul Pain, Death, and Healing* (New York: Scribner, 1996), pp. 155–156.

76 Emily Dickinson's poem "The Mystery of Pain." In *Poems: Including Variant Readings Critically Compared with All Known Manuscripts*. Thomas H. Johnson, ed. (Cambridge, MA: Belknap Press/Harvard University Press, 1955), pp. 501–502.

78 "Pain begins with a physical stimulus..." Adapted from Expert Advisory Committee on the Management of Severe Chronic Pain in Cancer Patients. *Cancer Pain: A Monograph on the Management of Cancer Pain* (Health and Welfare Canada, 1984), p. 6.

89 "Even if death is thought imminent..." Janet L. Abrahm. *A Physician's Guide to Pain and Symptom Management in Cancer Patients* (Baltimore and London: Johns Hopkins University Press, 2000), pp. 38–39, quoting the Church's position as stated first by Pius XII in 1957 and reiterated in the 1994 Catechism (*Catechism of the Catholic Church* 1994, Subheading I, Euthanasia, 2279).

Chapter 4: Being Touched, Being In Touch

98 "To Touch, to Heal" story from Mark 5:24–34, *New American Standard Bible* (La Habra, CA: The Lockman Foundation, 1960, 1962, 1963, 1968, 1971, 1972, 1973, 1975,1977, 1995).

98–99 "Gerasim smiled again..." Leo Tolstoy, "The Death of Ivan Ilych." In *The Death of Ivan Ilych and Other Stories* (New York: Penguin Books, 1960), pp. 136–137.

104–105 "The experience of body contact..." Aldo Carotenuto. *Eros and Pathos: Shades of Love and Suffering* (Toronto: Inner City Books, 1989), p. 53.

108 Study with a group of women who had breast cancer from David Spiegel, J. R. Bloom, and Irving Yalom, "Group Support for Patients with Metastatic Cancer," *Archives of General Psychiatry* 38 (May 1981): 527–533.

109 "Sometimes I have a terrible feeling..." Amanda Heggs, a woman with AIDS, was quoted in the *Guardian* (London, June 12, 1989).

109 "Working together in facing common problems..." Spiegel, p. 527.

110–111 "My father died at home..." George Soros. "Reflections on Death in America." Speech for the Alexander Ming Fisher Lecture Series at Columbia Presbyterian Medical Center, New York, 1994, p. 2. Available on the Web at http://www.soros.org/death/george_soros.htm.

111 "My mother's death was more recent..." Soros, p. 2.

111–112   "Touch is deeply reassuring..." Bill Moyers. *Healing and the Mind* (New York: Doubleday, 1993), p. 355.

112   Remen's work with touch and babies described in Moyers, pp. 355–356.

112   "The surface area of the skin..." Ashley Montagu. *Touching: The Human Significance of the Skin*, 3rd ed. (New York: Harper & Row, 1986), pp. 7–8.

113   "Infants deprived of ... maternal body contact..." Montagu, p. 97.

113   Information on death rates for babies abandoned to institutions also from Montagu, p. 97.

114   "The loss of physical contact..." Montagu, p. 265.

115   "Some people don't like being handled..." Lewis Thomas. *The Youngest Science: Notes of a Medicine-Watcher* (New York: Bantam Books, 1983), p. 56.

120   The ethical decisionmaking process is discussed in Albert Jonsen, Mark Siegler, and William J. Winslade. *Clinical Ethics*, 3rd ed. (New York: McGraw-Hill, 1992).

120   St. Paul's Hospital ethic committee guidelines described in David R. Kuhl and Patricia Wilensky, "Decision-Making at the End of Life: A Model Using an Ethical Grid and Principles of Group Process," *Journal of Palliative Medicine* 2, no. 1 (1999): 75–86.

Chapter 5: Life Review

138   The Garden of Eden story adapted from *The Pentateuch and Haftorahs: Hebrew Text with English Translation and Commentary*. J. H. Hertz, ed. (London: Soncino Press, 1960), pp. 8–13.

140   "The richest resource for meaning and healing..." Gary M. Kenyon and William L. Randall. *Restorying Our Lives: Personal Growth Through Autobiographical Reflection* (New York: Praeger, 1997), p. 2.

141   Structure for the process of life review from James E. Birren and Donna E. Deutchman. *Guiding Autobiography Groups for Older Adults Exploring the Fabric of Life* (Baltimore: Johns Hopkins University Press, 1991).

158–159   Emily Brontë's poem "Remembrance." In *Brontë*. Everyman's Library Pocket Poets ed. (New York and Toronto: Alfred A. Knopf, Inc. and Random House of Canada, Ltd., 1996), pp. 49–50.

162   "Reviewing their past helps..." Birren and Deutchman, p. vii.

Chapter 6: Speaking the Truth

166–167 "The Prisoner in the Dark Cave" story adapted from John Bradshaw. *Healing the Shame that Binds You* (Deerfield Beach, Florida: Health Communications, Inc., 1988), pp. 117–118.

173–174 "The confrontation with our own reality . . ." Alice Miller. *The Drama of the Gifted Child The Search for the True Self*, revised ed. (New York: BasicBooks, 1994), p. 41.

174 "Guilt" is defined in *The New Oxford Dictionary of English*, Judy Pearsall, ed. (New York: Oxford University Press, 1998), p. 817.

175 "[Recompense] only makes sense . . ." James Hollis. *Swamplands of the Soul New Life in Dismal Places* (Toronto: Inner City Books, 1996), pp. 26–27.

176 "Through life review . . ." Barbara S. Derrickson, "The Spiritual Work of the Dying: A Framework and Case Studies," *The Hospice Journal* 11, no. 2 (1966): 14–15.

179 "Whole" is defined in *The New Oxford Dictionary of English*, p. 2108.

179 "Heal" is defined in *The New Oxford Dictionary of English*, p. 846.

180 "Forgiveness is the means . . ." Robin Casarjian. *Forgiveness: A Bold Choice for a Peaceful Heart* (New York: Bantam Books, 1992), pp. 10 and 12.

180 "To pursue the path of healing . . ." Interview with Archbishop Desmond Tutu by Colin Greer, " 'Without Memory There Is No Healing. Without Forgiveness, There Is No Future.' " *Parade, The Sunday Newspaper Magazine* (*Washington Post*), January 11, 1998, pp. 4–6.

181 "It is necessary to know . . ." William A. Meninger. *The Process of Forgiveness* (New York: Continuum, 1999), p. 53.

181–182 "[The emotional umbilical cord] has grown out of a past of unmet needs . . ." Casarjian, p. 72.

182 Questions to guide the process of forgiveness from Casarjian, p. 76.

182 "[Unexpressed emotions seep] out at the edges of the personality . . ." Casarjian, pp. 50–51.

183 "Techniques that trigger awareness . . ." Casarjian, p. 54.

187–188 "What tormented Ivan Ilych most was the deception . . ." Leo Tolstoy, "The Death of Ivan Ilych." In *The Death of Ivan Ilych and Other Stories* (New York: Penguin Books, 1960), pp. 137–138.

Chapter 7: Longing to Belong

200   Naomi and Ruth story adapted from Ruth 1:1–18.

203   "[Without belonging, we experience] the pangs of loneliness . . ." Abraham H. Maslow. *Motivation and Personality*, 2nd ed. (New York: Harper & Row Publishers, 1970), p. 43.

207   "[Parents provide] a secure base . . ." John Bowlby. *A Secure Base: Parent-Child Attachment and Healthy Human Development* (New York: BasicBooks, 1988), p. 11.

208   "Children are driven unconsciously . . ." Carl Jung. "Marriage as a Psychological Relationship." In *The Portable Jung*, Joseph Campbell, ed. (New York: Penguin Books, 1971), p. 165.

210   "This pattern is promoted . . ." Bowlby, p. 124.

211   The infant's response when the absent mother returns from Bowlby, p. 124.

211   "A happier and more rewarding child . . ." Bowlby, pp. 126–127.

Chapter 8: Self-Realization: Who Am I?

224–225   "The Roar of Awakening" story from Heinrich Zimmer. *Philosophies of India*, Joseph Campbell, ed. (Princeton: Princeton University Press, 1957, 1969), pp. 5–8.

227   "Many people in the world . . ." Virginia Satir, John Banmen, Jane Gerber, and Maria Gomori. *The Satir Model: Family Therapy and Beyond* (Palo Alto, CA: Science and Behaviour Books, 1991), pp. 12–13.

231   Jung's "mask" discussed in Vivianne Crowley. *Thorsons Principles of Jungian Spirituality* (London: HarperCollins, 1998), p. 45.

231   Jung's "shadow" discussed in Daryl Sharp. *Jungian Psychology Unplugged: My Life as an Elephant* (Toronto: InnerCity Books, 1998), p. 47.

232   The mask and shadow distinguished in Sharp, p. 29.

233   "The world [makes] us into . . ." Frederick Buechner. *Telling Secrets: A Memoir* (New York: HarperSanFrancisco, 1991), p. 45.

233   "Whatever reality may be . . ." James Hollis. *The Middle Passage: From Misery to Meaning in Midlife* (Toronto: Inner City Books, 1993), p. 9.

236   "Much of personality development . . ." Roberta M. Gilbert. *Extraordinary Relationships: A New Way of Thinking About Human Interactions* (New York: Wiley & Sons, 1992), p. 199.

236   Tendencies of the female only child discussed in Gilbert, p. 205.

237   "Shame" defined in *The New Oxford Dictionary of English*.

237   "The shame that binds you . . ." John Bradshaw. *Healing the Shame That Binds You* (Florida: Health Communications, 1988), p. 10.

237   "The most paradoxical aspect of neurotic shame..." Bradshaw, p. 14.

239   "Fate provides the initial wounding..." James Hollis. *Tracking the Gods: The Place of Myth in Modern Life* (Toronto: Inner City Books, 1995), p. 67.

240   "In the developing fetus..." Roberta M. Gilbert. *Extraordinary Relationships: A New Way of Thinking About Human Interactions* (New York: Wiley & Sons, 1992), p. 181.

241   Techniques for effective mirroring adapted from Alice Miller. *The Drama of the Gifted Child: The Search for the True Self*, revised ed. (New York: BasicBooks, 1994), p. 53.

242   "[Despair is a] feeling that the time is short..." Erik H. Erikson. *Identity: A Life Cycle* (New York: W.W. Norton, 1980), pp. 104–105.

242   "[Integrity is defined as] the capacity to affirm..." Judith Herman. *Trauma and Recovery* (New York: BasicBooks, 1992), p. 154.

242–243   "[Meaning involves a] more honest encounter..." James Hollis. *Swamplands of the Soul: New Life in Dismal Places* (Toronto: Inner City Books, 1996), p. 15.

243   Metaphor of the triangle from James E. Birren and Donna E. Deutchman. *Guiding Autobiography Groups for Older Adults Exploring the Fabric of Life* (Baltimore: Johns Hopkins University Press, 1991), p. 11.

244–245   Questions to help recover personal integrity adapted from James Hollis. *Creating a Life: Finding Your Individual Path* (Toronto: Inner City Books, 2000), pp. 120–122.

246   The Moses story adapted from Exodus 2:11 and 3:1–11.

246–247   "Who Am I?" poem by Dietrich Bonhoeffer. *Letters and Papers from Prison: The Enlarged Edition* (London: SCM Press Ltd., 1953, 1967, 1971), pp. 347–348.

Chapter 9: Transcendence

250–251   "The Buddha's Enlightenment" story adapted from Liz Greene and Juliet Sharman-Burke. *The Mythic Journey: The Meaning of Myth as Guide for Life* (New York: Fireside, 2000), pp. 255–260.

252–253   "Little Gidding" from "Four Quartets" by T. S. Eliot. In *Collected Poems 1909–1962* (London: Faber, 1974).

253   "Transcendence" is defined in *The New Oxford Dictionary of English*, Its derivation is given in *The Oxford Dictionary of English Etymology*, C. T. Onions, ed. (New York: Oxford University Press, 1966).

254   "It is my belief that..." Howard Thurman. *For the Inward Journey* (Richmond, Indiana: Friends United Press, 1984), p. 152.

255–256   "Autobiography in Five Short Chapters" poem by Portia Nelson. In *There's a Hole in My Sidewalk: The Romance of Self-Discovery* (Hillsboro, OR: Beyond Words Publishing, Inc., 1993). Also available on the Internet at http://www.mhsanctuary.com/Healing/auto.htm.

259   "Let go of the dark..." Frederick Buechner. *Telling Secrets* (New York: HarperCollins, 1991), p. 92.

259–260   Monkey and coconut story from Jack Kornfield and Christina Feldman. *Soul Food: Stories to Nourish the Spirit and the Heart* (New York: HarperSanFrancisco, 1991), p. 323.

260   "Letting go is the essence of the spiritual life..." Kornfield and Feldman, p. 309.

261   "When I was a child..." I Corinthians 13:11–12.

261–262   "But that isn't the only way to interpret the passage..." Deepak Chopra. *How to Know God: The Soul's Journey into the Mystery of Mysteries* (New York: Harmony Books, 2000), pp. 50–51.

262–263   "Not everyone believes in a formal religion..." Sogyal Rinpoche. *The Tibetan Book of Living and Dying* (New York: HarperCollins, 1992), pp. 212–213.

272   "To a Hindu..." Zalman Schachter-Shalomi and Ronald S. Miller. *From Age-ing to Sage-ing: A Profound Vision of Growing Older* (New York: Warner Books, 1995), p. 127.

273   "As in a dream..." Jack Kornfield. *After the Ecstasy, the Laundry: How the Heart Grows Wise on the Spiritual Path* (New York: Bantam Books, 2000), pp. 26–28.

Conclusion: Embracing Life

291   "Eros" poem by Ralph Waldo Emerson. In *Early Poems of Ralph Waldo Emerson.* Introduction by Nathan Haskell Dole (New York, Boston: Thomas Y. Crowell & Company, 1899).

Appendix: Talking to Terminally Ill Patients: Guidelines for Physicians

293   "[Resurrect] the family doctor..." Sherwin B. Nuland. *How We Die* (New York: Alfred A. Knopf, Inc., 1993), p. 266.

Bibliography

Abrahm, Janet L. *A Physician's Guide to Pain and Symptom Management in Cancer Patients*. Baltimore and London: Johns Hopkins University Press, 2000.

Birren, James E., and Donna E. Deutchman. *Guiding Autobiography Groups for Older Adults Exploring the Fabric of Life*. Baltimore: Johns Hopkins University Press, 1991.

Bonhoeffer, Dietrich. *Letters and Papers from Prison: The Enlarged Edition*. London: SCM Press Ltd., 1953, 1967, 1971.

Bowlby, John. *A Secure Base: Parent-Child Attachment and Healthy Human Development*. New York: Basic Books, 1988.

Bradshaw, John. *Healing the Shame That Binds You*. Florida: Health Communications, 1988.

Bronte, Emily. "Remembrance." In *Brontë*. Everyman's Library Pocket Poets ed. New York and Toronto: Alfred A. Knopf, Inc. and Random House of Canada, Ltd., 1996.

Buechner, Frederick. *Telling Secrets: A Memoir*. New York: HarperSanFrancisco, 1991.

Carotenuto, Aldo. *Eros and Pathos: Shades of Love and Suffering*. Charles Nopar, trans. Toronto: Inner City Books, 1989.

Casarjian, Robin. *Forgiveness: A Bold Choice for a Peaceful Heart*. New York: Bantam Books, 1992.

Chopra, Deepak. *How to Know God: The Soul's Journey into the Mystery of Mysteries*. New York: Harmony Books, 2000.

Crowley, Vivianne. *Thorsons Principles of Jungian Spirituality*. London: HarperCollins, 1998.

Derrickson, Barbara S. "The Spiritual Work of the Dying: A Framework and Case Studies." In *The Hospice Journal* 11, no. 2 (1996): 11–30.

de Vries, B., J. A. Blando, P. Southard, and C. Bubeck, "The Times of Our Lives." In Gary M. Kenyon, P. Clark, and B. de Vries, eds. *Narrative Gerontology: Theory, Research, and Practice.* New York: Springer, 2001, pp. 137–158.

Dickinson, Emily. *Poems: Including Variant Readings Critically Compared with All Known Manuscript*s Thomas H. Johnson, ed. Cambridge, MA: Belknap Press/Harvard University Press, 1955.

Diggory, J., and D. Rothman "Values Destroyed by Death." In *Journal of Abnormal and Social Psychology* 63(1961): 205–210.

Dorland's Illustrated Medical Dictionary, 29th ed. (Philadelphia: W. B Saunders, 2000).

Eliot, T. S. "Little Gidding" from "Four Quartets." In *Collected Poems 1909–1962.* London: Faber, 1974.

Emerson, Ralph Waldo. "Eros." In *Early Poems of Ralph Waldo Emerson.* Introduction by Nathan Haskell Dole. New York, Boston: Thomas Y. Crowell & Company, 1899.

Erikson, Erik H. *Identity: A Life Cycle.* New York: W.W. Norton, 1980.

Eissler, K. R. *The Psychiatrist and the Dying Patient.* New York: International Universities Press, Inc. 1955.

Estés, Clarissa Pinkola. *Women Who Run with the Wolves: Myths and Stories of the Wild Woman Archetype.* New York: Ballantine Books/Random House, 1992, 1997.

Evslin, Bernard, Dorothy Evslin, and Ned Hoopes. *Heroes and Monsters of Greek Myth.* New York: Scholastic, 1967.

Expert Advisory Committee on the Management of Severe Chronic Pain in Cancer Patients. *Cancer Pain: A Monograph on the Management of Cancer Pain.* Ottawa: Health and Welfare Canada, 1984.

Gilbert, Roberta M. *Extraordinary Relationships: A New Way of Thinking About Human Interactions* New York: Wiley & Sons, 1992.

Goldstein, Joseph, and Jack Kornfeld. *Seeking the Heart of Wisdom: The Path of Insight Meditation.* Boston: Shambala Publications, 1987.

Greene, Liz, and Juliet Sharman-Burke. "Gilgamesh and the Tree of Life." In *The Mythic Journey: The Meaning of Myth as Guide for Life* New York: Fireside, 2000.

Greer, Colin. "'Without Memory There Is No Healing. Without Forgiveness, There Is No Future.'" *Parade, The Sunday Newspaper Magazine (Washington Post),* January 11, 1998, pp. 4–6.

Herman, Judith. *Trauma and Recovery.* New York: BasicBooks, 1992.

Hertz, J. H., ed. *The Pentateuch and Haftorahs: Hebrew Text with English Translation and Commentary.* London: Soncino Press, 1960.

Hollis, James. *Creating a Life: Finding Your Individual Path.* Toronto: Inner City Books, 2000.

————. *The Middle Passage: From Misery to Meaning in Midlife*. Toronto: Inner City Books, 1993.

————. *Swamplands of the Soul: New Life in Dismal Places*. Toronto: Inner City Books, 1996.

————. *Tracking the Gods: The Place of Myth in Modern Life*. Toronto: Inner City Books, 1995.

Jonsen, Albert, Mark Siegler, and William J. Winslade. *Clinical Ethics*, 3rd ed. New York: McGraw-Hill, 1992.

Jung, Carl. "Marriage as a Psychological Relationship." In *The Portable Jung*, Joseph Campbell, ed. New York: Penguin Books, 1971.

Kearney, Michael, M.D. *Mortally Wounded: Stories of Soul Pain, Death, and Healing*. New York: Scribner, 1996.

Kenyon, Gary M., and William L. Randall. *Restorying Our Lives: Personal Growth Through Autobiographical Reflection*. New York: Praeger, 1997.

Kornfield, Jack. *After the Ecstasy, the Laundry: How the Heart Grows Wise on the Spiritual Path*. New York: Bantam Books, 2000.

Kornfield, Jack, and Christina Feldman. *Soul Food: Stories to Nourish the Spirit and the Heart*. New York: HarperSanFrancisco, 1991.

Kuhl, David R., and Patricia Wilensky. "Decision-Making at the End of Life: A Model Using an Ethical Grid and Principles of Group Process." *Journal of Palliative Medicine* 2, no. 1 (1999): 75–86.

Maslow, Abraham H. *Motivation and Personality*, 2nd ed. New York: Harper & Row Publishers, 1970.

Meninger, William A. *The Process of Forgiveness*. New York: Continuum, 1999.

Miller, Alice. *The Drama of the Gifted Child The Search for the True Self*, revised ed. New York: BasicBooks, 1994.

Montagu, Ashley. *Touching: The Human Significance of the Skin*, 3rd ed. New York: Harper & Row, 1986.

Moyers, Bill. *Healing and the Mind*. New York: Doubleday, 1993.

Nelson, Portia. "Autobiography in Five Short Chapters" in *There's a Hole in My Sidewalk: The Romance of Self-Discovery*. Hillsboro, OR: Beyond Words Publishing, Inc., 1993. Also available on the Internet at http://www.mhsanctuary.com/Healing/auto.htm.

New American Standard Bible. La Habra, CA: The Lockman Foundation, 1960, 1962, 1963, 1968, 1971, 1972, 1973, 1975, 1977, 1995.

New Oxford Dictionary of English, The. Judy Pearsall, ed. New York: Oxford University Press, 1998.

Nuland, Sherwin B. *How We Die*. New York: Alfred A. Knopf, Inc., 1993.

Oxford Dictionary of English Etymology, The. C. T. Onions, ed. New York: Oxford University Press, 1966.

Reinhart, Melanie. *Chiron and the Healing Journey: An Astrological and Psychological Perspective.* Arkana Penguin Books, 1998.

Rinpoche, Sogyal. *The Tibetan Book of Living and Dying.* New York: HarperCollins, 1992.

Satir, Virginia, John Banmen, Jane Gerber, and Maria Gomori. *The Satir Model: Family Therapy and Beyond.* Palo Alta, CA: Science and Behaviour Books, 1991.

Schachter-Shalomi, Zalman, and Ronald S. Miller. *From Age-ing to Sage-ing: A Profound Vision of Growing Older.* New York: Warner Books, 1995.

Sharp, Daryl. *Jungian Psychology Unplugged: My Life as an Elephant.* Toronto: InnerCity Books, 1998.

Singer, Peter A., Douglas K. Martin, and Merrijoy Kelner, "Quality End-of-Life Care: Patients' Perspectives." In *Journal of American Medical Association* 291, no. 2 (January 13, 1999): 163.

Soros, George. "Reflections on Death in America." Speech for the Alexander Ming Fisher Lecture Series at Columbia Presbyterian Medical Center, New York, 1994. Available on the Web at http://www.soros.org/death/george_soros.htm.

Spiegel, David, J. R. Bloom, and Irving Yalom. "Group Support for Patients with Metastatic Cancer," *Archives of General Psychiatry* 38 (May 1981): 527–533.

Thomas, Lewis. *The Youngest Science: Notes of a Medicine-Watcher.* New York: Bantam Books, 1983.

Thurman, Howard. *For the Inward Journey.* Richmond, IN: Friends United Press, 1984.

Tolstoy, Leo. "The Death of Ivan Ilych." In *The Death of Ivan Ilych and Other Stories.* New York: Penguin Books, 1960.

"Tutu Says Life with Cancer Has Added 'New Intensity.'" In *The Globe and Mail* (Toronto), April 16, 2001, p. A2.

Wilber, Ken. *Eye to Eye: The Quest for the New Paradigm.* New York: Anchor Press/Doubleday, 1983.

Yalom, Irvin D. *The Yalom Reader: Selections from the Work of a Master Therapist and Storyteller.* New York: BasicBooks, 1998.

Zimmer, Heinrich. "The Roar of Awakening." In *Philosophies of India,* Joseph Campbell, ed. Princeton: Princeton University Press, 1957, 1969.

Permissions

Index

PublicAffairs is a publishing house founded in 1997. It is a tribute to the standards, values, and flair of three persons who have served as mentors to countless reporters, writers, editors, and book people of all kinds, including me.

I. F. STONE, proprietor of *I. F. Stone's Weekly*, combined a commitment to the First Amendment with entrepreneurial zeal and reporting skill and became one of the great independent journalists in American history. At the age of eighty, Izzy published *The Trial of Socrates*, which was a national bestseller. He wrote the book after he taught himself ancient Greek.

BENJAMIN C. BRADLEE was for nearly thirty years the charismatic editorial leader of *The Washington Post*. It was Ben who gave the *Post* the range and courage to pursue such historic issues as Watergate. He supported his reporters with a tenacity that made them fearless and it is no accident that so many became authors of influential, best-selling books.

ROBERT L. BERNSTEIN, the chief executive of Random House for more than a quarter century, guided one of the nation's premier publishing houses. Bob was personally responsible for many books of political dissent and argument that challenged tyranny around the globe. He is also the founder and longtime chair of Human Rights Watch, one of the most respected human rights organizations in the world.

For fifty years, the banner of Public Affairs Press was carried by its owner, Morris B. Schnapper, who published Gandhi, Nasser, Toynbee, Truman, and about 1,500 other authors. In 1983, Schnapper was described by *The Washington Post* as "a redoubtable gadfly." His legacy will endure in the books to come.

Peter Osnos, *Publisher*